THE CAPITAL/LOGIC DEBATE

Studies in Critical Social Sciences Book Series

Haymarket Books is proud to be working with Brill Academic Publishers (www.brill.nl) to republish the *Studies in Critical Social Sciences* book series in paperback editions. This peer-reviewed book series offers insights into our current reality by exploring the content and consequences of power relationships under capitalism, and by considering the spaces of opposition and resistance to these changes that have been defining our new age. Our full catalog of *SCSS* volumes can be viewed at https://www.haymarketbooks .org/series_collections/4-studies-in-critical-social-sciences.

THE CAPITAL/LOGIC DEBATE

ANDY BLUNDEN

Haymarket Books
Chicago, IL

First published in 2025 by Brill Academic Publishers, The Netherlands
© 2025 Koninklijke Brill NV, Leiden, The Netherlands

Published in paperback in 2026 by
Haymarket Books
P.O. Box 180165
Chicago, IL 60618
773-583-7884
www.haymarketbooks.org

ISBN: 979-8-88890-799-3

Distributed to the trade in the US through Consortium Book Sales and
Distribution (www.cbsd.com) and internationally through Ingram Publisher
Services International (www.ingramcontent.com).

This book was published with the generous support of Lannan Foundation,
Wallace Action Fund, and the Marguerite Casey Foundation.

Special discounts are available for bulk purchases by organizations and
institutions. Please call 773-583-7884 or email info@haymarketbooks.org for more
information.

Cover design by Jamie Kerry and Ragina Johnson.

Printed in the United States.

Library of Congress Cataloging-in-Publication data is available.

Contents

Preface

My aim in joining the debate about the relation between *Marx's Capital* and Hegel's *Logic* is not to just make a contribution to political economy as such. It just so happens that Karl Marx had devoted 25 years of his life to this important topic, and I know that Marx's approach to political economy was strongly informed by his reading of Hegel's *Logic*. Further, the other writer whose ideas have shaped my own theoretical development, the Soviet Psychologist Lev Vygotsky, had in turn used Marx's *Capital* to appropriate Hegelian methods for his development of Psychology. So a study of the Hegelian elements of Marx's *Capital* would provide me with an opportunity to bring together the shared insights of these three great writers. My ultimate aim is to determine general principles which remain applicable for understanding any social phenomena or problem, drawing on their shared methodological insights.

In 2023, I set about writing my own commentary on the Hegelian elements of Marx's *Capital*, having already arrived at a somewhat negative view of the current literature on the topic. However, my first effort went down like a lead balloon. Issues which seemed obvious to me were met with flat denial by others working in the field. Obviously, it was not viable to carry on with this task without first immersing myself in the current literature on the topic and gaining an understanding of where present-day Hegelian-Marxists (if any really exist) were coming from. It would not be enough to make counterclaims to those of contemporary writers, I would have to exhaustively refute what they had written before formulating and presenting my own view and expecting a serious response. Further, I wanted to understand how others who wanted to bring Hegelian ideas to the study of Marx's work had come to the views they held. And, quite frankly, I still had a lot to learn about *Capital*.

In what follows I examine present-day attempts to identify the relation between Marx's *Capital* and Hegel's *Logic* under four different categories, before summing up and anticipating my own answer to the question.

Chapter 1 deals with those who took as their subject matter the relation of Hegel's *Logic* to Marx's 1858 manuscript, the *Grundrisse*, effectively Marx's first economic manuscript. This is relevant to the *Capital/Logic* debate because the *Grundrisse* is widely characterised as "the first draft of *Capital*," and has been found to contain frequent explicit references to Hegel's *Logic*. Whereas I aimed to engage only with living writers in the present-day *Capital/Logic* debate, I wanted to include Hiroshi Uchida, who had written a book on this topic back in 1988 but had unfortunately died in February 2024. Parallels drawn between the *Grundrisse* and the *Logic* remain a major factor in how present-day writers think about the relation between *Capital* and the *Logic*, so this remains a current and relevant topic. However, the *Grundrisse* does raise the question of the extent to which an author's early work is a better guide to understanding the author's intentions rather than their mature work.

Parallels between the *Grundrisse* and the *Logic* are largely based on philological connections, that is to say, similar words and expressions which appear in both works. The most far-reaching case of this claim is that made by Mark Meaney who claims to find more than 200 philological connections linking the entire span of the *Science of Logic* from The One (near the beginning of the *Logic*) up to Life (effectively the final chapter of the *Logic*), to the *Grundrisse* beginning from after the Introduction to the end of the manuscript.

Now, you can believe this or not, but what is the significance of this parallelism if it is true? Within a couple of months of completing the *Grundrisse*, Marx began writing the *Contribution to the Critique of Political Economy*. This manuscript begins with "The Commodity," clearly anticipating the final structure of *Capital* and completely different from the structure of the *Grundrisse* which began with "The Chapter on Money."

Perhaps Marx was engaged in some exercise, using a reading of the *Science of Logic* to stimulate reflections on political economy or exploring arguments from the *Logic* which he could use? In any case, he did not decide, on the basis of this exercise, to continue with crafting the published versions of his political economy as "mirrors" of the *Logic*. After reading the efforts of others to show that *Capital* was a "reflection" of one or another section of the *Logic*, and the *diversity* of such claims amongst themselves, I have become inclined to treat such claims with considerable scepticism.

What had been demonstrated by those who studied the *Grundrisse*, however, was that Marx had indeed put Hegel to use in his study of political economy, just as he had put Hegel to use as a youth in his study of ancient Greek natural philosophy and in his last years in his study of the Calculus. But the question remained open: how much and *how* did Marx use Hegel in writing *Capital*?

Chapter 2 deals with Geert Reuten's effort to "update" *Capital* so that it would be adequate to capitalism as it is found today in the OECD countries. In itself this is a very interesting project and much of what Reuten has to say retains its validity even though his claim to take Hegel and Marx as his teachers is based on misconceptions. But the effort of extracting the methodological principles from *Capital* and the *Logic*, and then applying these principles to what is effectively a new problem, is exactly what I want to be able to do.

The study of Reuten's work gave me an important opportunity to examine the question of what these principles are and how one could go about using them, in the context of an overview of issues in present-day political economy. Reuten went to the opposite extreme from Meaney in basing himself on methodological principles he claims come from Marx and Hegel, and applying them in a new context, rather than simply following philological connections without having to justify each claim logically or scientifically. Reuten was prepared to depart from Marx in the word in order to be true to Marx in the method.

Reuten's work raises the question of structuralism versus historicism. That is, what role, if any, does the study of the past history of a social formation play in understanding its political-economic structure? Does it matter where some law or custom came from, or is it only the role it plays in supporting the existing structure which is important? In recent decades we have witnessed Althusser's Structuralism and American Functionalism give way to Post-Structuralism and "Third Way" theories. Why are we seeing a resurgence of anti-historicism in this debate in the new millennium?

Chapter 3 deals with three claims that *Capital* "mirrors" one of the books of the *Logic*. The first group sees *Capital* as reflecting the Essence Logic, the second group sees the early chapters of *Capital* as reflective of the Logic of Being, the second rejects such homologies and sees the influence of Hegel in matters of detail.

I will presently provide some explanation of the structure of the *Logic*, but for now I will put it simply like this:

– The Logic of Being is first Book of the *Logic*, and its chapters are Quality, Quantity and Measure – all the concepts arising in a quantitative analysis of a phenomenon.
– The second Book of the *Logic* is the Essence Logic. Its chapters are Reflection, Appearance and Actuality and it deals with all the concepts required for building a theory of a phenomenon based on existing theories and new data given in the form of Measure. Being and Essence together constitute the genesis of the Concept, and
– The third Book of the *Logic* is the Concept Logic which represents the development of a concrete concept, or science of the phenomenon, the unity of Being and Essence. Its chapters are Subject, Object and the Idea. The first chapter of the Concept Logic, the Subject, has three moments: Universal, Particular and Individual.

Tony Smith is the most influential and well-known advocate of the position that *Capital* exhibits the Essence Logic, but Smith has cited Arash Abazari to support this claim so I will deal with Abazari first. The feature of the Essence Logic which these writers find most significant is what I will call the Form-Content relation. In this discourse, it is more common to refer to the Appearance-Essence relation, but there is no such relation in Hegel's Essence

Logic. But in any case, the Essence Logic certainly is characterised by pairs of concepts which all reference the idea of looking behind what is immediately given, from Form to Content, from Effect to Cause, etc.

Thus these writers see *Capital* as describing the logical genesis of capital from the commodity, through money, to capital as such. Smith recognises that Marx himself saw capital as a Subject, but Smith believes that Marx was mistaken in this belief, and that *Capital* more closely resembles the Essence Logic. Thus Smith takes a position different from those writers who believe that when Marx wrote the *Grundrisse* he was self-consciously mirroring the *Logic*. The claim was no longer that Marx was *self-conscious* in his use of Hegel's *Logic*.

The second group is best represented by the work of Chris Arthur. Arthur claims a very close alignment between the first three or four chapters of *Capital* with a selected series of concepts in the *Logic* from Determinate Being, very near the beginning of the Logic of Being, through the Essence Logic, up to the first concept of the Concept Logic. Arthur sees Marx's elaboration of value in the first Chapter of *Capital* as reflecting the concepts in the Logic of Being, except that Arthur thinks that Hegel was wrong to include Measure under Being. According to Arthur, value is the essence of a commodity and the emergence of money described in *Capital* reflects the Essence Logic.

The links to the Logic of Being seem plausible because it is easy to see that the objective social process in which every product of human labour assigns itself a monetary value is what could be called "practical abstraction." Material products seem to be doing arithmetical operations autonomously. The Logic of Being is where Hegel derives all the concepts of quantitative analysis and it is very easy to see these same categories in the early pages of *Capital*. On the other hand, Arthur does not claim that this parallel extends beyond the scope of the first few chapters of Volume 1 of *Capital*. If the first 3 chapters of *Capital* are indeed reflecting the Logic of Being and Essence, this still leaves the rest of *Capital* to be explained some other way. At this point, we haven't even arrived at surplus value and wage labour. Capital isn't even mentioned until Chapter 4. Arthur offers little guide as to how the *Logic* is reflected in the remaining 114 chapters of *Capital*.

Chapter 4 is devoted to the work of Fred Moseley, who sees *Capital* as reflecting the first chapter of the Concept Logic, the Subject, with its three moments: Universal, Particular and Individual. Moseley claims that Volume 1 of *Capital* corresponds to the Universal moment of capital, the first section of the Subject in the *Logic*, and that Volume 3 of *Capital* introduces the Particular moment, the second moment of the Subject. This captures the fact that in Volume 1 Marx determines the total sum of surplus value in an economy extracted from the working class, and in Volume 3 Marx shows how this value is shared between capitalist companies in proportion to their capital value. This takes place through the equalisation of the rate of profit, overlaying the principle of the equal worth of all human labour which characterises Volume 1.

I endorse Moseley's claim so far as it goes. Moseley does not lay claim to a familiarity with Hegel's *Logic*, but Moseley does give us an insight into Marx's meticulously logical analysis, the failure to understand which has produced the debate about the "transformation problem." I intend to go further than Moseley in tracing the Hegelian roots of *Capital*, however.

In summarising this section, I will review what has been determined through this examination of current discourse on Marx's *Capital* and Hegel's *Logic*, and try to get to the roots of how this topic has been so misunderstood.

I agree with Roberto Fineschi when he said:

> In spite of this similarity ... I do not think we have to look for analogies or homologies between Marx's theory of capital and Hegel's logic; ... a very non-dialectical attitude ... which Marx himself criticised
>
> 2014, p. 140

> My starting point is the assumption that Hegel's legacy in Marx is methodological; ... [Marx] is faithful to its fundamental principle: the unfolding of the matter itself.
>
> 2014, p. 141

The matter itself is political economy, not logic.

In Chapter 5 I will examine two figures from Soviet times: the philosopher Evald Ilyenkov and the psychologist Lev Vygotsky. Their work convincingly points to how Marx used Hegel's *Logic* in *Capital* while ensuring that the *content* of the concepts of *Capital* is political economy, not logic.

The essential point here is that in the penultimate chapter of the *Logic*, entitled The Idea of Cognition, and in particular the section entitled "The Idea of the True," Hegel explained how the principles of the *Logic* should be used in the natural and social sciences, different to the way the *Logic* itself was structured. The *Logic* had to be presuppositionless. That is, Hegel had to choose as its starting point an "empty concept" so that no positive content would be imported unacknowledged into logic and therefore into philosophy as a whole. This is not the case with any of the positive sciences, each of which begins with some simple fact or problem which must be explained.

This simple, distinctive fact constitutes the Individual moment of a concrete concept of reality otherwise composed of only Universals and Particulars. The *Logic* describes how the perception of this unique Individual moment brings about the reconstruction of the concrete concept of reality with the simple something making the starting point of the process and the source of content.

Everything comes down to the starting point of a science, the point at which the content of the science is apprehended.

The first writer I deal with in Chapter 5 is Evald Ilyenkov, an opposition Soviet philosopher, who wrote a number of important books in the 1960s which were published posthumously in the West in the 1980s. In particular, I focus on *The Dialectics of the Abstract and Concrete in Marx's Capital* (1960/1982). Ilyenkov was part of a line of Soviet thinkers which was initiated by the Soviet psychologist, Lev Vygotsky.

Vygotsky founded a current of Psychology methodologically based on his reading of Marx's *Capital*. Vygotsky's knowledge of Hegel was secondhand and in his short career he never studied Hegel personally, but his close reading of *Capital* enabled him to grasp the methodological principle which, I believe, Marx adopted from Hegel. Vygotsky was able to apply this principle to as many as five different fields of Psychology, leaving us very clear directions as to the fruitfulness of Hegel's ideas as applied by Marx in *Capital*. Vygotsky's Psychology remains very influential across the globe to this day.

Because this book takes the form of a series of "book reviews", there will necessarily be repetition as the same issue will arise with more than one writer. I have not tried to limit this because the repetition gives me the opportunity to emphasise important themes.

Acknowledgements

In particular I wish to acknowledge the encouragement given to me in this exercise by Tony Smith, despite the fact that Tony knew well that what I would write would be critical of his own position on this topic. In addition, I remain indebted to him for the work he did in compiling and editing with Fred Moseley the Volume, *Marx's Capital and Hegel's Logic*, Brill 2014. I also thank Fred Moseley for his useful inputs in a series of private email exchanges. Likewise, I appreciate a short exchange of messages with Terrell Carver.

I also wish to thank Brill for having published a number of contributions in this discourse and in some instances made the manuscripts available for free download on the internet. I thank in particular my series editor, David Fasenfest, who helped me work through how to present this work, eventually offering me the opportunity to spread the work across two separate volumes.

In this volume I restrict myself to critically reviewing the existing literature on the relation between Marx's *Capital* and Hegel's *Logic*. In a second volume I will simply set out my own reading of *Capital* and its roots in Hegel's *Logic*.

Tables

The *Grundrisse/Logic* Debate

1   Lenin's Annotations on Hegel's *Logic*

Present-day images of Lenin as the imperious revolutionary leader some-what jar with the fact that it is *Lenin* who is responsible for twentieth century Marxists taking a serious interest in Hegelian philosophy. True, Lenin's own teacher, Plekhanov, was also a student of Hegel, but Plekhanov had continued to convey the impression, already created by Engels, that Hegel was impor-tant as a historical figure, but that Marx had thoroughly surpassed Hegel and serious Marxists did not need to pay too much attention to Hegel. If it was just Lenin's published speaking and writing then this impression would not have changed significantly. However, while in exile in 1914 in Bern, Switzerland, Lenin had closely studied both the *Shorter Logic* and the *Science of Logic*, and in 1929 his annotations on Hegel's *Logic* were published in Moscow, and these had a significant impact on the Russian Marxists.

In particular, while reading the first section of the Concept *Logic*, the Subject, Lenin wrote in his annotations:

> *Aphorism*: It is impossible completely to understand Marx's *Capital*, and especially its first chapter, without having thoroughly studied and under-stood the whole of Hegel's *Logic*. Consequently, half a century later none of the Marxists understood Marx!!
>
> LENIN, *CW, v. 38*, p. 180

His annotations also show that while he skipped over many of the passages in the *Science of Logic* on the Concept Logic, he did read closely the section enti-tled "The Idea of the True," and it is *this* section which is most important in the project of appropriating Hegel's *Logic* for the practice of natural and social sci-ence. However, this section is entirely ignored in the present-day *Capital/Logic* debate.

What effect did the revelation of Lenin's advice have on Marxists in Russia? For the most part, the debate over "dialectics" in Russia remained at an extremely primitive level, to be honest. This was true even among the support-ers of Abram Deborin, leader of the "Dialecticians" faction in its debate with the "Mechanists" and editor of the important theoretical journal, *Under the Banner of Marxism*, at the time when Lenin's annotations were published.

But one person who *did* study Lenin's annotations at the time and did take them seriously was the Soviet Psychologist, Lev Vygotsky. There are six references to Lenin's annotations on Hegel's *Logic* between 1929 and 1934 to be found in Vygotsky's six-volume *Collected Works*. In particular, Vygotsky indicated what he had taken from Lenin's advice with his own aphorism:

> In order to create such intermediate theories – methodologies, general sciences – we must reveal the *essence* of the given area of phenomena, the laws of their change, their qualitative and quantitative characteristics, their causality, we must create categories and concepts appropriate to it, in short, we must create our *own Das Kapital*.
>
> It suffices to imagine Marx operating with the general principles and categories of dialectics, like quantity-quality, the triad, the universal connection, the knot [of contradictions], leap etc. – without the abstract and historical categories of value, class, commodity, capital, interest, production forces, base, superstructure etc. to see the whole monstrous absurdity of the assumption that it is possible to create any Marxist science while by-passing by *Das Kapital*. *Psychology is in need of its own Das Kapital.*
>
> VYGOTSKY, 1927/1997; my emphasis

and referring to Marx's reference to the commodity as an "economic cell-form" in the Preface to the First German Edition of *Capital*, he goes on:

> Marx says essentially the same when he compares abstraction with a microscope and chemical reactions in the natural sciences. The whole of *Das Kapital* is written according to this method. Marx analyses the "cell" of bourgeois society – the commodity form of value – and shows that a mature body can be more easily studied than a cell. He discerns the structure of the whole social order and all economical formations in this cell. He says that "to the uninitiated its analysis may seem the hair-splitting of details. We are indeed dealing with details, but such details as microscopic anatomy is also dealing with" [1867, Preface]. He who can decipher the meaning of the cell of psychology, the mechanism of one reaction, has found the key to all psychology.

By the time of his early death in 1934, Vygotsky had completed the work which was posthumously published as *Thinking and Speech*, a study of the development of the intellect, his most well-known and influential work. But this was only one of several paradigmatic works *based on this principle* – the principle which he learnt from Hegel, via Marx's *Capital*, thanks to Lenin's advice, and applied to the foundations of Psychology.

I am not sufficiently familiar with the other Marxists of that period, but, for example, I.I. Rubin (1886–1937) wrote in his *Essays on Marx's Theory of Value*:

> This is the basic characteristic of the commodity economy, of its "cell structure," so to speak. The theory of value examines the process of formation of the productive unity called a social economy from separate, one might say independent, cells. It is not without reason that Marx wrote, in the preface to the first edition of the first volume of *Capital*, that the "commodity form of the product of labour or the form of value of the commodity is the form of the economic cell of bourgeois society." This cell structure of the commodity society represents, in itself, the totality of equal, formally independent, private economic units.
>
> RUBIN, 1972/1928, Ch. 17

It was this specific view of the methodology of *Capital* which was still advocated by Vygotsky's successor in philosophy, Evald Ilyenkov, in 1960, and by the British Trotskyists who were my early teachers on the interpretation of Marx's *Capital* in the 1980s. One did not need to know that the "analysis by units" approach to science came from Hegel because Marx was explicit about using this method in the Preface to *Capital*. However, knowing that this idea has its roots in Hegel – an insight for which we have Lenin to thank, Marx never having said so himself – makes it more likely that the method can be correctly and consistently understood and explained. It is only in the *Logic*, specifically the section of the *Science of Logic* entitled "The Idea of the True," that this idea is explained in full, albeit in almost impenetrable style.

However, this insight has played no part in the present-day debate about the connection between *Capital* and the *Logic*, so for the first four parts of this volume, I will have little more to say of it. I will return to this approach in Chapter 5. The topic before us now is the *present-day Capital/Logic* debate. We must begin, however, with the debate about the relation of the *Grundrisse* to Hegel's *Logic*.

2   Publication of the *Grundrisse*

The young Karl Marx completed his PhD on Epicurus's philosophy of nature in 1841 and became increasingly involved in radical political circles, including the Young Hegelians and a variety of utopian socialists, anarchists and communist insurrectionists in Paris. As a radical journalist he railed against censorship, autocracy and inequality in the peculiarly philosophical style of political rhetoric which young German radicals favoured at that time. In 1859, reflecting back on those times, he wrote:

> When [in 1843,] the publishers of the *Rheinische Zeitung* conceived the illusion that by a more compliant policy on the part of the paper it might be possible to secure the abrogation of the death sentence passed upon it, I eagerly grasped the opportunity to withdraw from the public stage to my study.
>
> The first work which I undertook to dispel the doubts assailing me was a critical re-examination of Hegel's *Philosophy of Right*; the introduction to this work being published in the *Deutsch-Französischen Jahrbücher* issued in Paris in 1844. My inquiry led me to the conclusion that neither legal relations nor political forms could be comprehended whether by themselves or on the basis of a so-called general development of the human mind, but that on the contrary they originate in the material conditions of life, the totality of which Hegel, following the example of English and French thinkers of the eighteenth century, embraces within the term "civil society" (*Bürgergesellschaft*, bourgeois society); that the anatomy of this civil society, however, has to be sought in *political economy*.
>
> The study of this, which I began in Paris, I continued in Brussels, where I moved owing to an expulsion order issued by M. Guizot.
>
> MARX, 1859, Preface

Marx was deeply involved in the revolutionary wave which swept over Europe in 1848, publishing the *Communist Manifesto* and his agitational newspaper, the *Neue Rheinische Zeitung* daily, sometimes even twice in one day, until the paper was finally banned in May 1849. By November 1849 Marx had fled to Britain with his family. In Britain, Marx felt isolated in an exile community which in any case he largely held in contempt. Cut off from the opportunity and necessity for political agitation, in May of 1850 Marx began writing, reflecting on the intense political experiences of the 1840s, but this work was disrupted by involvement in political affairs, journalism and family tragedies. It was the outbreak of a worldwide economic crisis in the spring of 1857 that finally impelled Marx to immerse himself in his political economic studies, beginning in August 1857. The authoritative *Marx-Engels Gesamtausgabe* (*MEGA*) includes 16 volumes of his political-economic writings and three volumes of letters between 1857 and 1867, culminating in the publication of *Capital*. This was an immense effort and one from which Marx suffered physically.

The first part of this series of manuscripts became known as the *Grundrisse* or "Foundations." It was first published in full in Moscow in 1939, but is particularly well-known and studied thanks to its translation into English by Martin Nicolaus, published by Penguin in 1973. The other well-known precursor to *Capital* was entitled *Contribution to the Critique of Political Economy*. It was published in Berlin in 1859 so it has been well-known from the beginning. The *Contribution* was the first published outcome of Marx's economic studies and already exhibited the basic structure which would later appear in the early chapters of Volume 1 of *Capital* when it was published in German in 1867.

The *Grundrisse*, on the other hand, was not immediately recognisable as an early draft of *Capital*, though it has since been described as just that: "the first draft of *Capital*." In 1973, thanks to Nicolaus's excellent translation, the publishing power of Penguin and the reach of an English translation at a moment when Marxism was reaching new audiences, the *Grundrisse* had a big impact.

There was one feature of the *Grundrisse* which was to attract particular attention. According to Louis Althusser, Marx had undergone an "epistemological break" separating his "humanist" writings of the 1840s from his "scientific" writings in *Capital* and its 1859 precursor. This was alleged to reflect Marx putting behind him his youthful interest in Hegelian Philosophy. Whether or not you subscribed to Althusser's views, this did express a widespread if tacit opinion along the same lines among Marxists broadly. The *Grundrisse* however was riddled with references to Hegel's *Logic* which the translator had noted. If this was the "first draft of *Capital*," how could this be? Lenin's more or less forgotten aphorism received renewed attention and there was a surge of interest in discovering *how* Marx was using Hegel in the *Grundrisse*. As it happens, the 1981 publication of Marx's *Mathematical Manuscripts* from 1881 (two years before Marx's death), established that Marx's inclination to turn to Hegel as the starting point for approaching any new project was a life-long habit.

In a letter to Engels in January 1858, first published as long ago as 1913, written whilst in the midst of penning the *Grundrisse* manuscripts, Marx confirmed his use of Hegel and opened new questions:

> I am, by the way, discovering some nice arguments. E.g. I have completely demolished the theory of profit as hitherto propounded. What was of great use to me as regards *method* of treatment was Hegel's *Logic* at which I had taken another look by mere accident, Freiligrath having found and made me a present of several volumes of Hegel, originally the property

of Bakunin. If ever the time comes when such work is again possible, I should very much like to write two or three sheets making accessible to the common reader the *rational* aspect of the method which Hegel not only discovered but also mystified.

MARX to ENGELS, 16 January 1858, *MECW v.* 40, p. 249

Research has confirmed that it is was indeed a copy of Hegel's *Science of Logic* to which Marx was referring. As a Young Hegelian from the 1840s who had already, even in his study of Epicurus, been engaged in criticising Hegel, there can be no doubt that Marx was already a Hegel aficionado. What was it in the *Logic* which was "of great use" to Marx in working out his theory of profit?

Other clues to how Marx used Hegel would have to be divined from a study of his commentary and references to Hegel's *Logic* in the *Grundrisse*, because by the time of the 1859 *Contribution*, explicit references to Hegel had been expunged from the text. You would have to know your Hegel well to recognise the Hegelian influence on *Capital* without these explicit references which, however, could still be noted in the so-called "first draft of *Capital*."

3   The Multiple Drafts of *Capital*

According to Fred Moseley (who makes no claim to be a Hegel scholar, but is a meticulous and observant Marx scholar) has identified six drafts or partial drafts of *Capital* in the Manuscripts of the 1850s and 1860s. Like everyone else, Moseley sees the *Grundrisse* as the first draft. However, in February 1858, immediately upon finishing the *Grundrisse*, Marx prepared a manuscript which was published in 1859 as the *Contribution to the Critique of Political Economy*. Unlike the *Grundrisse*, the *Contribution* is notable by making its beginning from the commodity. The *second* draft of *Capital* according to Moseley was the *Manuscript of 1861–63* (an enormous manuscript of 23 notebooks). The Manuscript of 1864–65 is the third draft of all three Volumes of *Capital*, and the final draft of Volume 1 was published in 1867. In addition, the Manuscripts contain multiple plans and drafts of separate chapters, parts and volumes of *Capital* during this period.

The manuscript of 1861–63 even contained an outline of Volume 3 with the "price of production" theory of the price of products under capitalism which is absent from the *Grundrisse*.

I note also that in the *Grundrisse*, Marx never settled on what is meant by an "individual capital." At one point, Marx refers in passing to an individual enterprise, while at another point Marx interprets the individual capital as a single share. Particular capital Marx connected at this time with fixed or circulating capital. A *different* take on the Particular moment of the Concept, which Moseley believes to be the basis of Volume 3 of *Capital*, is based on markets for different products which are more or less labour intensive.

Moseley has drawn my attention to the section in the *Grundrisse* (p. 275) where Marx tries to render the "three moments of the Subject" from Hegel's Concept Logic in economic terms, by means of nested triads. Nowhere does Hegel use nested U-P-I triads, but Marx had in mind that if each of the moments of the concept of capital is itself a concept, then each moment could be represented again with the same three moments. In this excerpt from the *Grundrisse*, the Individual capital is to be analysed as "capital and profit, capital and interest, and capital as value" (three ways in which capital generates wealth) and in addition he takes individual capital as "Capital as credit, capital as stock, and capital as money market" (three forms of existence of capital). This is, to me, evidence that Marx was *exploring* possible relations between capital and Hegel's *Logic* in the *Grundrisse*; he did not start this exercise with this relation already worked out. Logic is logic, not economic relations; it is not at all obvious *how* to *use* the Logic here.

My point here is only that giving the *Grundrisse* the status of a "first draft" of *Capital*, despite the *Grundrisse* making its beginning from consideration of the three moments of Production, Distribution and Exchange rather than the Commodity Form. Further, lacking the "production price theory" of prices elaborated in Volume 3 of *Capital* indicates that *essential ideas* of *Capital* were lacking in the *Grundrisse*, I don't believe that "first draft" is an appropriate characterisation of what the *Grundrisse* is. It lacks *essential* aspects and the structure of Marx's mature theory.

A final preparatory note. One thing which all the commentators discussed here are in agreement on is that Marx treated commodities, their circulation in the market, money, capital and credit all as *forms of value*. Both *Capital* and the *Grundrisse* are about value and its forms. This theme is rightly *common ground* in all the studies of Marx's economic work to follow.

4   Hegel References in the *Grundrisse*

In his 1973 translation, Nicolaus noted frequent references to Hegel, which he interpreted as Marx "showing signs of humanism and the influence of Hegelian dialectic method." He noted about ten allusions to Hegel, mostly to the *Science of Logic*, in his editorial notes.

In his 1976 article "The Logic of Marx's Capital," the Hegel scholar Richard Winfield claimed that the *Grundrisse* and *Capital* "complete the critique of political economy originally outlined by Hegel in his discussion of the 'System of Needs' in the *Philosophy of Right*," though Winfield did not at this time publish an extended study of the *Grundrisse*.

In *The Making of Marx's Capital*, first published in 1977, Roman Rosdolsky described the *Grundrisse* as making "massive reference" to Hegel's *Science of Logic*, and this claim spurred others to identify and interpret these references.

The Marx scholar Terrell Carver took issue with the enthusiasm this project engendered, but I will come back to Carver's comments later. In any case, what followed from these observations were concerted efforts to "map" the linkages of the *Grundrisse* to the *Logic*. In order to make sense of the discussion which follows it is essential that the reader be familiar with the structure of the *Grundrisse* and the *Logic*; I have provided the structure of each in the table below. "Structure" is probably too grand a word for the *Grundrisse*, but the *Science of Logic* may be the most structured work of literature ever published. Everything Hegel says must be taken in the context of *where* in the Logic it is uttered. In the table, there is absolutely no suggestion of correspondence between the two columns. The two outlines are placed side-by-side only for convenience.

5 Hiroshi Uchida's Analysis of *Grundrisse* and *Logic*

5.1 *Introduction*

In 1988 Hiroshi Uchida published "*Marx's Grundrisse and Hegel's Logic*," which first argued the claim that the *Grundrisse* "mirrored" the *Logic* comprehensively and systematically. I will do my best to outline the correspondences that Uchida claimed to unearth, but this will unavoidably be somewhat confusing. Refer to the table of contents for the *Grundrisse* and the *Logic* below.

Hiroshi Uchida's commentary was published in 1988, but commentaries on the *Grundrisse* had been published by Japanese Marxists as early as 1974. Uchida was not only a scholar of Marx's political economic writing, but also a scholar of Hegel and Aristotle. In the *Grundrisse*, according to Uchida, Marx was criticising the Political Economists by means of a critique of Hegel because "Hegel adopts the standpoint of modern political economy" (Marx, 1844). Further, Uchida shared with Hegel and Marx an admiration for Aristotle, but according to Uchida, Marx accused Hegel of deforming Aristotle (1988, p. 4), while Marx used Aristotle against Hegel particularly in order to develop his own philosophical materialism.

TABLE 1   Structure of the *Grundrisse* and Hegel's *Logic*

Outline of the *Grundrisse*	Outline of *Science of Logic*
Introduction	**Introduction** (*Where to begin?*)
Production in general	**BEING (Quality)**
Production, distribution,	1. Determinateness (Being, Nothing,
exchange and consumption	Becoming, Something)
Method of Political Economy	2. Determinate Being
Forces and Relations of	3. Being-for-Self, the One
Production	**Quantity**
	Measure
	Transition to Essence
Chapter on Money	**ESSENCE**
	1. Reflection (Identity, Difference, Diversity,
Chapter on Capital	Opposition, Contradiction, Ground)
Section 1. Production Process	2. Determinate Being
of Capital	3. Being-for-Self
Surplus Value and Profit	**Appearance**
	Form and Content
Section 2. Circulation Process	**Actuality**
of Capital	Cause and Effect
Surplus Value becomes capital	Possibility and Necessity
	Reciprocity
Original accum'n of capital	**CONCEPT**
Theories of Surplus Value	**Subject**
	Univ'l, Part'r. & Indiv'l.
Miscellaneous	Judgments
Value	Syllogisms
Bastiat and Carey	**Object**
	Mechanism
	Chemism
	Organism
	The Idea
	Life
	The Idea of Cognition
	The Absolute Idea

As Uchida tells it, however, in the course of criticising Hegel, Marx appropriates much of Hegel's *Logic*. In particular, Marx learns from Hegel how capital
reproduces the presuppositions for its own existence, and in that specific sense
is an organic system. However, Marx's central aim is to show how Hegel (and
the Political Economists) obscures the *historical* origins of the conditions of
existence of capitalism and the limits on its development. *When cast in terms
of logical categories, the social relations of capital appear for Hegel to be natural and eternal realities of human life.* In fact, they are products of past history
and are sowing the seeds of their own extinction. This is summed up in Marx's
logico-historical method. What later appears as the "tendency of the rate of
profit to fall" appears in the *Grundrisse* in a form anticipating the theme of
"expropriation of the expropriators" and the preparation of the conditions for
Socialism.

In the *Grundrisse*, then, Marx's debt to Hegel is quite explicit, whereas in the
later economic manuscripts references to Hegel are much reduced, evidently
for the purpose of making the economic critique more accessible. Uchida
takes the reader through large swathes of the *Grundrisse* seeking to show
paragraph-by-paragraph the textual links to the *Shorter Logic*.

According to Uchida:

> [Marx's] task in the *Grundrisse* therefore consists in demonstrating that
> the genesis of value and its development into capital are described in
> the *Logic*, albeit in a seemingly closed system which reproduces itself,
> and overall [Marx's] work is directed towards transcending capitalism in
> practice.

and

> the *Logic* is the most abstract philosophical expression of the bourgeois
> spirit or consciousness of value. This consciousness of value forms the
> basic economic relation of bourgeois society.
>
>   1988, p. 4

Uchida observes Marx tracing the development of value through the *Grundrisse*,
from product, to commodity, to money in its successive guises as measure of
value, means of exchange and hoard to merchant capital and industrial capital
and gets as far as "constant" and "variable" capital, taken to be the *particular*
forms of capital – and finally the abolition of capital by the transformation of
capital into a single planned economy.

What is intriguing in Uchida's retracing of the path of value from product to industrial capital is how the forms of value are mapped against the three books of the *Logic*. The various transitions are not neatly located in separate books of the *Logic*, however, contrary to what is suggested by the titles of Uchida's chapters.

5.2   *The Chapter on Money*

Chapter 1 of Uchida's book is entitled "Doctrine of the Concept," and deals with the Introduction to the *Grundrisse* and, according to Uchida, Hegel's "Doctrine of the Concept." The next chapter in the *Grundrisse* is Chapter 2 on Money and, according to Uchida, Hegel's "Doctrine of Being." This is followed in the *Grundrisse* by the extensive "Chapter on Capital" which Uchida deals with in his third chapter subtitled "Doctrine of Essence."

We could briefly illustrates Uchida's mapping as follows:

TABLE 2   Uchid's mapping of the *Grundrisse* on the *Logic*

Uchida	Grundrisse	Logic
Chapter 1	Introduction	CONCEPT
Chapter 2	Money	BEING
Chapter 3	Capital	ESSENCE

That is, according to the *titles* Uchida assigns to his chapters. But when we look at the *content* of each chapter, the material Uchida places under each chapter heading does not match the location in Hegel's *Logic* suggested by the chapter heading.

I will deal with Hegel's advice on *where to begin* last. These are questions Hegel raises in an Introduction to the *Science of Logic*, but only answers in the last passages of the *Logic*, "The Idea of the True," devoted to a discussion of the method of the *Logic* and its application to the sciences, even though both Uchida and Marx deal with these questions first. Otherwise, I will follow Uchida's sequence.

The first section heading in Uchida's Chapter 2 on "Money and Being," reads "Product, commodity and money, and 'identity, difference, opposition and contradiction.'" However, "Identity, Difference, Opposition and Contradiction" are the "Moments of Reflection" in the *Logic*, concluding with "Ground". These are the first moments of the first chapter of the Doctrine of Essence, Reflection, and are very much *not* part of the Logic of Being. In fact, the moments of Reflection are the analytical moments of Essence and set out the form of movement which is characteristic of the whole of the Essence Logic.

Hegel's chapter on Reflection is concluded with the pair Form-and-Matter, laying the basis for the second chapter, Appearance, and the third chapter, Actuality, each of which are marked by *pairs* of concepts respectively Content-and-Form, and Cause-and-Effect. The moments of Reflection are the *analytical* moments of the Doctrine of Essence, just as 'Being, Nothing, Becoming, Determinate Being and the One' are the analytical moments of the Doctrine of Being. But Uchida says that the Moments of Reflection are the "transition from being to essence" (1988, p. 31). But there is a section Hegel entitled "Transition into Essence" in the *Science of Logic* and it is *not this*. Reflection definitely falls under Essence. Being is *immediate*, and Reflection is *relative*.

The form of movement we see in Reflection is where one concept pushes another to the side and overtakes it, so to speak, but rather than extinguishing the former, it includes it. Eventually, the resulting contradictions are resolved into Ground, which proves to be only a deeper contradiction, and the movement displayed in Reflection gives way to a succession of *pairs* of concepts, each in turn pushing the other into the background. In Appearance, the middle chapter of Essence, the pair is form-and-content *explicitly understood to be a contradiction*, entailing a succession of forms being endlessly overtaken by their content, each constituting a new form. The third and final chapter of Essence, Actuality, is similar in structure inasmuch as when Ground is shown to be an Effect, it is disclosed in turn as a Cause with new effects, again in an endless series of cause-and-effect which never gets to the bottom of matters, a "bad infinity." This bad infinity is characteristic of the Logic of Essence. Essence ever fails to grasp the totality.

As Uchida continues examining this chapter of the *Grundrisse*, he continues to reflect on the Moments of Reflection (even though he claims to be linking the text in the *Grundrisse* to the Logic of Being!) and cites a further link to the same section at the beginning of the Essence Logic. After five pages, Uchida does move back to the early moments of Being with the transition to Quantity, in which he makes a plausible logical link between Marx's use value and exchange-value and Hegel's Determinate Being and Being-for-itself, but no evidence of an actual textual link. In Uchida's narrative, Marx continues to talk about money as the substance of exchange-value, and then refers again to "contradiction." Indeed, Hegel speaks here of "contradiction," but only the "contradiction" entailed in the *limit* implied in singling out one determinate being from another. Hegel's next mention of "contradiction" is extensive and repeated and is found in the Moments of Reflection in the Logic of Essence, and it is here that Uchida should rather have been connecting to the contradiction arising with the reflection of the exchange value of a commodity in money, another particular commodity. There *are* grounds, however, to say that Marx was here inspired by the Chapter on Measure. Uchida continues for some time along the same theme until citing Hegel again, this time in The Idea, the last chapter of the Doctrine of the Concept. Uchida now devotes himself to Marx's comments on Substance, one of the last phases of Essence before the leap to the Concept.

Uchida then covers "Price and Quantum." Quantum is indeed a category of Quantity in the Doctrine of Being, along with a number of other categories dealt with by Hegel in that same chapter, and Uchida cites the relevant passages. "One and the Many" dealt with next is indeed under Hegel's "Being-for-Self." After several pages still plausibly connected to Being, Marx returns (apparently) to the Moments of Reflection under Essence. Later there are references to the *Phenomenology* (a Preface to the *Science of Logic*), before citing Marx on Substance (part of Actuality) and The Idea (the final chapter of the *Logic*).

And so on. For the remainder of this chapter, Uchida finds cause to cite a couple of paragraphs near the end of the Doctrine of Being, but even more from the chapter on Reflection in the Essence Logic.

It is indeed hard to talk about the quantification of commodities as values, or the transformation of value into money, without finding some relevant quotes from the Logic of Being, especially Measure, the last chapter of the Logic of Being. However, the transformation of value from product to commodity to money is also clearly relevant to Essence, and Reflection in particular. Assuming that Marx was indeed inspired by the Hegel passages Uchida points out, insofar as Marx was talking about money, what we see is that Marx was mostly interested in Reflection. The Doctrine of Being nonetheless would have attracted Marx's attention in relation to the emergence of money as a measure of the value of commodities, Measure being the final chapter of the Doctrine of Being. But from Uchida's examination, it seems that in his work on money, Marx took inspiration from *every section* of the *Logic and* the *Phenomenology*. I see no basis in what Uchida has written for the Chapter heading linking Money to Being. The first form of value is the "commodity" itself, but Measure (such as "= 5 yards of linen"), the last chapter of Being, is not yet money. Measure generates the contradictions which then give rise to Reflection and the successive changes in the Form of Value. When we say: "5 yards of linen = 2 pounds" that is equally linkable to Measure or Reflection. Take your pick.

The reason for making these admittedly rather tedious points is that in recent times the question of *which* section of *Capital* reflects *which* section of the *Logic* has become the central matter of dispute. From the *actual evidence*

Uchida provides, if the Chapter on Money "corresponds to" any section of the *Logic* at all, it is Reflection, not Being. As money changes from a measure of value to a means of circulation to commercial capital to industrial capital, without abolishing the previous form of value, this is classic Reflection in Hegelian terms. But Uchida's claim is that the section on Money reflects not Essence but Being.

5.3   *The Chapter on Capital*

Chapter 3 of Uchida's book is titled "The Chapter on Capital and the Doctrine of Essence," but the title is immediately followed by the subheading: "Part One. The Generality[1] of Capital." A later subheading refers to "Substance," and "Relation of Substantiality" explicitly referencing the second and third chapters of Essence. About halfway through the Chapter there is another subheading "Component Parts of Capital and 'the whole and the parts'", and then "Force and its Manifestation". All the Hegel quotes confirm this connection. But after the subheading about "Force" (from the Essence Logic) we see Marx taking up the Particularisation of capital, which in the *Grundrisse* is based on what later became "variable" and "constant" capital (referencing the Concept Logic), and "surplus capital" enters the narrative along with primitive accumulation. Uchida continues to connect Marx's concerns about the forms of capital and cites sections mainly from the Essence Logic (Actuality as Cause-and-Effect and Substance). Thus, he says, Marx's "critique of political economy is the genesis of the two 'forms', value and capital" (p. 93).

And Uchida comments:

> In economic relations, according to Marx, results or effects turn into presuppositions or causes. His model of an organic system of circular self-reproduction depends on Hegel's account of 'causality'.
>
> 1988, p. 99

However, Uchida does not see that capital's systematic reproduction of its own presuppositions is what is characteristic of an *organism*, and it is the Doctrine of the *Concept* which represents the logic of an organic *system*, in the Subject and in its transition from Subject and Object to the Idea. This crucial idea about

---

1   The same German word, *Allgemeine*, may be translated as "general" or "universal." Hegel did distinguish the concept referred to here from that of "allness," that is, of some attribute which applies to each individual singly. See the comment on Rousseau on p. 132.

capital as a self-reproducing whole is *not* that of the bad infinity of Causality represented in the Doctrine of Essence.

The final section of the book is an outline of the three critiques of Hegel's *Logic* which Marx has explored in the *Grundrisse*. I will return to this later.

What we see in the Chapter on Capital are, I think, plausible links to the latter parts of Essence, but there are also clear allusions to the first two moments of the Concept, Universality and Particularity, though these moments arise in the narrative in a manner clearly relevant to the main lines of the argument for "transition from money to capital".

Overall, Uchida's claim that the *Grundrisse*'s theme is the transition from product, to money to capital, is confirmed by his textual analysis. Consequently, in the main, both chapters 2 and 3 "correspond" to the Logic of Essence, with the proviso that Being is relevant to the first phase, in which a product acquires various forms of value, while the transition from substance to Concept necessarily entails a reference to the logic of the Concept as the outcome, not itself part of the Logic of Essence.

5.4   *Introduction to the* Grundrisse

Chapter One of Uchida's book is titled: "The Introduction to the *Grundrisse* and the 'Doctrine of the Concept.'"

Uchida is undoubtedly correct to begin from the Concept Logic in his study of the *Grundrisse*. Hegel recommends that the logical order of proceeding is to begin the "synthesis" of the phenomenon from a product of analysis in the form of a "universal individual" and to proceed from there to particularity. Uchida's path which I have followed above, from product to capital, which Uchida claims is Marx's main theme in the *Grundrisse*, bears some resemblance to the path of cognition in the *Logic* from Being to Essence to Concept. This, however, puts me at odds with Uchida's own order of presentation.

When we look at the content of the Logic of the Concept, it is really only the first chapter of the Logic of the Concept (the Subject) in which we would expect to find ground-breaking work on capital, because the second Chapter of the Logic of the Concept (the Object) is to do with the interaction of capital with *other* activities, and the final two chapters of the Idea outline the methodology of the *Logic* and then summarise the whole of the *Logic*. So only the first section of the Concept, the Subject, could represent capital as such.

So what topics does the Introduction to the *Grundrisse* actually deal with? I will follow Uchida's commentary here.

Marx begins by defining the subject matter as production in general which Uchida connects to the main, first section of The Idea, Life, which concludes the systematic unfolding of the Idea which Hegel has traced throughout the *Logic*. As Uchida points out, Marx is here laying out his main line of critique of Hegel and the Political Economists: they all treat the activities of individuals in abstraction from the *historically* determined social context, namely capital. Marx further alleges that Hegel treats the human being as simply a "being," without taking account of the human mind, as if mind and body were separate. In fact, Hegel deals with both these issues in what he sees as the appropriate place, not in the *Logic* but in the "Objective Spirit," in his *social* theory. Hegel *never claimed* that the *Logic* was about social relations. But Marx's point rests on his claim that, unconsciously, both Hegel and the Political Economists have *naturalised* logic as if it were a *timeless* reflection of "human nature." Hegel does naturalise a range of social behaviours, including gender relations, divisions of labour and private property, but in the *Philosophy of Right*. According to Uchida, this rupture between the mental and the material is reflected both in the vulgar materialism of Adam Smith and David Ricardo, and in Hegel's Idealism. Hegel's Idealism leads to Hegel *adopting* the capitalists' value-consciousness and expressing this consciousness in logic, with value as an active and knowing Subject.

Uchida writes: "As we will see later in detail, the 'subject' in the Doctrines of Being and of Essence is an ideal subject *par excellence*" (1988, p. 13). "Subject" is not a category in Being and Essence (the Objective Logic) which constitute the "*genesis* of the Concept" and which figure throughout Uchida's analysis of the remainder of the *Grundrisse*. The Subject is the first chapter of the Concept. One could claim that there is an ideal subject implicit in the Objective Logic, but it is certainly odd to describe such a subject as "ideal *par excellence*" given that is not yet self-conscious and is not mentioned in these sections of the *Logic*. Self-consciousness is what characterises the Subject, which is in the Concept Logic.

In the Introduction to the *Grundrisse*, Marx proceeds to critique the fundamental concepts of political economy in a pair-wise fashion, such as exchange-and-production, demonstrating how each of the Political Economists grasp these pairs in a one-sided way, reflecting the standpoint of different sections of the capitalist class. In this trope, Marx is unquestionably utilising Hegelian techniques of criticism as illustrated in the Doctrine of Essence, while drawing from his own work in the 1840s. Marx goes on to criticise Hegel's conception of "Life", the last chapter of the Idea.

5.4.1   The Method of Political Economy

Uchida considers the section entitled "Method of Political Economy" to be very important in identifying the method of ascending from the abstract to the concrete as reflecting the method of the earliest writers such as William Petty and reflective of Hegel's *synthetic* method as described in the penultimate section of The Idea, and the method of Adam Smith and the later Political Economists, of building a *system* of political economy, by ascending from the simplest, most abstract determination to a concrete, conceptual representation of the whole. This distinction is explained in the penultimate section of the Idea, in "The Idea of the True." Marx says that the synthetic method is the "scientifically correct one," and (referencing the three moments of the Subject in the Doctrine of the Concept) Uchida remarks:

> In Marx's work this is reflected in the triadic composition of the Chapter on Capital in the *Grundrisse* as I. Generality of Capital, II. Particularity of Capital, III. Individuality of Capital.
>
> 1988, p. 21

and that

> What Hegel says in 'the development of the moments of the concept' signifies for Marx that reality is mentally reproduced and appropriated as the concrete concept. This is a totality of manifold determinations in the mind, so categories in the *Doctrine of Being* become presuppositions of the notion of capital, and categories in the *Doctrine of Essence* develop from generality or the 'concept' itself, towards particularity or judgment, and up to individuality or syllogism. Marx thus turns the two doctrines of the objective logic [i.e., Being and Essence] into objective moments of the mental reproduction of the concrete. This reflects Hegel's triad – generality, particularity, individuality – in the *Doctrine of the Concept*.
>
> 1988, p. 21

This is confusing. First, Uchida agrees that the correct method is Hegel's synthetic method, but this is reflected in the *Grundisse*'s Chapter on Capital, which Uchida has characterised as Reflecting the Logic of Essence, and *then* states (correctly) that these are moments, not of Essence, but of the Concept, while falsely stating that the moments of the Subjective Concept fall under Essence. Further, Marx has agreed that these moments reflect real *historical* moments and uses them himself in his logical representation of the capitalist system. Uchida does not recognise the "leaps" in the *Logic* from Being to Reflection (as part of the Essence Logic), or from Essence to Subject (as part of the Concept Logic). Effectively, he shifts each boundary one chapter forward from where Hegel put it, ignoring the significance of the "leap" entailed in each transition.

Uchida's criticism here is that, according to Marx, Hegel thinks that the real process of development of the concrete follows the same path as the logical development of the concrete in the mind. Both writers take it that the object exists outside of the individual mind. However, Hegel takes it that the objectification of the ideal is a natural social process, whereas Marx sees the process of subjection of individuals to these bourgeois relations through a social division of labour in which the mental rules over the physical. Hegel is not aware that the universal process of objectification under the rule of capital becomes alienation and is itself an *historical* form of this division of labour. Smith and Ricardo, on the other hand, "unconsciously reify or transubstantiate value-consciousness into material products" as "vulgar materialists" (1988, p. 23).

Marx follows Adam Smith in defining the "simplest" categories as "exchange-value, possession, money, exchange and labour in general," but he traces the *historical* origins of these through the pre-capitalist development of the form of value, chiefly money.

Here Uchida points to Hegel's view of development as a "circle"; the starting point of the "simplest determinations" is also the endpoint of the analysis, the conceptual concrete. Uchida reminds us that the German word for Essence, *Wesen*, is the past tense of Being (*Sein*), "was." Uchida sees here a reference to the cycle: capital – product – commodity – money – capital; i.e., forms of existence of value, capital withdrawn from circulation and then returned to circulation. Uchida takes this as affirmation of the characterisation of the movement of capital as *Essence*. Uchida says that the question which arises for Marx, however, is whether the first pre-positing was made by capital (as would be consistent with Hegel's notion of a "circle") or whether on the contrary the presuppositions of capital were first posited by pre-capitalist formations. Is capital a "self-moving subject" or is it historical (and therefore transitory) in form? He does not consider whether it could be both.

As Uchida has shown, Marx adopts a *logico-historical* method which is concerned with the historical origins of the presuppositions of bourgeois society. Later on in the Chapter on Capital, Uchida points out that Marx investigates primitive accumulation and the changing form of money from means of circulation, hoards, and finally capital. Uchida expresses this in summary:

> Marx reads the *Logic* as the phenomenology or genesis of the value-consciousness described in the *Chapter on Money* and the *Chapter on Capital* in the *Grundrisse*.
>
> 1988, p. 25

Hegel saw his *Phenomenology* as the preface to his system as outlined in the *Logic* and the *Encyclopaedia*. It seems that Uchida invites us to see these two chapters of the *Grundrisse* in the same way. These chapters correspond to Being and Essence according to Uchida, which Hegel calls the "Objective Logic," or the *genesis* of the Concept, logically prior to the Subject becoming self-conscious. By simply participating in exchange, buyers and sellers unconsciously share their value-consciousness and reify value as money.

Further, Marx's logico-historical method leads to Marx's speculative reflections on the developing consciousness of the working class. Uchida follows on here in the Introduction through his analysis of tendencies he sees within the capitalist system itself. These reflections belong within a *logical, speculative critique* of the concept of capital. I believe that Uchida fails to adequately distinguish between the historical pre-conditions of capital (including the logical genesis of the concept of capital by the Political Economists) and analysis of the concept of capital itself including the critique of the concept. Equally, he has failed to distinguish between Being which is serial and *immediate*, Essence in which everything is *relative,* and the Concept which is *organic* development. As it was Marx's first manuscript in a ten-year long labour to produce *Capital*, there was no reason for Marx to separate out these aspects of his work into separate chapters reflecting these distinctions, but I think it is incumbent on later commentators to make such distinctions explicit, based on the textual evidence, if they are to make these claims.

Uchida points out that the plan drawn up by Marx at this point reflects Hegel's method in that it begins from the general and simple, through "external considerations," to Particularity. He then remarks that this structure is "manifested throughout the Chapter on Capital," contradicting his claim in the final chapter of his book that the Chapter on Capital in the *Grundrisse* is reflective of Hegel's doctrine of Essence. Perhaps the fact that he was using the *Shorter Logic* made his task more difficult? Much of what Uchida has to say about what Marx is doing in the *Grundrisse* has merit, but his efforts to pin the development of Marx's argument to Hegel's *Logic* is utterly confused. In that sense, Uchida prefigures this entire debate about the relation between the *Logic* and *Capital*. Uchida differs from present-day authors however in the priority he gives to historical critique as opposed to 'systematic dialectic'.

5.5 *Marx's Critiques of Hegel*

Uchida sums up his analysis of the *Grundrisse* by outlining three principal lines of Marx's critique of Hegel, which he entitles the Generality, Particularity and Individuality of Capital, mimicking Hegel's Moments of the Concept.

5.5.1 Generality of Capital

Marx's first line of critique of Hegel (and by implication, of the Political Economists) is whether capital generates a closed circle in the form of an eternal circular chain of causality or whether the conditions for the existence of capital are historical products which are eventually *negated* by capitalism itself. Marx agrees, he says, with Hegel's view of "circular causality" (Reciprocity and Absolute Necessity – in fact the final phase of the Doctrine of Essence). He likens the emergence of value-consciousness associated with the changing forms of value to Hegel's *Phenomenology*. The demise of capitalism is anticipated in the growing self-consciousness of the proletariat arising from contradictions within the logic of capital.

The transition from money to capital is mediated by the pre-capitalist economic formations in which Marx traces the origins of the presuppositions for capital:
- free exchange,
- free labour-power,
- free funds and
- the accumulation of money.

He says that Marx shows that "capitalism is a logico-historical system that is open," in contrast with Hegel's logical system that is closed and timeless. Uchida likens the historical emergence of capitalism to Hegel's *Phenomenology* and Hegel's Objective Logic: Being and Essence.

Uchida however has blurred the distinction between Essence, which can go no further than an infinite chain of causality, and the Concept which transcends this bad infinity, with the character of an Organic, self-reproducing whole with its three Moments. According to Uchida, Marx agrees that capital is such a self-reproducing whole, but its capacity for self-reproduction is *finite*, and its presuppositions were first produced by *pre*-capitalist formations and primitive accumulation.

In Hegel's defence, I would say that although neither Hegel's *Logic* nor the *Philosophy of Right* make any suggestion of the demise of a social formation, *all* the books of the *Encyclopaedia* end with a transition to a higher sphere which is at the same time a return to its own origins. That is how the "circle of circles" is formed. The demise of social formations rightly belongs in his *Philosophy of History*.

Note also, that regarding the "Method of Political Economy," both Uchida and Marx at this point have overlooked the fact that Hegel's *Logic* is *both* synthetic and *analytical*. Synthesis presupposes analysis; analysis presupposes synthesis. As a result, the problem of *how* the starting point for the synthetic development exhibited in *Capital* is to be determined was never clearly explained nor is it understood in our day.

5.5.2   Particularity of Capital

Following this consideration of the "generality" of capital, Uchida moves to the particularity of capital which Uchida identifies in Marx's distinction between

fixed and circulating capital, and again, we see Marx showing that the presuppositions for this particularisation are found in pre-capitalist formations, and
the extinction of these conditions found in the logic of capital. Here the particularity leads to the social accumulation of large amounts of surplus or "dispos-
able time," a concept which Marx appropriated from an 18th century economist.
Thus Marx also identifies the appearance of the concept of *relative surplus value*
and the prospect of a decrease in the general rate of profit, and with this, the
education of the working class and the growing redundancy of the capitalist.

Again we see a combination of historicism (absent from the *Logic*) and
logical analysis, appropriated from the *Logic* but with Marx highlighting the
contradictions within the supposedly closed system of capital, which lay the
preconditions for socialism.

5.5.3   Individuality of Capital

When Uchida refers to "III. The Individuality of Capital," he cites various sections of the last Notebook which are indexed by the translator mostly under
"Miscellaneous." It could be related to the historical origins of industrial capital identified by Marx: the transformation of independent producers into
wage-labourers, the organisation of wage labourers into manufacture, and the
transformation of merchant capital into industrial capital, and subsequently
its own abolition.

Thus, Uchida may see "Individuality of Capital" as referring to capital moving "from 'a whole' to 'one determinate totality' [revealing] the real possibility of practical transcendence," and the final outcome of this logic-historical
development of capital in which the proletariat takes political power and
plans economic development. So, the "Individual" moment of capital refers to
the capitalist system's final destiny as a single planned economy controlled by
the working class.

According to Uchida, the drift of Marx's critique of Hegel dealt with in this
section is this: that "Hegel's idealism is not merely philosophical speculation,
but rather a real expression of the relations of modern private property – a
philosophical expression of its own economic background, i.e. the relation of
value and capital, the basic relation of modern bourgeois society" (1988, p. 138).
Consequently, the relations which Hegel takes as belonging to moments of
cognition, Marx sees as characterising *real* moments of the development of
value. Marx sees a metaphor which shows how this is possible:

> Marx critically suggests that Hegel's *Logic*, in which an ideal subject or
> 'idea' appears to posit itself and all other objects, is similar to political
> economy, in which value and capital do likewise.
>
> 1988, p. 138

In Marx's own words:

> Therefore, to the kind of consciousness – and this is characteristic of the
> philosophical consciousness – for which conceptual thinking is the real
> human being, and for which the conceptual world as such is thus the
> only reality, the movement of the categories appears as the real act of
> production ... this is correct in so far as the concrete totality is a total-
> ity of thoughts, concrete in thought, in fact a product of thinking and
> comprehending; but not in any way a product of the concept which
> thinks and generates itself outside or above observation and conception;
> a product, rather, of the working-up of observation and conception into
> concepts. The totality as it appears in the head, as a totality of thoughts,
> is a product of a thinking head, which appropriates the world in the only
> way it can, a way different from the artistic, religious, practical and men-
> tal appropriation of this world. The real subject retains its autonomous
> existence outside the head just as before; namely as long as the head's
> conduct is merely speculative, merely theoretical. Hence, in the theoreti-
> cal method, too, the subject, society, must always be kept in mind as the
> presupposition.
>
> MARX, 1973/1858, p. 101

5.6   *Conclusion*

Uchida has shown how extensively Marx was both appropriating and criticising Hegel's *Logic* and developing his philosophical materialism while engaged
with the Political Economists. However, to figure out from this work which
parts of the *Logic* are implicated in which parts of his critique of political
economy it is necessary to look closely at which paragraphs of the *Logic* Marx
is referencing as they do not correspond to what is implied by Uchida's chapter headings. Equally, the chapter headings of the *Grundisse* do not map on
to what became the volumes, parts or chapters of *Capital*. However, Marx's
plans for *Capital* constantly changed over the ten years between writing the
Grundrisse and writing *Capital*.

Uchida claims that Marx is aiming to disclose the dynamics of capital by
means of a logico-historical tracing of value from product to commodity to
money to capital and subsequently to different components of capital and,
speculatively, to the transformation of value to a single social whole following
the overthrow of capital. This claim is well made.

Marx's lines of critique of Hegel are well established by Uchida, viz.,

– that, by naturalising human practice and ignoring the genesis of practice which *produced* the presuppositions of both capital *and* the *Logic*, Hegel mistook historical product for an eternal circle of reproduction of capital.
– that while revealing real dynamics of human practice in his *Logic*, Hegel failed to realise that these practices are products of history, and in turn the source of the philosopher 's abstractions.
– that Hegel has failed to identify the contradictions in the capitalist "organism," but which Marx was able to reveal by appropriating Hegel's logical method.

Mapping the *Grundrisse* on to the *Logic* was already widely discussed by the time Uchida wrote this book, but I think his was the first really comprehensive attempt to complete the task. Uchida is unique among commentators in this discourse in seeing Marx's text as criticising the ahistorical stance of both Hegel and the Political Economists. Hegel's views on political economy were uncritically adopted from the Political Economists, so it is not surprising that he shared their views. Others who have followed Uchida in this study see the opposite: that Marx was adopting Hegel's ahistoricism.

I will now consider one other, even more comprehensive effort to interpret the *Grundrisse* as a commentary on Hegel's *Logic*.

6   Mark Meaney's Analysis of *Grundrisse* and *Logic*

Mark Meaney published his PhD thesis, *Capital as Organic Unity: The role of Hegel's Science of Logic in Marx's Grundrisse*, in 1991 and it was republished by Springer in 2002.

By my count, Meaney finds over 200 links to the *Science of Logic*. A helpful synopsis included in the text lists 66 links, in order, in each case with Meaney's précis of the meaning of each passage, from the beginning to the end of both the *Logic* and the *Grundrisse*.

The *Grundrisse's* Chapter on Money is mapped to the Logic of Being; Section I of the Chapter on Capital linked to the final sub-chapter of Being, and through the Logic of Essence. Section II on the Circulation of Capital and the material following this is linked to the Concept Logic – Subject Object and Idea.

Meaney says that the Introduction to the *Grundrisse* is a critique of Hegel, but the rest of the *Grundrisse* closely follows the logic and text of the *Science of Logic*. After a brief consideration of the Introduction, he matches one-to-one the entire text of the *Grundrisse* to corresponding passages in the *Science of Logic*, paragraph by paragraph, in the same order in which they appear in the

TABLE 3   The Mapping of the *Grundrisse* on to the *Logic*, according to Meaney

Meaney	*Grundrisse*	*Logic*
Chapter 2	**Money**	BEING
Chapter 3	**Capital** Section I	Transition to Essence
		ESSENCE: Reflection
Chapter 4	**Capital** Section I cont.	Essence: Appearance
	Section II	Essence: Actuality
Chapter 5	**Capital** Section II cont.	CONCEPT: Subject
Chapter 6	Theories of Surplus Value	Concept: Object
	Miscellany, Value	Concept: Idea, Life

Logic. We know that Marx was reading the *Science of Logic* at the time and Meaney's matching with the *Grundrisse* is far more extensive and consistent than that identified by Uchida's 1988 book, for which Uchida used the *Shorter Logic*. The two writers also disagree somewhat on the way the correspondence plays out.

Meaney begins by linking the passage on the One (where the synthetic development of the Logic of Being begins) to a point early on in the Chapter on Money.

The Hegel passage:

> Being-for-self is thus a being-for-self, and since in this immediacy its inner meaning vanishes, it is the wholly abstract limit of itself – the One. ... as essentially self-relation, the other is not indeterminate negation as the void, but is likewise a *one*. The one is consequently a *becoming of many ones*.
>
> HEGEL, 1816, pp. 163 ... 168

Meaney parses this as "The one is a result of activity, and it is possible to conceive of it as a *quantity*," and claims that

> Marx employs these categories when he contends that the quantitative determination of the "immediate product" is a function of the real possibility of conceiving of it as an "amount of time."

Meaney then continues in this way to map the Chapter on Money to the Doctrine of Being, through to the Measureless, almost at the end of the Doctrine of Being.

When Marx remarks:

> In direct barter, every article cannot be exchanged for every other; a specific activity can be exchanged only for certain specific products. Money can overcome the difficulties inherent in barter only by generalising them, making them universal. ... When money enters into exchange, I am forced to exchange my product for exchange value in general or for the general capacity to exchange, hence my product becomes dependent on the state of general commerce and is torn out of its local, natural and individual boundaries. For exactly that reason it can cease to be a product.
>
> MARX, 1973/1858, p. 149

Meaney connects this to Hegel's moment of the Measureless, the last category before the Becoming of Essence:

> The exclusive measure, even in its realised being-for-self, remains burdened with the moment of quantitative determinate being and is therefore open to movement up and down a scale of fluctuating ratios. Something, or a quality, based on such a ratio is impelled beyond itself into the *measureless* and is destroyed by the mere alteration of its magnitude. Magnitude is that side of determinate being through which it can be caught up in a seemingly harmless entanglement which can destroy it.
>
> HEGEL, 11816, p. 371

I will not continue to present the relevant passages which Meaney claims to link. It is hard to prove or disprove any of them, even with the aid of his useful synopsis at the end, as Meaney always expresses Hegel's and Marx's thought in his own words, without precise citations, and it takes work to hunt down passages on which Meaney could have reasonably based his précis.

For Meaney, the Chapter on Capital begins with the Becoming of Essence, actually the last category of the Doctrine of Being, and continues through Reflection, Appearance and Actuality (the three divisions of the Doctrine of Essence).

The section which is entitled "The accumulation of capital" in the *Grundrisse* corresponds to the beginning of the Doctrine of the Concept, according to Meaney. He traces the linkage through the three moments of the Subject and the moments of the Object Mechanism, Chemism and Organism, continuing this latter category to the first section of the Idea – the Living Individual, and the Life Process. And there, with the concept of a self-reproducing whole, reproducing itself through the death and birth of new individuals, ends the exposition. Thus Meaney maps the entire development of the *Logic* from its beginning in the One up to its conclusion in the Life Process to the entirety of the *Grundrisse* following the historical/methodological Introduction.

The final two methodological chapters of the *Science of Logic*, "The Idea of Cognition" and "The Absolute Idea," are not connected to the *Grundrisse* by Meaney.

Meaney has the following to say about why Marx had reason to think that the *Science of Logic* might be open to an interpretation as a coded exposition of capital.

> Marx came to the conclusion that Hegel could conceive of the interrelation among nature, society, and thought in terms of a distinction between nature and thought that gives primacy to thought, precisely because of the principles and laws that govern the conditions of production of bourgeois society. Hegel could conceive of this dialectical opposition as well as its supersession in the self-development of Absolute Spirit, precisely because of the dialectical structure of capital.
>
> If Marx's critique of Hegel's system in general includes a demonstration that the self-development of Absolute Spirit is an ideal expression of capital, then the *Science of Logic* could not be for Marx what it is for Hegel. It could not be an absolute method that comprehends the eternal structure of all that is, but merely a method for exploring the dialectical structure of capital. The categories of the *Science of Logic* could not be the presentation of the general laws of movement of each part of reality, and their unity together. Whether or not they are for example applicable in the comprehension of the laws of movement in nature would be strictly an empirical question.
>
> Hegel's reflections on the general laws of movement take place within a specific, historical form of the conditions of production, i.e., capitalism. The systematic elaboration of the dialectical structure of the thought-determinations of the *Science of Logic* is therefore expressive of the conditions of production of capital. It would follow for Marx that the systematic elaboration of the dialectical structure of movement in general could be used legitimately only in an exposition of the dialectical structure of capital. In fact, a systematic elaboration of the structure of capital that uses the Hegelian method to order the material in a critical presentation of it would amount to a critique of the *Science of Logic*.
>
> MEANEY, 1991, pp. 10–11

I do not intend to look further into Meaney's reasoning for how this correspondence between Hegel's *Logic* and early-19th century political economy comes about. I will just note a couple of points about the linkages he found.

In my view, beginning from the passage on the One in the *Science of Logic* is significant, and this starting point *seems* to be preserved in the final draft of *Capital* itself. There is nothing about "Being, Nothing and Becoming" in Marx. And there is sense also in finishing with the first division of the Idea, because the final two sections are not part of the immanent critique by means of which Hegel elaborated all the preceding passages of the *Science of Logic*. If Marx stopped there, it would make sense because the proper place to respond to these sections would be in the Introduction to the *Grundrisse*, as indicated by Uchida. Marx placed his reflections on method mostly at the beginning of the *Grundrisse*, not the end. The problem is that I think it is exactly this passage of the *Logic* which Meaney did not connect to the *Grundrisse*, the chapter of the *Logic* following Life, which is the crucial element which Marx *did* appropriate from the *Logic*, though not by "mirroring" it.

I have no concern with whose mapping is correct. After all, they are not all that wide apart. But the thing is: both writers claim that Marx was self-consciously "mirroring" the *Logic*, so surely they should be identical, and they're not.

I do accept though that it is reasonable to assume from this work that Marx *was* engaged in a study of Hegel while he wrote this manuscript. There are, after all, a number of direct quotes. It is no wonder then that we find so many lucid observations by Marx about methodology scattered through the pages of the *Grundrisse*, and I will have cause to cite such passages in the remainder of this book.

The point is that the Logic is a *logic of enquiry*, generating the concepts which arise as the activity of enquiry develops, and there is considerable lee-way in how these concepts can be useful in any science. Marx may well have been engaging in some exercise of this kind in 1857–8, but Uchida and Meaney were deluding themselves if they find any more significance in these corre-spondences than evidence that Marx engaged in this as some kind of *exercise*. It is surely wrong to see the *Grundrisse* as a "first draft" of *Capital*. More likely it was a preparatory exercise. And if the *Grundrisse* was a "copy" of the *Science of Logic*, then it follows that *Capital* was not, because the structure of *Capital* is quite different from that of the *Grundrisse*.

7   Terrell Carver on the *Grundrisse* and the *Logic*

Before Uchida and Meaney wrote, as early as 1976 Marx scholar Terrell Carver commented that:

> As a master key to Marx's work, 'Hegel's *Logic*' has been over-rated, but as a methodological source-book for Marx it has been lamentably under-researched.
>
> CARVER, 1976, p. 58

German Idealism arose because Science had come to an impasse in the 18th century, beset by a number of irresolvable conflicts between scepticism and dogmatism, rationalism and empiricism, etc., and Immanuel Kant correctly judged that it was only by renovating the *concepts* used by Science that a way through the crisis could be found. Marx was among those who recognised Hegel's *Logic* as the foremost achievement of that program.

One of the unresolved problems of political economy was the source of profit. If commodities were exchanged at their value, how was it possible to make a profit? Surely one person's profit is another's loss. Solving this problem was a central problem for Marx's economic work, and Marx indicated its importance and the use he had made of Hegel's *Logic* in the 16 January 1858 letter to Engels already cited. Preparatory to solving this central problem of political economy Marx made a critical study of the *concepts* and *logic* of this Science. The *Grundrisse* is the manuscript where this preparatory work is found.

Carver examined *one* somewhat arcane logical argument in the *Grundrisse* in which Marx follows very closely Hegel's discussion of "the finite" in the *Science of Logic* (See Marx, 1973/1858, p. 270). Hegel sees a quantity, which is always a *specific* amount must be "in contradiction" to its quality, which must exist in *unlimited* amounts. Marx adduces from this an argument to the effect that "There lies in its [money's] nature a continual driving beyond its own limitation." Carver rightly argues that such a logical argument is a very thin basis for establishing that the drive for profit is inherent in capital.

This point can be illustrated by an example Meaney has, similar to the one Carver cites:

> The contradiction that arises within the quantum results in the 'quantitative infinite'. Since the determination of each is a function of its relation to every other, the quantum is finite "as impelled beyond itself, as being determined in an other (Hegel, 1816, p. 226). This infinite progress is therefore an expression of contradiction."
>
> MEANEY, 1991, p. 65

I would compare this to an argument that legislating a minimum age for the drinking of alcohol creates under-age drinking. From the point of view of *logic* this is true. There is no "under-age drinking" without a minimum age for drinking. But legislating a minimum drinking age does not make people drink at a younger age. Logic is not Economics or Law, or any other science. Logic has its own truths distinct from those of any of the sciences, natural or social.

Carver continued that arguments based on appeals to "human nature" were also of no use to Marx since such arguments serve to prove that capitalism is a transhistorical aspect of human behaviour. But Marx could have argued, and eventually did argue, on the basis of economic arguments, that the tendency of capital to expand is independent of the will of its individual owners.

Carver argues that this "otherwise puzzling exposition of views in the *Grundrisse*" (1976, p. 64) is behind those expressed in *Capital*.

> [In *Capital*] the necessity for ever-increasing profits is simply assumed to be an immanent law of capitalist production. ... Unlike the text of the *Grundrisse*, however, the argument in *Capital* proceeds without an analysis of the relevant 'simple determinations'.
>
> It is likely that the Hegelian exposition in the *Grundrisse* had confirmed Marx in his view that 'expansion' is inherent in the 'fundamental definition of capital' [and Carver reasons that] a polished version of his work on 'simple determinations' in the *Grundrisse* was an unnecessary and possibly confusing step in putting his case to the reader of *Capital*.
>
> CARVER, 1976, p. 64

That is:

> For Marx the dialectic was a useful part of his repertoire of logical methods for critically analysing and re-presenting the categories of political economy.
>
> CARVER, 1976, p. 66

Carver claims that crucial to the success of the application of Hegel's logical arguments in any science is what Carver calls "a restricted selection of source-material" (p. 68). This is exemplified by Marx's decision to begin his analysis of capitalism with an analysis of the *commodity* relation. Carver concludes: "Neither 'the dialectic' nor 'Hegel's *Logic*' represents a master key to Marx's work" (p. 68). My response to this observation is simply that Hegel makes exactly this point in his *Logic*. That is, that the content of a science is first determined by the selection of its starting point, and for any science other than Logic, this starting point will be some fact or problem which requires explanation. But none of the participants in this discussion have observed this. Picking out his starting point from the background noise is the first and decisive step in building a science.

I remain of the view that Hegel's *Logic* was indispensable for the writing of *Capital*, and I agree that:

> As a master key to Marx's work, 'Hegel's *Logic*' has been over-rated, but as a methodological source-book for Marx it has been lamentably under-researched.
>
> CARVER, 1976, p. 57

8   Conclusion to Chapter 1

Whenever new manuscripts or translations of the early works of a great writer come to light there is always a lot of excitement among academics. A new opportunity to discover what the writer "really meant" will be revealed in their youthful work. Alas, I think this is rarely the case. Sometimes an author's early work reveals a moral commitment which may be less obvious in later work. But in general the early work is where the writer was sorting out their thoughts and trying to extricate themself from the prejudices of their age. Rachmaninoff's Concerto No. 1 will never be in the same league as his Nos. 2 and 3. The *Grundrisse* did not set off from the commodity, the simplest and historically first form of value. It began by playing with ideas that Marx had already worked out in the 1840s. I think there is enough evidence that he was doing *something* with Hegel's *Logic* while writing the *Grundrisse* but isn't it more reasonable to take it as a kind of "exercise"?

According to Roberto Fineschi (2014), between 1857 and 1864 Marx wrote not only six different versions of *Capital*, but thirteen different plans or partial plans reflecting the changing structure and scope which he was contemplating for *Capital*. Marx changed his mind about what would become the structure of *Capital* frequently during this decade.

Marx put a great deal of effort into composing, editing and proof-reading the final draft of *Capital*. I think we should pay him the respect of accepting it as the first part of the definitive presentation of his economic ideas which was only finally completed by Engels from Marx's notes in 1894.

Geert Reuten's "Updating" of *Capital*

1   Introduction

From works concerned with a textual analysis of Marx's early work on political economy, I now move to the opposite focus, an effort by an economist to "update" *Capital* for our times: *The unity of the capitalist economy and state: A systematic-dialectical exposition of the capitalist system*, by Geert Reuten, Brill, 2019.

I hope that in reviewing Reuten's book I will be able to further my understanding of present-day political economy as part of my project of learning how to understand complex social processes in general. Political economy is itself of considerable interest to all socialists, but it is not my principal aim to enter into the discourse on economics. I am an outsider to the specialised domain of political economy, and have no standing in many of its aspects. But in other aspects of the Marx-Hegel relation I do have standing and my criticisms of Reuten's book outlined in the seven "issues" below ought to be taken seriously.

One of the interests socialists have in political economy is to understand what are the contradictions in present-day capitalism which threaten crisis – either the collapse of capitalism altogether or drastic change. And Reuten delivers on this, pointing to at least six contradictions in the present-day configuration of political economy which herald the approach of impossible situations, situations for which there is no apparent solution within the existing social and economic arrangements. Only a drastic transformation of the world economy or its collapse is possible. Capitalism has met such contradictions before and overcome them, but these situations are of central interest to those who hope to one day transcend this system entirely.

The book also contains a wealth of material about the kind of day-to-day economic and political issues which fill the pages of serious newspapers, and Reuten deals with a host of such issues based on the fundamentals laid out in earlier chapters of his book.

Further, examining this effort to appropriate the principles of *Capital* and the *Logic* (rather than a textual analysis) will give me an opportunity to clarify in a relevant context just what these principles are.

1.1   Overview of Reuten's Book

From 2007 to 2015, Geert Reuten was a member of the Senate in the Netherlands representing the Socialist Party and in that position had to publicly defend his economic views against, among others, those responsible for running capitalism in that country. In addition, he is a member of the ISMT (International Symposium on Marxian Theory) which includes Geert Reuten, Tony Smith, Fred Moseley, Christopher Arthur, Martha Campbell, Patrick Murray, Guglielmo Carchedi, Paul Mattick Jr., Riccardo Bellofiore, Nicola Taylor, Roberto Fineschi, Andrew Brown and Guido Starosta. Each of these has defended their own line on *Capital* and the *Logic*, all different, and they have met once a year since 1991 for discussion. Reuten also teaches Economics at the University of Amsterdam. Reuten himself has been continuously working on this book since its first version was published in 1989. In the light of this background, the book has to be taken seriously.

Reuten defines his relation to Hegel and Marx in the following terms:

> Although the systematic-dialectical method used here sometimes deviates significantly from that of Hegel and Marx, I nevertheless proceed in their scientific tradition and am greatly indebted to these authors.
>
> 2019, p. 9

Reuten does indeed deviate very considerably from Marx's treatment, and I will deal with these issues below as they arise. But it is right and proper that a present-day writer would differ from Marx; capitalism itself has changed a great deal over the 150 years since *Capital* was written, as has the bourgeois science of political economy of which his book should be an immanent critique. Differing from Marx is no sin; my criticism relates only to when Reuten differs from Marx to the detriment of the science.

What makes Reuten's book unique is his claim to apply the systematic-dialectical method to the capitalist economy *and the capitalist state* together. He claims, correctly, that no economy can exist without the support of a state which grants and enforces rights supporting the given economic formation. In the case of capitalism this means specifically *bourgeois right*, that is, the right to own private property in the Earth, the right to appropriate the product of the labour of others who use means of production which you own as private property, as well as the right to existence and public security core to any state. In fact, a capitalist state is the sine qua non of a capitalist economy. Hegel's treatment in *The Philosophy of Right* likewise deals with civil society and the state in a single dialectical reconstruction. But in writing at a time when the bourgeoisie had a monopoly of political power in Britain, Marx took it as given that the state granted rights as demanded by the development of the capitalist economy and dealt only with tendencies immanent in the economy.

The publisher, Brill, has made a PDF of Reuten's book available for free download at https://brill.com/display/title/38778 and I urge the reader to take advantage of this offer and read the book. I also urge the reader to make their own study of Marx's three volumes of *Capital* which are available at https://www.marxists.org/archive/marx/works/1867-c1/index.htm, especially the first few chapters. In the end, you have to make your own judgment.

Reuten claims to have produced a systematic-dialectical reconstruction of capitalism as it is instantiated today in the 27 core OECD countries. In *Capital*, Marx presented a systematic-dialectical reconstruction of the capitalist economy as it was essentially manifested in Britain, at the time the most advanced capitalist country. I use the word "reconstruction" alluding to Marx's words: "the method of rising from the abstract to the concrete is only the way in which thought appropriates the concrete, reproduces it as the concrete in the mind" in "The Method of Political Economy" in the *Grundrisse* (p. 100). In any such reconstruction the writer distinguishes between *contingencies* – features of the formation which are accidental and are not necessary for the social formation to function, and *necessities* – the focus of the reconstruction, those features of the object which are necessary for the ongoing reproduction of the social formation.

Reuten is at pains to point out that *Capital*, Hegel's *Philosophy of Right* and his own book are *logical*, or *structural*, reconstructions of the concrete, integral whole of a modern capitalist society, beginning from one simple and indisputable initial fact. The sequence in which the categories are presented and derived is quite different from the sequence of their appearance in the *history* of the social formation. (This claim turns out to be not as simple as it sounds, but more of that later.) For Reuten, the dialectic at work in history is something distinct from the dialectical analysis of a social structure at some given moment and the object is taken to be a systemic whole (rather than some hybrid). I dispute this claim insofar as it pertains to *Capital*.

The systematic-dialectical presentation, as it is conceived by Reuten, makes reviewing the work difficult, because social formations are posited which at the given point in the reconstruction are not only counterfactual, but untenable and never did or could have existed historically. The same is actually true of *Capital*, but not to the same extent. The exposition itself is driven by addressing contradictions in a given conception of the social formation, identifying how they are overcome, in turn uncovering new contradictions in the modified formation, and so on. The reconstruction is complete and tenable only at the end of the book – "in which thought appropriates the concrete, reproduces it as the concrete in the mind" (Marx, 1973/1858, p. 101).

Given my aim in writing this review, and Reuten's immersion in political economic theory, I am inclined to take Reuten as an authority in the matter of political economy. But that does not oblige me to believe anything he says about the matter of "systematic-dialectics" or methodological issues, any more than I would take the advice of *any* economist on those questions.

I will now provide a brief overview of the eleven chapters of Reuten's book.

Chapter 1: The starting point of the logical reconstruction presents what Reuten takes to be the meaning of "capitalism" in its barest essentials, the schema which "captures the essence of the entire system" (2019, p. 15): one class of the population owns all the means of production, including relevant elements of Nature as their private property through *enterprises*, and the rest of the population lives in *households* lacking access to any means of production. The enterprises can produce nothing unless labour capacity (this is the term Reuten uses in lieu of Marx's "labour-power") can be acquired to operate the means of production. Meanwhile, those living in households can only live if they can gain access to the products produced by the enterprises.

Reuten calls this situation "dissociative," meaning that it is a situation which cannot sustain itself as an ongoing form of human life. There is no suggestion that such a dissociative society ever existed even in some marginal way, or that capitalism grew out of a situation of this kind.

Now we see how the exposition unfolds.

Reuten asserts that the only way, and the way evidently adopted by capitalist nations, for this social formation to exist, is that there is *trade* between the households and the enterprises (and the enterprises with each other). The enterprises will pay a price for labour capacity solely depending on the value the enterprise can realise by its use. The cost of living of working-class households is irrelevant to the price of labour power and Reuten rejects of Marx's concept of the value of labour-power.

The households buy the goods they need to sustain their lives and the enterprises hire the labour capacity created in the households to operate the enterprises' means of production. Reuten further claims that this trade is only possible if there is money. Only by means of money can products be brought into relation with each other universally and take on a value for the purpose of exchange. So, the conclusion of Chapter 1 is that *given* the above "dissociation," logically, *then there must be* money, and goods and labour capacity *must* take the social form of commodities.

It should be noted that Reuten takes value to be expressed in the dimension of money, the unit being euro, dollar, or whatever. "Socially necessary labour time" does not figure in his analysis.

The chapters alternate between the economy and the state, so the book can be read in order, Chapters 1, 2, 3 etc., following the development of the economy first and then the state in Chapters 6, 7, ..., or in a zig-zag fashion 1, 6, 2, 7, etc., so that we can follow the logic of the state, side by side with that of the economy it supports. I will follow the latter sequence.

In *Chapter 6*, beginning the conceptual reconstruction of the state, we learn that the economy in itself has no means of creating and enforcing the *rights* which are implied in this formation – only a state can protect private property. In addition to securing the right of persons to exist, including public security and ensuring that others do not interfere with persons exercising such rights, it is down to the state to see to it that enterprises have the right to appropriate elements of Nature (insofar as this is possible) and appropriate the entire product arising from the application of labour capacity to the means of production they own. Therefore the state must enforce these latter rights, the "core economic entitlement claims" (2019, p. 303) on which capitalism rests.

Chapter 2, continuing the discourse on the economy, is confronted by the problem of: where is this money to come from? There must be money because otherwise there could not be commodity exchange. Reuten does not accept the idea of money as a commodity. Nor does he see the state as having an essential role in creating money. Long story short: money is created by commercial banks.

If there is to be dissociation there must be commodities, and if there are to be commodities there must be money and if there is to be money there must be banks.

So this chapter must posit the existence of banks as entities distinct from production enterprises. A bank creates money when it speculatively gives credit to an enterprise (which in turn acquires a debt to the bank, thus keeping the bank's books balanced) betting that by using this money the enterprise will make a profit, i.e., extract a surplus from the use of labour capacity after paying the labourer for its use. By this means, the bank can recover its initial investment and a share of the surplus, and production continues on an expanded scale. Now that we have banks, money is not only a medium of exchange, supporting markets, but also a medium of credit, facilitating investment and the accumulation of capital.

Investment does not arise out of savings. Savings are in fact a *drag* on capital accumulation. The banks create money *ex nihilo* (2019, p. 103) on the basis of trust. In short, enterprises require three conditions for the realisation of surplus value: money, labour capacity and Nature. There can be no production without investment by a bank. Capital always begins from a sum of money.

Chapter 7 confronts the fact that the state has been required to do all this work in order to enforce capitalist rights claims, and has somehow to acquire money to do that work. Reuten claims that it must therefore collect taxes, and has in fact historically done so. Taxing the capitalists is an infringement on the very rights that the state was there to protect, so here we have the beginning of sources of political conflict between the state and the class whose interests it protects. Over and above this, the vast majority of the population might see that the state, which claims to represent the "general interest", is in fact furthering the exploitation of the majority of the population, so we see also the source of conflict with the working population. However, the function of the state in ensuring the specifically bourgeois rights claims is generally invisible to the broad population of a country.

The state must also regulate the monetary system, imposing a common standard on the money issued by banks, be in it euros or dollars, and ensure that banks make adequate provisions against bad loans, etc., activity which entails making decisions which inevitably favour one group against another, whatever they do, generating more possibility for conflict.

Chapter 3 deals with the finance system. Quite frankly I am way out of my depth in this chapter. It is a world which is foreign to me. I can only recommend Reuten's exposition to the reader.

Chapter 8 concerns the state's expenditure, and here we meet an important theme. The state has to *legitimate* itself, that is, the state must see to it that the *vast majority* of the population accept the laws and regulations laid down and enforced by the state. Were it to fail to achieve this, then economic and social life would become impossible – laws would be flouted, law and order would break down and the capital accumulation would cease. The state may achieve legitimation by brute repression alone or by open and democratic deliberation on its activity, no matter, but a state with a deliberative legislature is the most efficient if it can carry it off.

However, here arises the largest component of state expenditure, the social security system, including pensions and transfers of all kinds, which ensure that all those for whom capitalism cannot provide a living can nonetheless live a decent life, and as a result will in practice consent to the existing order. It also supports Reuten's claim that the cost of living for a working-class family does not affect wage levels, because if the employers cannot provide profitable employment, the workers can go on welfare. The need for legitimation which drives social security expenditure continues to be a factor in all which follows.

By this point, Reuten has completed what he calls the *"conditions of existence"* of capitalism. What follows he calls the "concrete *manifestation of capitalism*" particularly its realisation through market interaction. In the first chapters, we see the positing of untenable, abstract formations from which the writer concludes that this or that institution must therefore exist, because otherwise there could be no capitalist system (i.e., a tenable system essentially conforming to the initial model). Now we move to a situation where the relevant contradictions, i.e., "impossible necessities" (2019, p. 506), do arise in really existing social formations, and the officials of the state self-consciously make whatever innovations are necessary to survive the given contradiction. The theoretical cognition of the writer is now replaced by the real-time political calculation of real actors in the capitalist state and its enterprises and banks. The analysis of these manifestations, explaining *why* the state, banks and enterprises *must* take the actions which they in fact do, rests on the work of the early chapters which have already set the chief features in place. Different state officials will propose different policies, but Reuten argues his case on the basis that the necessities arising from the political-economic theory laid out in the first three chapters will inevitably be agreed upon.

Chapter 4 describes how competition actually takes place in a modern capitalist society. This was new to me, but the simple idea of price or quality competition is evidently mistaken. Reuten paints a picture of a sector of production in which each firm has more or less outmoded *and* more or less up-to-date technique, and they compete by means of a price leader deliberately over-producing, forcing inefficient producers out of the race. What results is a rotation of innovation and price-leadership. This is an engaging chapter and I fully accept that it gives a truer picture of how competition happens than the usual naïve conceptions. The results are pretty much the same however.

In *Chapter 9* we learn how the state formulates its own conception of "proper competition" and imposes a competition policy avoiding the formation of monopolies. Again, the resulting conflicts of interest demand measures to ensure legitimation of the state which frequently entails the delegation of state functions to purportedly "independent" authorities, such as the Central Bank. Here we learn how the state (or a surrogate) obliges a monetary policy which determines "creeping inflation" (see 2019, p. 344). This creeping inflation is vital for several reasons. First, it avoids capitalism slipping into stagnation, which would otherwise occur; second, it enhances the accumulation of capital, especially its concentration in financial institutions, essential for expanded accumulation; and third, it puts the working class constantly on the back foot, having to fight for wage increases just to maintain the same real wage. The same situation affects small savers. Creeping inflation effectively socialises the losses of all those who cannot secure a rate of profit greater than the rate of inflation while privatising the gains with those who can.

Chapter 5 deals with the ever-expanding demands for regulation of all kinds: the business cycle, the concentration of capital, the quality of products, the supply of labour capacity and its quality, the fierce rivalry between capitalist firms. Every new regulation generates a dozen new loopholes, and the cycle is then repeated on an expanded scale as governments try to plug loopholes. We find that the demand for more and more regulation is unlimited; already the leaders of large financial institutions do not know what they own or what they are legally allowed to do! A number of openings for terminal crises appear at this point which I will summarise later.

In *Chapter 10* Reuten deals with the "reach" of the state, the ever-increasing proportion of GDP absorbed by social security transfers, the appearance of banks too-big-to-fail (that is, were such a bank to fail, no state would be able to save it and it threatens a chain reaction). Regulation has become so complex and provisions so complicated that no one understands them. More on this later.

In *Chapter 11* we learn that the state must exist in a world side-by-side with *other* states, something hitherto unaccounted for in the reconstruction. This chapter deals with international trade, including the complexity and fragility of the international transport infrastructure supporting that trade, international regulation of trade and production, the flight of capital, and the movement of production into and out of nations, depressing the conditions of the more advanced economies when production is moved off-shore to low-wage economies which in turn enjoy improved conditions, (provided the state can provide satisfactory security and basic capitalist economic rights). Thus, the tendency for the movement of capital to very gradually equalise economic conditions for workers in countries around the globe. Imperialism is not on the horizon here and there is no consideration of non-economic issues between states, such as warfare or migration.

And beneath all of this is the impending climate crisis which the uncontrollable destruction wrought by capitalism makes inevitable. In fact, despite the claim of being a "dialectical reconstruction," these crucial features are derived from *observation of historical* tendencies in capitalist development, rather than as logical consequences of the foregoing construction: the secular growth of the cost of welfare spending, the secular growth in the extent and complexity of regulation, the ever-increasing risk of runaway bank failure and ever-increasing international trade.

2 Issues with Reuten's "Dialectical Reconstruction"

2.1 *The Starting Point*

"Every beginning is difficult, holds in all sciences" (Marx 1867, Preface). In Reuten's words:

> The idea of a systematic-dialectical methodology is that one can best present a system in a layered movement that begins with *general-abstract concepts* of the (putative) system, gradually developing these into more concrete complex ones. ... the starting general-abstract concepts should capture key characteristics of the system as a whole.
>
> 2019, p. 29, my italics

That starting point is, he says, "a concept that captures the essence of the entire system." Reuten says that for Marx the starting point is "commodification." This is not true. I will defer a full explanation to the companion volume, but briefly, "commodification" entered the English language in 1977. The general idea is to be found in Marx's work as early as the *Communist Manifesto*, but he *never used the word*. It is a Latinised, societal process word which arises from within the theory as an effect of capitalist development, and as such *cannot* be the starting point of a dialectical reconstruction, either Hegelian or Marxist. Marx began from "the commodity," an everyday word indicating an artefact which mediates exchange of labour and is the substance of wealth.

In Reuten's case the starting point is "dissociation" – a whole society bifurcated into two classes: enterprises and households. This Reuten calls a "general abstract" characterisation.

By "general-abstract" Reuten means a feature of the social formation which characterises the whole system in its barest essentials. "Dissociation" is taken to be this concept:

> the formal starting point of this chapter is Division 1 (on 'dissociation'), which establishes that a key characteristic of the capitalist system is its structural-institutional separation between households and privately owned enterprises.
>
> 2019, p. 29

Private households (where the reproduction of human life is conducted) and private enterprises (in which goods are produced) are taken as given. The starting point is the *separation* of households and privately-owned enterprises, that is, the *bifurcation* of society into two classes one of which owns the enterprises as private property and the other a class of free labourers who have only labour-capacity to offer but no means of labour. What remains to show is how such a bare-bones capitalist social formation can and has maintained itself in existence, though not how it came into existence.

The dissociation has been resolved (the first step in the systematic reconstruction) by the exchange of goods produced by enterprises and labour-capacity created in households, all as *commodities*, which in turn requires money as a universal measure of value. Any historically outmoded means of exchange is irrelevant to the logical reconstruction of modern capitalism. Reuten does not consider any other possible resolution to the dissociation other than commodities and money, and indeed it is hard to imagine any other resolution of that impossible situation. The ration cards issued in wartime were a very inefficient means of distribution. Money and markets may be necessary given the starting point of dissociation. Nor does he inquire into how and on what basis dissociation itself has been established. Simply that *if* it exists, *then* exchange of goods and labour-capacity is *needed*, and thus money is *needed*. Where money comes from and how the dissociation is maintained is the work of successive moments of the reconstruction.

So Reuten's starting point is a vision of an entire society as a system of the two basic classes and institutions, *already a capitalist society in its bare bones*. All production is already in the hands of one class to the exclusion of all others, who are already "free," propertyless workers – a situation which would better be regarded as a *product* of capitalist development, rather than its presupposition. He goes on in this book to show us how all the institutions found in modern capitalist societies are necessary given this logical starting point of a society already bifurcated between owners of enterprises and sellers of labour capacity, using as his empirical reference point the contemporary OECD countries.

2.1.1   Marx's Starting Point

Marx made his starting point the *commodity*:

> The wealth of those societies in which the capitalist mode of production prevails, presents itself as "an immense accumulation of commodities," its unit being a single commodity. Our investigation must therefore begin with the analysis of a commodity.
>
> *Capital*, opening words

He introduced money and private enterprises in the next stage. Money is derived from being a commodity in the next couple of chapters and capital – buying and selling for a profit – comes only in Part 2 of Volume 1, beginning with Chapter 4.

So it is clear enough that Reuten's starting point is very different from that of Marx (and Hegel). Reuten took a minimal, abstract conception of an entire capitalist system. Marx took a *universal individual relation* (commodity) which long *predated* capitalism albeit only as a marginal activity, but which provided the fertile soil on which capitalism grew. Reuten, on the other hand, posited an extreme and already essentially capitalist but unviable *social system* from the outset. Which is not to say that Reuten is wrong, but simply that he contradicts his own claim to be using the method of Hegel and Marx:

> Hegel and Marx also produced the chief paradigmatic examples of a social-scientific systematic dialectic, that is, the method that is adopted in this book.
>
> 2019, p. 9

Hegel described the starting point of a science in the following terms:

> The progress, proper to the Concept, from universal to particular, is the basis and the possibility of a *synthetic science*, of a *system* and of *systematic cognition*.
>
> The first requisite for this is, as we have shown, that the beginning be made with the subject matter in the form of a *universal*. In the sphere of actuality, whether of nature or spirit, it is the concrete individuality that is given to subjective, natural cognition as the *first*.
>
> But in cognition that is a *comprehension*, at least to the extent that it has the form of the Concept for basis, the first must be on the contrary *something simple*, something *abstracted* from the concrete, because in this form alone has the subject-matter the form of the self-related universal or of an immediate based on the Concept.
>
> HEGEL 1816, p. 801. The italics are Hegel's.[1]

Note that the first for Hegel is something simple, a self-related universal, an immediate based on the Concept – not a "general-abstract concept." It is widely recognised that Marx was following Hegel's advice in choosing the commodity as the starting point of *Capital*. For comparison, Hegel began his *Philosophy of Right*, in which he outlined his vision of a constitutional monarchy, with

---

1 Note that most of the participants in the current *Capital/Logic* debate fail to grasp this. Because the topic presupposes *Capital* mirroring the *Logic* in some way, they mostly believe that Hegel's advice is to begin from a contentless concept like Being.

"abstract right," which in modern terms means more or less the right to private property, rather than *exchange* of products or a bare-bones constitutional monarchy.

The social arrangements implicit in Marx's starting point are a society of simple commodity exchange, since nothing else is prefigured, neither bifurcation nor capital. Of course, no society has ever existed in which exchange of commodities was the sole economic relation; distribution of goods and labour has always been regulated in some way by *some* state-form, and commodity exchange was marginal in the past. But it is Marx's *logical* starting point. It is empirically *universal* in modern capitalist society and *historically* capitalism emerged from commodity exchange on the peripheries of ancient societies. Reuten's starting point, on the other hand, presumes a terminally developed capitalist society, already ruptured absolutely between free labourers and capitalist owners, which is of course an idealisation of reality, an idealisation which could exist only in the imagination of the writer.

One of the effects of choosing a *system* (households without means and privately owned enterprises) as the starting point is that it relieves the writer of explaining how it comes to be that households have no means of production and are dependent on the sale of labour capacity for a living, which is logically and historically a *result* of capitalist development, not its presupposition. Indeed, it is not posited that any such configuration did or could exist in the absence of the other elements. Reuten *deduces* the commodity from the hypothesised total bifurcation of society. "Deduces" in the sense that given that bifurcation exists, therefore there must be commodities, but there is no sense of precondition or causality here. It is *solely a movement of theoretical cognition*. It is not the claim that bifurcation *created* commodity production because it *needed* commodity exchange. Like Sherlock Holmes, the *writer* needed commodity production in order to *rationalise* the already hypothesised bifurcation, to make it plausible that such a society continue to exist. And of course, the writer could see that commodity markets did indeed exist in the reference group of OECD countries. These markets are now "explained" by the hypothesised bifurcation.

Further, whilst Marx derived wages and money as special forms of commodity, Reuten firmly rejects the idea of money as a commodity. Marx took pains to "derive" money from the logical-historical development of commodities, whereas Reuten simply declares that money is necessary for commodity exchange, therefore money must exist. Reuten says that Marx took money as a special commodity because that was the norm among the Political Economists of the time whose theory he was critiquing. Reuten instead embraces the modern theory of money as bank credit. Bank credit and paper money were common enough in Marx's day, too.

If one is going to understand the problems of finance and economic planning in a modern economy, it makes a lot of sense to embrace the idea of money as credit issued by a bank, and I will return to this later. However, the conception of money as bank credit should not *exclude* the conception of money as a commodity any more than Marx saw the conception of money as a commodity as limiting money to its historical origins in gold or silver coins, etc., or excluded his discussion of bank credit in later volumes of *Capital*. His aim was always to come to bank-money at a later stage in the analysis as the need for bank-money emerged, logically and historically, rather than simply posit it at the outset because it is logically necessary to explain commodity exchange.

In the *Grundrisse* (Marx, 1973/1858), Marx prefigures beginning the dialectical reconstruction of bourgeois society from "value," but by the time he came to write *Contribution to the Critique of Political Economy* (1859), he began from an historically specific *social form of value*, the commodity: "something simple, a self-related universal, an immediate based on the concept" of value (Hegel, 1816, p. 801). Value might fit the description of a "general-abstract concept," which Reuten says must be the starting point, but commodities certainly do *not*. A commodity is a "universal individual." Commodities appear to the denizens of bourgeois society as immediately given, discrete, everyday objects: anything which is available for purchase or exchange is a commodity. Marx does not posit "general-abstract" concepts, like "value," or "bifurcation" or "commodification" at the outset. The first chapter of *Capital* is an exploration of value beginning with an examination of the commodity, abstracted from its historical conditions. He begins from "the simplest social form in which the product of labour presents itself in contemporary society, and this is the '*commodity*'" (Marx, 1881). The commodity is *universal* in the sense that it encompasses all the products of labour which can be passed to another to meet the other's needs. It is characteristic of bourgeois society, i.e., bourgeois society is essentially a market place. And this is still the case to this day (even if working class people pay their bills from their bank accounts using their phones). The commodity relation is abstract in the sense that it is taken *in abstraction from* the multifarious shapes in which commodities appear, and the multifarious conditions which are presupposed by the ubiquity of the commodity relation, but it is as concrete as any socially-constructed thing could be. But it is not abstract in the sense which we can say of "value." Value is not given in perception; it is a social property of an artefact, meaningful only within a specific theory or form of society (not including, as it happens, economic science for most of the 20th century). "Commodity" is a concept shared alike by every-day bourgeois consciousness as well as all theories of economics. It is a secure starting point for a science, rooted in the natural consciousness of the practice it reflects. Bifurcation, on the other hand, is not a "self-related simple some-thing" as Hegel suggested, but an abstract *system-attribute*.

There *is some* sense in starting the enquiry from the bifurcation. After all, commodities existed for millennia without the development of industrial capitalism, which began (in Britain) only after the Enclosures created a class of labourers without access to means of production which could be exploited by industrial capitalists, but the transformation of the labour process which would come to be the basis of industrial capital came later. The Enclosures themselves presupposed conditions in which a landed aristocracy was domi-nant. The point is that industrial capital *regenerates* the bifurcation on which it continues to rest. It is not so much a precondition of capital as its product.

Commodities, like capital, existed even in feudal societies, but it was mar-ginal. It was trade in commodities which opened the door for capital, eroded the traditional relations and this was the principal reality which eventually *brought about* the (relative) bifurcation of society. Commodities were both logically and historically prior to the bifurcation of society which is taken by Reuten as the starting point. Capitalist society could not develop on the basis of commodity exchange alone, but required a propertyless class of labourers and a class who owned capital. That came later, both logically and historically.

By beginning with the commodity, Marx began with a simple, easily under-stood fact. All the books of Hegel's *Encyclopaedia* begin from a "germ cell" (*der Keim*) like this: in Hegel's Physics he does not begin from Space (the subject matter of the first section of the Philosophy of Nature), but from the point, and in turn the line, the surface and the volume, all simple forms of space.

The fact that dissociation, and all the other features which figure in Reuten's reconstruction, are found in all the OECD countries is far from proving that these features are *necessary* and not contingent with respect to capital accu-mulation. A logical and historical investigation would be necessary to prove this. These nations share a long history throughout which they have acted upon one another; all the present-day OECD countries have developed under the sway of the World Bank, IMF, United Nations and with the USA as the dominant capitalist power, within the arrangements established in the wake of World War Two. Reuten says however that he is "not concerned with the possible economic impact of one country on another" (2019, p. 328). In real-ity, none could choose an independent road, nothing was spontaneous. Any reconstruction which represents each moment as it is *actually found* is of inter-est, but it does not necessarily provide a comprehension. For example, China cannot simply be dismissed as "underdeveloped" or in some way defective. It is an *alternative* to what is found in the OECD countries, and in a sense the most modern, having developed only in the past few decades. These countries do not *have to* be as they are. They have been *made* that way.

That Reuten began from an abstract-general system attribute rather than a simple universal individual relation does not prove that Reuten's representation of capitalism is wrong. In fact, Reuten builds a masterful representation of the capitalist economy and state in this book and identifies crucial problems at the current moment in its development. But as Hegel says, the point of a dialectical synthesis is to provide a "cognition that is a comprehension" (Hegel, 1816, p. 801), and by making his *beginning* from what is *already* a bare-bones capitalist system, and then finding that all the existing institutions are necessary, Reuten fails to provide that comprehension. It was assumed at the outset. What the system seemed to *need* to survive is not the same as what it essentially is.

For me, it is more the point to understand how a society came to be divided between owners of enterprises on one hand, and free, propertyless labourers, on the other, and whether and how it can be otherwise once this has become the case. Marx identified that commodities created the conditions for the development of capitalism, which had emerged historically and become ubiquitous *despite* the efforts of feudal states to suppress them. Marx did not take a bifurcated class society as the logical or historical precondition for commodity production, but on the contrary showed how such a rupture occurs on *a foundation created by commodities*, subject to some other conditions.

2.2   *Functionalism*

Reuten does not speculate at all about a form of society in which bifurcation is not evident. That is a matter for the historian or the novelist. He shows that bifurcation exists (Essentially. Of course bifurcation is nowhere complete even now and as a matter of fact, things are not even tending in that direction). He claims to have shown that all the necessary features found in modern capitalist states can be so arranged, beginning with the bifurcation, that each additional feature introduced makes the existence of otherwise untenable features already posited *explicable* and sustainable.

Bifurcation exists. How is the continuity of human life possible then? Only because there are commodities and money. Therefore commodities and money are necessary. Where does this money come from? Banks. And so on.

Historically, commodities and money existed before any significant bifurcation, so the historical order is here the opposite of the "logical" order of presentation. But under what conditions do we expect the logical and historical sequences to be opposite to one another, what exactly is meant by the histori-cal sequence, and under what conditions do the two sequences coincide?

2.2.1   Two Phases of Reconstruction

Reuten's systematic dialectic has two phases. Chapters 1 to 3 deal with the "con-ditions of existence" of the capitalist economy, setting out the fundamental institutions which make the accumulation of capital *possible*, and Chapters 4 and 5 deal with self-conscious *state responses* to "manifestations of capital-ist accumulation" which arise from market interaction. My criticism here is directed at the first phase: "conditions of existence," as the situation is quite different in Chapters 4 and 5.

Here is the procedure: Reuten identifies a contradiction (a defect or impedi-ment to the continuity of social life, an impossible situation) and then identi-fies the "grounds" (the conditions in which the continuation of human life is possible *despite* the existence of the contradiction) such that the defect is sub-lated (cured, overcome, transcended, but not obliterated). This condition in turn invariably reveals further contradictions which *must have been* sublated were social life to continue, and they indeed *do* exist. Each step "proves" that the given existing formation exists in order to overcome a defect which would otherwise have been present. This is the basic structure of the systematic dia-lectic as Reuten sees it. It is an avowedly logical presentation, not an historical review. Apples exist because people need apple pie.

It seems to me that this sequence, from "contradiction" to "ground" in turn uncovering a new and deeper contradiction, might be the basis for Reuten claiming (as he does) that his systematic dialectic builds on the logic of Hegel's Essence Logic (*Shorter Logic*, §112 to §122). On pp. 614–615, including foot-note 16, Reuten claims in fact that the second part of his book (which I have not come to yet), "would be a further development of Hegel's 'actuality'" (i.e. *Shorter Logic*, §142 to §159, also part of the Essence Logic). And indeed there is some merit in this claim with respect to the *latter* part of the book (which I will come to later). Reuten cites the support of Tony Smith in the claim that it is Hegel's Logic of Essence which provides the "model" for his dialectical reconstruction; Smith in turn cites Arash Abazari for proving it. Both insist that the dialectical reconstruction is irrelevant to the Concept Logic (the outcome of the Essence Logic). There is no reference to the Logic of Being in Reuten's book, though others, such as Chris Arthur (2015), establish a strong likeness to that section of the *Logic*. So, I will proceed on the basis that Reuten sees the first part of his book as mirroring Hegel's Essence Logic, in particular, the earlier section ("Essence as the Ground of Existence") as the basis for what

Reuten calls the presentation of the "conditions of existence" of the capitalist economy and state.

2.2.2   Hegel's Essence Logic

The movement Reuten has alluded to is the Essence Logic, a movement of cognition. The Essence Logic begins with Reflection, beginning in turn from the moment of Identity and culminates in the infinite regression seen in the latter moments of Actuality, and Ground is one moment in this process (*Shorter Logic* §121) which, like all the moments of the Essence Logic, *falls short* of the "*causa finalis*," the Concept (*Shorter Logic* §160–§244).[2]

Hegel's *Logic* is the logic of a cognitive process, a process of *enquiry*. Although it can be read to reference the thinking process of an individual investigator, its *objective* basis is that *social processes are themselves practical critiques of existing activity*. "Thought" for Hegel is human activity (i.e., social practice) not an internal mental process, and activity is a process of self-change and self-comprehension, an objective process which an individual thinker is able to observe and mentally reconstruct, but alas only rarely anticipate. This is why Marx said: "The real subject retains its autonomous existence outside the head just as before" (1973/1858, p. 101).

Essence is the logic which responds to the question: what is the essential problem here? But when it eventually discloses that "essence," the *concept*, a new logic, the Concept Logic, takes over – a logic of development from abstract to concrete, the unity of Being and Essence, the conceptual reconstruction of what is.

In particular, the Logic of Essence is that phase of cognition which begins from something distinctive in the immediate qualitative/quantitative knowledge of a situation apprehended under existing beliefs and commitments (The Logic of Being, §§86–111). The Essence Logic (§112 to §159) is concerned with seeking a theoretical explanation of it, until a new concept emerges which captures the new situation in a nutshell (the Concept Logic §160–§244) and concretises that concept. The Essence Logic is manifested for instance in the history of the sciences, social movements, practical critiques of existing conditions, as well as spontaneous social processes such as the development of aspects of bourgeois society. The Essence Logic is the logic of the development

---

2 Hegel does not use the word "essence" for any of the moments of this process; "Essence" refers to the *whole process*. The final outcome, the moment which most corresponds to the intuitive idea of "essence," is the Concept – the next division of *Logic* and the outcome of Essence.

of specific practices (and/or theories) and there is a sense in which the history of a single form of practice (and/or ideology), once it comes into existence, abstracted from the impact of other processes, follows the sequence whose concepts are exhibited in the Essence Logic, until it reaches the form in which it can be institutionalised in a new Concept.

Once a form of practice "breaks through" into the existing formation, every part of that existing formation begins to be *transformed*, and the new practice is itself transformed by successive such "critiques." This is exhibited in the Concept Logic. It is *here* that the *historical first* becomes the *logical last*. However, for Hegel and Marx, the most recent, dominant concept (e.g. industrial capital) is first grasped as a universal individual (the capitalist employer), *not* as an abstract general feature, far less as a systemic whole or system. It *becomes* a system only at the very end of the story.

The movement of the Concept Logic which follows is one of the movement from the simple-abstract to the systematic, concrete whole. The second phase of Reuten's reconstruction is relevant to capital once it has established its own state which then responds to *other* processes as they arise and accommodates them.

"The history of a science is a part of the science itself," said Goethe (1988, p. 161) correctly, but mainly so as to give advance explanation for the selection of the starting point of the logical exposition of the science. *Pace* Goethe, the history of a science is not generally included in the logical exposition of the science. *Capital* begins from the *outcome* of the history of Political Economy – with the simplest, discrete social form of value, the commodity, not with properties of the capitalist system as a whole.

In the *Philosophy of Right* (1821), Hegel refers the reader to the *Logic* for the method, and begins with private property, in his terms, "abstract right" – individuals with the right to private property – not with a system of constitutional monarchy or with the Crown, not with an abstract system characteristic. Hegel began with private property, Marx began with exchange of property. The historical first, but the last dominant relation – the relation which existed all along and only became dominant at the end.

2.2.3   Essence, Diagnosis and Remedy

So the difficulty we face in assessing Reuten's claim to follow Hegel's Essence Logic, is this. It proceeds through successive remedies of an initially simple but flawed social arrangement, becoming more and more complicated, generating further contradictions awaiting sublation – "too big to fail" banks, escalating and impossible demands for regulation, the climate crisis. This infinite regression is indeed *appropriate* for the Essence Logic. The Essence Logic begins on the basis of a completed quantitative/qualitative analysis of Being (an "economic almanac" of the OECD nations) and concludes with mounting contradictions, infinite regressions and possibilities to be realised. There clearly are *echoes* of the Logic of Essence in Reuten's exposition of his dialectical reconstruction. But according to Hegel, the Logic of Essence is not a systematic dialectical representation of a science but of the logical *genesis* of its essential principle.

> Thus the *dialectical movement* of *substance* through causality and reciprocity [the final moments of Essence] is the immediate *genesis* of the *Concept*, the exposition of the process of its *becoming*. But the significance of its becoming, as of every becoming, is that it is the reflection of the transient into its *ground* and that the at first apparent *other* into which the former has passed constitutes its *truth*. Accordingly the Concept is the *truth* of substance.
>
> HEGEL, 1816, p. 577

Reuten, starting from an absolutely bifurcated society, does not present a genesis, logical or historical, of either political economy or capitalism itself in the first three pairs of chapters. "Genesis" implies growth, or self-development. Reuten "assembles" the system from outside like an Architect.

And yet, Reuten's exposition both *resembles* the Essence Logic *and appears* to be a reconstruction of the concrete whole (a Concept Logic). How is this possible?

I grant three of Reuten's claims. (1) His exposition *resembles* the structure of Hegel's Essence Logic, particularly the Logic of Reflection from contradiction to Ground, and in its overall trajectory: beginning from analysis of a fundamental contradiction and concluding with a contradiction-ridden structure marked by infinite regression; (2) His exposition is a good representation of the object, capitalism as it is manifested in modern OECD countries and it contains elements which are a comprehension; (3) In the course of his exposition he identifies important contradictions – unresolved problems threatening the continuity of social life.

The question is: *is this a cognition which is a comprehension?* I say it isn't, (1) because the starting point is already an *abstract-general* concept of the whole as a system, as a capitalist system; it is already something *which needs explaining* and that explanation never comes; (2) because the form of movement is actually the *mirror* (i.e., inverted) *image* of the Essence Logic; (3) when he comes to the "interesting bits," he departs from his synchronic method by *historically* reflecting on mounting tendencies. Which he must, because they are as yet unsublated contradictions. Most of the insights in the latter part of his exposition result from a diachronic, not a logical investigation. He doesn't know what new institution will step into the breach, if any. Capitalism might indeed collapse.

As to (1), bifurcation is a systemic feature which is taken at the outset as a self-related fact (just as Marx took the ubiquity of wealth in commodities as a self-related fact), and Reuten has arranged all the given features of the object in order such that each feature performs a function *without which the feature just described would be inexplicable*. This is not a comprehension, it is *Functionalism*, a *pseudo-rationalisation*. It could just as well be claimed that the condition of existence of bifurcation is the possession of an entrepreneurial spirit or a capacity for delayed gratification or inheritance of capital or 'social capital'. Any given fact has many grounds (Hegel, 1831, §121, note). One ground should not be arbitrarily selected so as to prove what one wants to prove. There have to be self-evident premises and an essential logic to it. Many different grounds have been proffered for bifurcation in the history of political economy. Marx found the ultimate ground in the concept of bourgeois society, value, and *derived* from that the concentration of wealth in the hands of the bourgeoisie thanks to the commodity form.

2.2.4   A Metaphor

Owing to the difficulty of explaining Hegel's Essence Logic and the fact that few people are really familiar with this book at all, the book which Hegel called "the most difficult branch of the Logic" (1831, §114), I will resort to a metaphor.

Like most of the concepts of the Essence Logic, "Ground" is an ambiguous term. (1) The ground for a doctor claiming that a patient has hypertension may be a simple blood pressure measurement using an inflatable cuff, and the doctor can prescribe a beta blocker. (2) But the ground of the patient's hypertension may rather be said to be the patient's diet, and the doctor may refer the patient to a dietician. Already we can see two opposite paths of enquiry and treatment.

In either case, if revelation of the ground fails to produce a solution to the problem, the same method may be repeated. Along one route a series of pills and procedures could keep the patient alive, along the other route, the root cause may be found to be economic inequality and poor public health education and ultimately, capitalism. In the latter case, which follows the logic of Hegel's Essence Logic, the doctor would *then begin* a treatment program based on an understanding that the patient's illness was primarily a result of their social position in a capitalist society. Exactly *how* he would proceed would depend on other aspects of the patient's situation. There the doctor would be realising Hegel's Concept Logic. In the former case there is no transition to a remedy, no Concept Logic, but merely a succession of cures based on diagnoses of the current condition that may drive the patient deeper and deeper into ill-health while keeping them alive. That is the path of Functionalism.

Both types of logic lead to some kind of understanding of the object and some kind of corrective action. Both set off from some feature of the object, potentially the same feature. The first line of enquiry leads to a cure of sorts; the second line of enquiry leads to a concept of the root condition underlying the observed feature which can inform an effective treatment program. Only the second follows the Essence Logic. Only the second constitutes a *comprehension*.

2.2.5 The Place of Essence in Systematic Dialectic

Hegel and Marx did use "Essence-like" Logic in their analysis of the structure of modern society, inasmuch as the logic paralleled historical development, but only in a *subordinate* way. (By "Essence-like," I mean transitions in which each new form incorporates the content of the preceding concept, incorporating it, but not abolishing it.) The overall structure of the analysis is that of the Concept Logic, a systematic reconstruction of a concrete concept "rising from the abstract to the concrete." For example, in the *Philosophy of Right* section on Contract (§§72–81), Hegel demonstrates the *genesis* of Contract from Gift using an Essence-like Logic. But the transition from Abstract Right to Morality is of a wholly different character because morality has *independent roots* relative to abstract right, and likewise the logic of the transition from Family to Civil Society or from Civil Society to the State – each has *separate roots* (For example, the Norman kings of England had no role in civil society in the land they conquered, and the two existed side by side for several centuries). There is a difference between the autonomous unfolding of an institution according to its own logic in a given context (e.g. Contract), on one hand, and on the other hand, the concrete development of an institution as it comes under critique from *other* practices having their own independent roots, such as the impact of the State on civil society and vice versa, which must draw on the Concept Logic.

In the above I say "Essence-like Logic" rather than "Essence Logic" because the logic which arises from critique of the concept and practice of Gift *cannot be the same* as the logic which arises from critique of the concept of Identity. Contract has external, social content; Essence does not. It is a logical concept. But the Essence Logic is the archetype of such critiques.

2.2.6   Theory and Social Practice

Reuten's cognitive process begins with an abstract-general feature of the system in which life would actually be impossible (the bifurcation) and selects a feature (commodities and money) thanks to which social life nonetheless could continue. Reuten is modelling the capitalist society as successive remedies to remedies to bifurcation. This resembles the point of view of an Architect of capitalism. But (in the first three chapters) the "remedy" (commodities) historically preceded the "disease" (bifurcation). The "movement" in Reuten's construction is entirely in the head of the writer. It does not correspond to any social-historical process at all. If anything, it reflects the point of view of the *capitalist state* applying remedies to crises as in the latter part of the book, not that of the scientist or the socialist revolutionary.

Commodities are *not* a practical critique of a bifurcated society as proposed, but in fact have proved to be a practical critique of an *un*bifurcated society, drawing it *towards* bifurcation. For Reuten, commodities are a *theoretical* response to an *unviable conception* of a society, rather than a fix for an increasingly *unviable society*. The movement from bifurcation to commodities is a purely theoretical move which set off from a mental characterisation of the system. It is by no means immediately given, but rather is abstracted from a *relatively* bifurcated society and *deemed* to be essential. It is only a relative truth, and is selected from the concrete conception of the object arbitrarily *so as to* provide a basis for "deducing" commodities and money. "Bifurcation" is an extreme, abstract characterisation of a system which has *already* been determined as a capitalist economy (all means of production are privately owned, the labourers have nothing to sell but their labour capacity). It presumes what is to be proved, and in fact what may never come about, as all really-existing capitalist states are only partially bifurcated. It is an unviable theoretical construct not an immediately given fact (as was the starting point of *Capital*). And facts and *real* problems are surely the starting point of *all science* and *all* social action.

The term "abstract general" is not a term which Hegel uses in his *Logic*; perhaps "abstract universal" is intended – some feature held in common by all. Reuten takes it to mean a concept of the object (an OECD economy) which "abstractly captures the totality of the capitalist economy." But characterising a totality is no simple matter. Hegel, for example, derived his starting point for understanding bourgeois society to be private property, from the *Philosophy of Subjective Spirit* (his study of the human psyche), which preceded the *Philosophy of Right* in his system.

Now, admittedly, the above observation seems picky. Surely propertyless labourers, capitalists and a state enforcing bourgeois right exist, and how could capitalism exist otherwise? The point is that all the other institutions "derived" in this book have the same status: such-and-such an institution exists, therefore such and such problems must arise and indeed have arisen, and these problems had to be overcome by such-and-such novel institution and have been so overcome. So, given that you have "free labour" and private ownership of the means of production, then this institution is serving such-and-such a function. Every institution is shown to have a specific *function* in facilitating capital accumulation by maintaining conditions for capitalist accumulation. The function does not make its existence comprehensible.

For example, Chapter 7 claims to prove that the exercise of law *requires* taxation. But this is not necessarily true. Post World War Two Britain made extensive inroads into the market economy which provided plenty of opportunity to generate government income without imposing taxation and without generating the need for legitimation which taxation creates, but violated the postulate of bifurcation. State-owned industry is not a modern, exceptional invention, but has an ancient lineage. Likewise, many petro-states fund state activity with oil revenue, as does Norway, which uses taxation mainly for income redistribution. And in no way do these measures *impose* on private enterprises. So we know the *function* of taxation, but this by no means proves the *necessity* of taxation or tells us about the *conditions* under which taxation is appropriate and sustainable or by what *motivation* of which *actors* we have taxation.

And it is not as if the 30-odd OECD countries are independent natural experiments which have all produced substantially the same results. The histories of these nations are all deeply intertwined and the post-World War Two Bretton Woods arrangements *imposed* common features on to all European countries. An isolationist USA in 1945 would surely have led to a different Europe and there is nothing in the Functionalist reconstruction of the status quo which could prove otherwise.

At the starting point of his exposition, Reuten:

> sets out condensed-abstractly how the capitalist economy appears in empirical reality. However, the starting point does not reveal *how* it can have 'existence in' concretely interconnected relations between these households and enterprises.
>
> 2019, pp. 34–35

It merely sets a problem, so to speak, which has yet to be provided with a solution. This is how Reuten sees the systematic dialectical reconstruction proceeding. Labour capacity and the means of labour are the property of two distinct classes. How is life possible in such a system? The solution in fact adopted by the OECD countries is not necessarily the only solution possible.

The commodity is a really existent relation and it does *not* presuppose bifurcation *or* capital. Bifurcation would be the final result of considerable development. By taking bifurcation as the presupposition, Reuten is *describing* existing capitalist societies in such a manner that he can claim at each moment it is all *necessary*. For socialists, the implication is that if you are to transcend capitalism, then you must abolish the bifurcation of society into households owning only labour capacity and private owners of enterprises, but that could have been said without writing the book; it's essentially a truism.

Reuten points out that Marx's beginning ("The wealth of those societies ...") "on the one hand, refers to everyday perception," but on the other hand is the "abstract perception" of the *resolution* of this initial bifurcation, i.e., the formation of markets to mediate between producers and consumers. He observes that: "If so conceived, Marx's starting point may not be fundamentally different from the current one" (2019, p. 39). Marx's starting point, wealth in commodities, is more consistent with Proudhon's imagined society of independent producers, not a bifurcated society; Marx introduced capitalist employers only in Part 2 of Volume 1, and exchange of commodities between enterprises only comes in Volume 3. It is not essentially the same at all.

In England, centuries passed from when commodity production first emerged in early mediaeval times till the misnamed Glorious Revolution in 1688 created a constitutional monarchy suited to bourgeois rule, and still more centuries passed before "full-blown" capitalism was achieved in England. This suggests that a lot of work was required to produce the preconditions for "full-blown" capitalism. At the very beginning of commodity production in England, a monthly court had to be convened to certify a purchase (Loyn, 1984). A bourgeoisie had to be created – a class of people who trusted each other in the buying and selling of commodities, and were able to accumulate capital, supervise labour, and adapt to market demand. And the bourgeoisie also had to withstand interference by the landed aristocracy, notwithstanding the nobility's armies and landed wealth.

Much of the work of creating the conditions for full-blown capitalism was to create the proletariat by separating the workers from the means of production that they needed to live. The Enclosures were crucial in creating a proletariat in England and this was achieved by wholesale *theft*. For several centuries after the Norman Conquest, the state did not intervene in civil society at all, but I grant that the creation and maintenance of a proletariat presupposes the existence of a state of some kind, so maybe a capitalist state supervising civil society could be logically deduced from the existence of a bourgeoisie and a proletariat, but the Enclosures were carried out in defiance of the state at the time.

In summary, Reuten's Functionalist exposition of the capitalist economy and state is a *rationalisation*, not a comprehension. It expresses the practice of those who govern capitalism, but it doesn't help those who seek to comprehend it and overthrow it.

2.3   *The Logical and Historical Sequence of Categories*

The Structuralists and Functionalists, Reuten, and many Marxists claim that to understand any social phenomenon it must be analysed "synchronically," while "diachronic," i.e., historical analysis can contribute nothing to that synchronic analysis. Now it is true that structural analysis of the existing state of affairs here and now before our eyes is the most important result, but this by no means proves that historical analysis has no role to play in understanding a social formation. The current arrangements for international trade and finance make no sense, for example, unless you happen to know that in 1945 alongside the USSR, the USA was the supreme power and the People's Republic of China did not even exist and most of the world were colonies of one of the Allied powers.

Marx famously explained in the *Grundrisse* how the reconstruction of the complex whole always begins from "the simplest determinations" such as "labour, division of labour, need, exchange value. ..." whether in Marx's own work or in that of the earlier Political Economists.

> [The concrete] appears in the process of thinking, therefore, as a process of concentration, as a result, not as a point of departure, even though it is the point of departure in reality and hence also the point of departure for observation. ...
>
> the method of rising from the abstract to the concrete is only the way in which thought appropriates the concrete, reproduces it as the concrete in the mind. But this is by no means the process by which the concrete itself comes into being. ...
>
> MARX, 1973/1858, p. 101

Marx then reflects on the sequence in which the categories come into existence historically, as compared to the sequence in which they are taken up in the logical presentation:

do not the simpler categories also have an independent historical or natural existence pre-dating the more concrete ones? *That depends.* Hegel, for example, correctly begins the *Philosophy of Right* with possession, this being the subject's simplest juridical relation. But there is no possession preceding the family or master-servant relations, which are far more concrete relations. ... the simple categories are the expressions of relations within which the less developed concrete may have already realised itself before having posited the more many-sided connection or relation which is mentally expressed in the more concrete category; while the more developed concrete preserves the same category as a subordinate relation. ... the simpler category can express the dominant relations of a less developed whole, or else those subordinate relations of a more developed whole which already had a historic existence before this whole developed in the direction expressed by a more concrete category. To that extent *the path of abstract thought, rising from the simple to the combined, would correspond to the real historical process.*

> MARX, 1973/1858, p. 100, 102, my emphasis

So the logical development from simple relations may correspond to the historical sequence, or not. *It depends.* As the entire, concrete social formation develops, either the simple relation develops as an expression of the more developed ones or it is incorporated and subordinated within a more concrete relation.

But the same does not necessarily apply to more concrete relations, in particular entire sectors of the economy and *which* sector of an economy will "determine the relations of all other branches as well ... as though light of a particular hue were cast upon everything, tingeing all other colours and modifying their specific features" (Marx, 1859).

where agriculture predominates, as in antiquity and the feudal period, even industry, its organisation and the forms of property corresponding thereto, have more or less the character of landed property. ... The *reverse* is the case in bourgeois society. Agriculture to an increasing extent becomes merely a branch of industry and is completely dominated by capital. ... Capital is the economic power that dominates everything in bourgeois society. It must form both the point of departure and the conclusion, and must be analysed before landed property. After each has been considered separately, their interconnection must be examined.

> MARX, 1973/1858, p. 44

As it turned out, Marx did not make capital the point of departure, he started from the simplest social form of value, the commodity, but he did make analysis of capital logically prior to the analysis of rent, etc.

When such *concrete institutions* come to be analysed in the context of a more developed social formation, the logical order of the categories is the *reverse* of their sequence in prior history:

> It would therefore be inexpedient and wrong to present the economic categories successively in the order in which they played the determining role in history. Their order of succession is determined rather by their mutual relation in modern bourgeois society, and this is quite the *reverse* of what appears to be their natural relation or corresponds to the sequence of historical development. The point at issue is not the place the economic relations took relative to each other in the succession of various forms of society in the course of history, ... Rather, their order within modern bourgeois society.
>
> MARX, 1973/1858, pp. 107–108, my emphasis

The sequence of the subject matter in history, on one hand, and in a logical presentation on the other, may be from the least to the most developed or from the most developed to the least, according to the writer's intent in taking up a specific category. *It depends.*

Much like Hegel's treatment of Gift and Contract in the *Philosophy of Right*, in §3 of Chapter 1 of *Capital* Marx takes up the various concepts of money in historical sequence using Essence-like Logic, in order to demonstrate the essential nature and multiple roles played by money in pre-capitalist societies and finally, in a capitalist economy. The form of money continues to develop within the subsequent development of capitalism. I will return to this specific question later in respect to the appropriate conception of money for a dialectical reconstruction of capitalism.

The importance of these reflections is seen when we come to determine the starting point for a dialectical reconstruction of the capitalist economy. We have seen above that we must begin from a "simple relation," rather than from an abstract characterisation of an entire system. There are many relations which could be selected as the "ground," however. It is the history of political economy and the history of the *theories* of political economy which provide the resources from which a choice of the starting point can be made. All economic *systems*, including those of Marx's predecessors, begin from simple relations. The problem is: *which* of these simple relations "such as labour, division of labour, need, exchange value" (op. cit., p. 100) truly corresponds to the essential nature of the whole, and in what *sequence* should other simple relations be introduced to modify it. The Political Economists whose work Marx criticised generally started from the trinity: land, interest and profit. The first problem that the dialectical reconstruction faces is the choice of this simple relation from which to begin the logical exposition of the whole. In the course of this exposition, the sequence of categories may follow the historical sequence in which the relation was dominant, or may be the reverse of that order. Hegel, for example, saw the state as an organism, each organ of which had had its own history separately from the state before being subordinated and transformed into organ of the state (*Philosophy of Right*, §269). Consequently, the nature of those various organs of the state depended upon the character of the state and would be different in different historical eras when they might even have functioned as independent institutions altogether separately from the state.

In short, the sequence of categories in the dialectical reconstruction of a social formation depends on conclusions which can only be drawn from a study of the *history* of political economy, principally seen through the eyes of its theorists, the Political Economists, *and* a study of the history of economic life, but "to develop the laws of bourgeois economy, it is not necessary to write the real history of the relations of production" (Marx, 1973/1858, p. 460), it can be written merely in outline such as in a 'genealogy' of a given relation.

In any case, it is simply impossible to perceive something as complex as the political economy of a country without recourse to historical documents and theories which are the products of historical processes. Impossible. The sequence in which concepts are introduced into a conceptual reconstruction may correspond to the historical order of their appearance or not. It depends. The kind of historiography which is required is more like genealogy.

2.4   *The State as an Epiphenomenon of the Economy*

On p. 307, Reuten correctly points to the fact that the feudal state in England "collaborated" with the bourgeoisie, having been obliged to chiefly because of the exigencies of war against other states, making it possible for capitalism to develop even whilst the feudal state remained in place. As a result, the pre-existing feudal state was gradually *transformed into* a state serving the interests of mercantile capitalism. These developments took place in a Europe in which states were perpetually at war with one another. My point being that there is more to the state than the demands of bourgeois economy.

A remarkable feature of Reuten's book is that it claims to derive both the capitalist state and the capitalist economy *as a unity*, rather than, as Marx had done, first abstracting economic activity from the state, family, science, religion, etc., and dealing only with the tendencies inherent in the economy. Marx never found the opportunity to write his theory of the state. The closest he came was in his journalism in which he developed his theory of Bonapartism and Imperialism (See Spencer, 2023), both of which were a far cry from the conception of a state as simply an instrument for clearing the way for capital accumulation, which he had described in 1843.

Reuten's argument seems plausible. For example, the bifurcation requires that a person has a right to own parts of the natural world (mainly land) as their private property and that a person has the right to appropriate the product of the labour of another in its entirety if that other uses means of production which they own. These practices emerged historically in a context in which they were novel, and consequently may have been objected to by those who missed out under such arrangements. Presumably factory owners had guards and supervisors just as landowners had gamekeepers. However, it is clear that, for the accumulation of capital to continue and be secure, the *state* must enforce these rights claims as law.

Reuten says: "to the extent that the state grants *these* (bourgeois) rights in particular, it is identified as a 'capitalist state', which constitutes a unity with the capitalist economy" (2019, p. 6).

Generally speaking, these needs arise from bourgeois economic activity; the state serves these needs. But the state has *separate roots*, as I have indicated, and the development of the state also has *its own* logic. For example, as Reuten highlights, taxation to fund the state's interventions requires an imposition upon the rights of capital. Consequently, the state faces the need for legitimation, and duly engages in activity which helps win consent to their right to extract taxes from everyone. *The capitalist state is the intersection of two separate lines of development*: a capitalist economy and a nation state. There is an internal contradiction there which cannot be theorised by assuming unity from the outset. The state has to be understood by first abstracting it from the economy and examining it in its own right, with its own history. It is a fundamental mistake to derive them both from the same origin in the bifurcation.

In the context of the Functionalist exposition Reuten makes abundant sense. After all, once the capture of the state by the bourgeoisie has been completed then we have ministers, civil servants and lobbyists who *self-consciously* diagnose the needs of capital accumulation and take legislative and administrative action to remedy any problems – just like the first doctor in my metaphor above. Self-conscious strategic management of a process is not the same as immanent tendencies in the spontaneous development of that process; rather it is a reaction to it.

Much about present-day capitalist reality makes no sense by these lights. For example, it is only in the last chapter that the fact of the state being one among many states appears in the analysis. This draws attention to the fact that the state – not a capitalist state, but a state of some kind – long pre-existed bourgeois society, and had reason to exist. The state, generally speaking, was the work of nobles who sought a monopoly over exploitation of certain people and resources, generally but not exclusively in some geographical domain, and was specifically motivated by rival nobilities (or tribal peoples) seeking to deprive them of that monopoly. In other words, before the state became a capitalist state it was already a national state as against other nation-states, and *remains so*. States are not merely trading partners.

Here is the problem of theorising the unity of two institutions which have separate roots by this Functionalist approach. Reuten points to the demand of the capitalists for certain services to be delivered by the state and their resistance to the state imposing on their free market activity in so doing. What in fact happened, is that the bourgeoisie first encountered the state as a protagonist which it had to plead with and bribe to get its needs met, and ultimately *captured*. The state had already made its relationship with its citizenry on the basis of historically *earlier* relationships, and had to be moulded to its will by the capitalists under conditions where a multiplicity of classes *competed for hegemony in the state*. Why bother with a Socialist Party otherwise?

Insofar as the state has been captured, and is compliant to the needs of capital accumulation and is well-advised, then we have a *class-subject*. In the extreme conception, the capitalist state is that self-conscious class-subject, incarnating the will of capital. But in actuality this is never quite the case. Government and even the state itself is ever the subject of contest by competing classes. And as a capitalist state it is, as the saying goes, holding a tiger by the tail.

Here is where the attempt to make the dialectical reconstruction by "building upon" Hegel's Doctrine of Essence is so wildly misconceived. The Subjective Logic (i.e., the Concept Logic) is the appropriate logic for dealing with the process where a subject develops while being continuously challenged by other subjects (institutions, practices), and entering into a process in which the various competing concepts in some way and to some degree *merge* with and accommodate one another. It seems to me impossible to develop a practical and realistic theory of the state on the flat, dogmatic assertion that it is a *capitalist* state. It is always necessary and wise to recognise the multiplicity of interests which are at play in the political sphere. Long gone now are the days when only property-owners voted and only the children of the wealthy held high office in the state. The state is *also* an *arena of class struggle*. To paint the state as an out-growth or even epiphenomenon of the process of capital accumulation is to disarm those who would seek another kind of state.

That said, I do not deny that Reuten's exposition of the various functions of the state, insofar as it is a capitalist state, are very helpful, well-informed and insightful. Producing a book which analytically separates tendencies which are immanent in the economy from phenomena which derive from the actions of a state is also immensely helpful in developing a theory of capitalism, whether it corresponds to a genuine dialectical reconstruction or not. The whole book in fact remains a treasure trove of insights into the working of modern capitalist nation states.

My disagreement lies mainly in the section on the "conditions of existence" of a capitalist state and Reuten's claims in relation to Marx and Hegel.

2.5   Households "Create" Rather Than Produce Labour-Capacity?
It is evidently important for Reuten that:

> The form of labour as the distinctive activity of production implies for workers that 'non-labour' takes the form of *revitalisation and recreation* at the site of households.
>
> 2019, p. 34

Reuten explains that Nature, the banks and the working class provide the necessary ingredients for enterprises to produce surplus. "A bank, for example, issues money that it creates 'ex nihilo'" (2019, p. 103). Enterprises are prepared to pay for these ingredients, if they must, so long as each factor can be purchased at a price equal to or less than its utility in producing surplus value under the prevailing conditions. Nature is in principle free, because it doesn't belong to anyone else; banks demand a share of the profits, but only the employment of labour capacity creates new, surplus value.

Reuten has his own way of explaining the origin of the capacity of workers to produce more than they need to just reproduce the capacity to work again the next day, while enjoying a standard of living which has been established as normal for their class.

> But the key point is that whilst labour-capacity is grasped by the monetary-value dimension (the wage), it is not 'produced' within the capitalist sphere of production as a commodity. Rather, it is *created* within the sphere of households. The price of labour-capacity (i.e. the wage) does not represent previous value-added and it has *nothing to do with the 'price of production' of labour-capacity*.
>
> 2019, p. 68, my emphasis

His difference with "conventional Marxist Theory" being:

> The thesis that the price of the capacity to labour (i.e. the wage) has *nothing to do with the 'price of production' of labour-capacity*, and that these terms are indeed incompatible, appears very un-marxian.
>
> 2019, p. 75, my emphasis

Indeed. And further:

> "value-added is in [no] way proportional to labour-time."
>
> 2019, p. 75

A footnote further explains:

> Labour-capacity is *created* in the private sphere of the household; what is involved is the activity of procreation – it is *not produced with a view to sale*. It is created within the household sphere, and used (exerted labour) in enterprises; (final) commodities are produced within enterprises and used within households. ... children are not produced for sale and hence do not have an actual price of production.
>
> 2019, my emphasis

No one suggests that children are born for sale (i.e., as slaves – an elision to which Reuten repeatedly resorts, obfuscating the distinction between selling a person and them hiring out their labour capacity). But to suggest that parents in a capitalist society procreate without having in mind that their children will *work*, have a career or profession and support themselves (by means of wage labour in the case of *working class* families) and their parents in their dotage, is *bizarre*. Where has Reuten been? Parents work hard to equip their children with the means of living. I have never in my life met a parent entirely indifferent to the capacity of their children to earn a living and contribute to their parents in some way upon reaching adulthood. And it was always so.

Reuten accepts that, as part of the legitimation of the state, the state must ensure that every citizen is able to live "decently" (2019, p. 364). But what underlies this is a many-generation-long *struggle by the workers' movement* to define and redefine what is meant by "decently."

And to suggest that raising children does not have a cost! Self-evidently, households are no longer mere *consumers* of goods (out-sourcing many caring services to the market), but *producers* of labour capacity and they need products to do so and have fought down the centuries to establish a standard of living consistent with the raising of children who will enjoy a life equal to or better than their own. This has gone on since mediaeval tradespeople apprenticed their sons and daughters into the trade to present-day immigrants who sacrifice everything so that their children get an education and go on to become doctors, etc.

It is interesting to compare this, what is to me, odd position which Reuten has taken with his observation that civil servants *do* produce surplus value (2019, p. 390). This value, he says, is distributed to the benefit of all citizens in the course of the state's activity. Isn't something similar happening in the domestic sphere? Domestic labour also produces a surplus product. Not surplus *value*, but a surplus *product* nonetheless. And this surplus product is not distributed; rather it is consumed by families in their enjoyment of a "decent" standard of living.

Granted it is not as simple as that. "Value" pertains only to products with use-value, i.e., usefulness which can be transferred to others, and only appears at the moment of sale. Wealth is not yet value. So it must be true that within Marx's terminology domestic labour does not have *value* even though it obviously is a form of wealth creation. And one could argue about whether the concept of "labour" in Marxist literature could or should include domestic labour, or whether "labour" has a more restricted meaning, but so what? Domestic labour does not produce *value*. But labour power *does have costs of production*, it is found only in capitalist society, and not in "wild nature," and entails the purchase and productive-consumption of commodities.

How does Reuten think wages are determined if it has nothing to do with the cost of living for workers and the cost of raising working class children?

> Whereas for straight commodities a *demand-induced* price increase evokes an increase in their production, demand-induced wage increases do not evoke an increasing 'production' of children [or increased participation?]. In this respect the 'labour market' – inasmuch as the 'money market' – is very different from ordinary commodity markets.
>
> 2019, p. 92, my emphasis

and

> Money and labour-capacity are similar in that it is merely their demand, not their supply, which mimics commodity markets. As to their supply they are similar in that they are not 'produced', but rather created.
>
> 2019, p. 93

It seems that working-class households as sources of labour-capacity are viewed by Reuten in much the same frame as natural resources: nature-given though privately owned. Nature creates, labour produces. The enterprise purchasing labour-capacity will pay whatever is asked up to the level of its "utility" in application to the production of profit at the going rate. The sellers conversely will push the price up until it reaches this level, whereupon they find that the buyers are no longer willing to pay. Thus the wage rate is *unilaterally* determined by its utility as a factor of production and the going rate of profit. Labour capacity no more has costs of production than the oxygen burning in the furnaces – it just has to be brought to the factory gates for use.

What advice does it give to the workers' movement? It tells them that wages cannot be increased because the capitalists are already paying as much for it as they ever will. Just go back to recreating and procreating and take a job when you can. How different from Marx's invitation to workers to fight to reduce the length of the working day!

On p. 94, Reuten speculates on how "in the limit case of an around subsistence wage, wages do have an indirect effect on population growth and the supply of labour-capacity." This misses the point that since *Les Misérables* and *Wealth of Nations* were written, the industrial, social and political struggles of the workers' movement have lifted their standard of living beyond the point where child starvation is the only factor reducing the supply of labour. Reuten accepts that as a problem of legitimation, the minimum wage will be set such that it provides a living; but what constitutes "a living" is very elastic. On the other hand, Reuten tells us that "an increasing rate of capital accumulation gives rise to an increasing wage rate," based on his utility theory of wages. Tell that to US workers.

In a system where entitlement to a profit is proportional to the total capital deployed in creating value, working-class households are entitled to no surplus value. They are paid only the value of commodities purchased from capitalist enterprises, consumed and the product passed on for the use of employers in the form of labour capacity. The labour of working-class households in creating labour capacity is not "productive labour" in the sense that it *does not produce surplus value*. *Owning* capital is precondition for entitlement to profit under the rule of capital. But under capitalism *every* seller is entitled to and *must* recover their costs of production. If the buyer can't pay that, then they can't buy. Equally, if an employer can't make the going rate of profit *given* the cost of labour capacity, then they go out of business.

2.5.1   Utility?

Reuten does not use the term "utility" because he is aware of its origins, but uses the term "usefulness" instead. For clarity, I will continue to use the term "utility" because it clearly indicates the implications of using this concept, rather than obscuring the implications by introducing a synonym like "usefulness."

Contra Adam Smith and Karl Marx, Reuten thinks that the standard of living of the working class, the life-time cost of raising new workers, does not exert any pressure on wages, determined *solely* (as it turns out) by the amount of value which use of their labour-capacity adds to products, its "usefulness" to the buyer in producing surplus value. Its *utility alone* in other words.

Why, and to what purpose, does Reuten insist on *"creation"* of labour capacity and not *"production,"* and that the capacity to work does not represent the expenses made in the course of their upbringing and education, and has *nothing to do with* the cost of living at a certain cultural level according to one's place in the given social formation – the result largely of past social and industrial struggles of the workers' movement?

It is of course integral to Marx's (and Adam Smith's) view that sustaining the life of a working-class family does indeed have a cost to them, and there is a minimum wage below which a worker cannot or will not present themself or their offspring to work in the next cycle of production and from time to time workers emphasise this point by striking. Like the capitalist, if the worker cannot recover her costs (so as to be able to live and work again the following day) then she stops producing the product. She might find another kind of work or emigrate, but she will not come to work.

It was the insight that wages were determined by workers' costs of living which was at the centre of the 1815 Repeal of the Corn Laws – to reduce the production costs of labour capacity at the expense of the landed aristocracy, which Reuten identifies as the benchmark for bourgeois economic domination of England. It is worth noting also that Reuten uses "rate of surplus value" as the characteristic of a single firm, and is thereby blind to the effect on the cost of living of the workers they employ resulting from economy-wide effects of innovation, length of the working day, etc.

Reuten's capitalists are realists, and do their calculations based only on the status quo here and now and the going market rate for their products; the effects which lead to changes in the economic environment are always *over the horizon* for them.

Humans produce a surplus product, and there is always a struggle over appropriation of that surplus and its valorisation as profit. The struggle to appropriate that surplus product is as old as class society. Capitalism provides the conditions for capitalists to exploit workers and appropriate that surplus product by means of the bourgeois legal norm which means that a worker's product is the property of whoever owns the means of production. The surplus product is transformed into surplus value by means of its sale, realising a profit subject to various technical and market conditions. Many workers nowadays produce in their domestic life more than the minimum needed to work. This is not surplus *value* because it is not valorised, it is simply consumed as their share of the social surplus. That right is the product of class struggle. Reuten has theorised the unity of the capitalist state and the capitalist economy, but he has neglected to include the workers' movement in that picture. That is, I imagine, a reflection of the times we live in.

Given access to socially average means of production, human beings work and produce more than they need to live day by day, and hope to live well by appropriating surplus product for themselves. To whom does the surplus product belong? Working in their own domestic sphere, workers appropriate what is over and above what they need to survive by living a decent life. But under bourgeois right, working for an employer, that surplus is appropriated by the employer.

Labour, Marx says, "is the first premise of all human existence" (1845a). It is not limited to conditions where it is exploited by an alien class. It is conventionally distinguished from consumption and domestic activity on one's own behalf or in friendly collaboration. However, this dichotomy has itself proved to be problematic in its failure to recognise the social and economic impact of the exploitation of women's *domestic labour*. Workers and their children can be recreated almost entirely through the market, the cost being the sum of the costs of the goods and services purchased, or, working-class families can perform the necessary work themselves. Import substitution. The saleable product, a quantity of labour capacity, is just the same. Workers need money to buy the goods and services needed to produce their labour-capacity and they will have to buy it on the market. Working-class life is social, human life, it is not merely a "part of Nature."

Reuten insists that it is in labour capacity's application to production, when wisely employed, that the value of labour capacity is *unilaterally* determined, and not its "price of production" (Reuten's quote marks). If so, then I believe this is a profound misunderstanding of *Capital*, not limited to the question of the determination of wages but extends to the problem of the value of *all* commodities.

In some circumstances, the total labour required to produce a given product may exceed what that product can bring on the market, in competition with other products meeting the same need, and its sale will not make a profit. It is always the *market* which determines the value realised, never mind what was actually spent in production. This is true of labour capacity as much as of any product. In the case of labour capacity, its utility is its capacity to realise value. So, yes, an employer will only pay what he can afford whatever difficulties a worker may face providing the required capacity. The employer is a *realist*. He is not interested in *how things got the way they are*. All that takes place *behind his back*. But if a given capitalist can't make a profit by employing labour he will be out of business.

There is a difference between scientific reason and the understanding of the players in a given practice. People do as they must, but why must they?

The point is that this contradiction (in Reuten's language, an "impediment to on-going sociation") that if the capacity to add value is less than it costs the worker to live at the socially established standard of living it will either destroy the working class or put capitalists out of business. In general, viewed momentarily, *the price is determined in two contradictory ways*: from the point of view of the seller and of the buyer, and monetary value is realised at the moment buyer and seller strike a price. But when the two *systematically* cannot strike a price *the entire economic system adjusts itself*. Capital flows from one sector to another, workers move to different districts, change jobs, new techniques are applied, firms go out of business, until finally (if ever) a dynamic equilibrium is recovered, and the values determined either way allow purchase and sale to provide the conditions for ongoing economic activity including the average rate of profit for capital invested in the given industry. Value is indirectly determined by processes which are not proximal to the point of sale or the point of production. All this is over the horizon for Moneybags. This is why *science* is needed to understand the economy.

However, because production includes a component, labour capacity, which expands its value in the process of being used, then when stability is restored, profit has not been wiped out by competition, but on the contrary, the rate of profit will have been equalised across the economy and sections of the capitalist class have appropriated surplus value. Outmoded techniques become marginalised, poorly skilled workers lose their jobs or suffer wage cuts.

This doesn't come into view in *Capital* until Volume 3 after Marx has taken into account the capital markets and the circulation of capital between particular industries. The "other things being equal" presupposition which Marx relies on in Volume 1 is also relied upon by Reuten, but it seems that Reuten wants the happenstance that maybe workers can indeed live on the going wage determined by the 'utility' of labour capacity for the enterprise, and elevates this seeming happenstance to a necessary, logical starting point. In the hypothetical world implied in Volume 1 of *Capital*, in which economically identical enterprises operate side-by-side in the same world that produced the present generation of workers and factories, it so happens that workers *can* just manage to live on wages corresponding to Moneybags making a profit. We have to wait till Volume 3 to learn about the *dynamics* of an *actual*, diverse economy which produces the tendency towards the equalisation of the rate of profit and an economy-wide basic wage rate, etc.

The value of labour capacity, he says, is determined by *demand only*; supply is free. No amount of mathematical equations (of which Reuten has many) can demonstrate that the value of labour capacity is determined solely by its capacity to generate surplus value irrespective of supply costs. Its value for the employer, at this moment, yes, but by what luck is it that this price is (as it usually is) also sufficient for the workers to "create" that labour capacity and live "decently"? Market savvy is not enough to answer that. Science is needed.

Reuten says that "price of the capacity to labour (i.e. the wage) has nothing to do with the 'price of production' of labour-capacity," and his theory of value has nothing to do with "so-called socially necessary labour-time" (p. 74). Reuten says that the product's price *is* its value. But the price is the *appearance* of its value.

> He [the vulgar economist] boasts that he holds fast to appearance, and takes it for the ultimate. Why, then, have any science at all?
>
> MARX, Letter to Kugelmann, 11 July 1868

There is, he claims, no difference in principle between price and value. How then does the labour market unilaterally determine the level of wages without reference to the cost of living? How is the monetary value of labour to be independent of the cost of living of those who provide the labour capacity. At any given instant, the buyer of labour capacity has no mind at all to workers' cost of living. But whether he gets applicants for the jobs he is advertising and whether his investment in capital is ever activated, certainly does depend on whether the wage he offers is a living wage.

I shall reflect in passing on some of Marx's concepts which Reuten chooses to give up.

2.5.2   Embodied Labour, Value and Price
I grant Reuten that there is something metaphysical about the idea of value being the number of working days of socially necessary labour "embodied" in a product. But give me a better way of expressing the fact that a commodity's value depends on the amount of social labour which is necessarily required under existing social conditions to bring the commodity to market – a non-sensory, social attribute of a product having nothing whatsoever to do with its physical properties. And yes, once a product is *sold* and its value is

finally disclosed, how much of that "embodied labour" was socially necessary *appears* and is now clear for all to see. But the question is: how did it get so expensive? Why does a house cost more than a work of art? That turns out to be a complicated story, but it *is* to do with a quantity of labour. There is no getting around the fact that (abstract) labour is the substance of value, and price is just the *appearance* of that value, to use the Hegelian term.

The basic point is that *value determines price* which is nonetheless realised subject to market conditions. But "market conditions" are totalising a wide array of social conditions, some quite distant from the point of sale. Value is the substance which takes on different forms in capitalist society, a commodity is the simplest form of value, price is the *appearance* of the value of a commodity. Another metaphor: a painting has no colour unless and until light is shed on it, and what is seen depends on the quality of that light. But we still understand that it is the pigment in the painting which determines the colour which is realised by the light; we don't say that only the observed colour is real and the colour of the pigment has no place in science!

Around the turn of the 20th century, under the influence of Positivist philosophy, economists started to eliminate "value" from their vocabulary. Early editions of the works of Alfred Marshall (1842–1924) talked about value, but later editions did not mention the word. It was now all just 'price' determined by supply and demand. In Economics, Science had given way to Positivism. But the determinants of value act *behind the backs* of the agents who meet in the marketplace, and *this* is the stuff of Political Economy. Value is also indispensable to understanding how the working class is exploited, but exploitation is not a concern of modern Economics.

When buyer and seller meet in the market there is the "leap" which transforms a value into a monetary price. But it is still value which appears as the price, still value which is the Substance of what appears, not the other way around. What is it that makes one product have more or less value than another prior to its appearance in the market? "The price of an entity is its monetary value" (2019, p. 44). Yes, and euros or dollars are an appropriate measure of value, but what is the *source*, the *substance*, of that value?

Reuten accepts "price" as *realised* value. But for example, during the course of the process of producing a product, "value" means the *expected* price. The means of production, we learn, also have a "current ideal value" (2019, p. 68) on the same basis. But we cannot take the hopes and opinions of an industrialist as objective scientific categories. The point is: what quantification *should* the industrialist use in *rationally justifying* her expectations? Would she refer to the total monetary value of "embodied labour," the "embodied monetary value," or the going rate on the market at the time? Being a realist, she would use the *going market price* and if she's smart, she would have ensured that her enterprise can make the product with that quantity of labour or less.

The value is determined by socially necessary labour time, and wages (the cost of labour-power) determine the share allocated to the working class. The proportion of the total value which accrues as surplus value to the capitalists is determined by Marx in *Capital* in Volume 1. Volume 2 explains how this value is shared with distributors, retailers and others who do not extract surplus value but claim a share in it and how the different components of value are realised. Volume 3, largely, determines how the industrial capitalists share this surplus value amongst themselves, and this includes goods being sold at *other than* their value. The industrialist is *not interested* in this two-stage view of how the total surplus value comes to be determined, only in how they get their share of it. The industrialist has no need of Marxist political economy. They have a business to run.

2.5.3   Measuring Working Time

Reuten says that the basic measure of labour is time, with coefficients for the skill and the intensity and efficiency of the application of labour capacity. Reuten chooses the unit of calendar year as the unit of time – full-time equivalent working years. That is, he measures only the *hours worked*, and standardises this to worker-years. Marx on the other hand, uses the *working day* as the standard of time by which labour is to be measured. It was up to the employer to keep workers at work as long as possible. This standard allowed Marx to examine the length of the working day. I think Marx's standard makes sense, especially in the light of the fact that the cost of living is largely measured per day, somewhat independently of how many hours are worked. It also, helpfully in the 1860s, focussed workers' attention on the length of the working day.

2.5.4   Abstract Labour

Reuten (2019, p. 51) says that in *Capital* "abstract labour is a placeholder for money" until money appears in the reconstruction. "Placeholder" is a trivialising word for a socially mediated relationship. As I see it, "abstract labour" is an ideal; but it is *also* the type of labour characteristic of fully fledged industrial capitalism: the same worker packs boxes for Amazon one week, skins chickens the next and then serves coffees for Starbucks the next, all for a basic wage. It is abstract labour because it is labour without quality (concrete skill, type). Basic wage work is uniform, simply measured in hours, consequently it is the mirror of money which is the equivalent of just that kind of labour. It is also the labour characteristic of a "society of independent commodity producers" who recognise each other as equals. Purely quantitative labour abstracted from any quality. Abstract labour is the *substance* of value and *appears* as money.

2.6   Rejection of "Embodied Labour" as Determinant of Value, for Price

As to commodities in general, I have tried and failed to find anything in the book which tells me what *creates* or *forms* value if not "embodied labour." "The actual market trade is the value *salto*, the value leap ... the price of an entity is its monetary value." Sure, but what makes me *rationally expect* that this diamond will be equal in value to that house? "The market," is the only answer Reuten gives. To "know the market" is to know where the answer is found, but tells us nothing about the process by which the answer was socially determined. "Value is the market price" is not a *theory* of political economy at all.

2.6.1   "Socially Necessary" and "Socially Average"

Reuten rejects any notion of "socially necessary labour time" as a determinant of value. Moreover, Reuten tells us (2019, p. 74) that "socially necessary" does not mean "socially necessary" but "socially average." In the context of the early chapters of *Capital*, what meaning can "average" have, and how is "average" manifested practically? How does "average" manifest itself as a "thing"? It is an artefact of the statistician and exists only in her imagination. *Total* has a material existence, but average does not.

"Socially necessary" refers to the fact that labour applied to a product which in the conditions of the times is in excess of what was necessary for production of the given use-value, has no value. If somewhere someone can produce the use-value for less expenditure of labour, they will be the price setter. Ideal labour not actual labour, that is, the amount of labour which is socially determined as necessary, is a *social property of a commodity*. And even the realist industrialist knows the difference between wasted labour and necessary labour.

Marx says, in broad terms, that something has value to the extent that the commodity requires for its production a certain quantity of labour at a basic wage, so long as that labour is not wasted in some way but is carried out according to what is socially necessary. The need met by the commodity cannot be met by some other commodity with less such labour – *but* value is realised only at the moment of purchase when it is realised as money and the quantity of labour expended in its manufacture is just history. No buyer, no value, and the labour was wasted. Consequently, if an enterprise believes that it has acted according to the best standards of the time and place, then a calculation of "embodied labour" of this kind can be compared with the going rate in the market. The going rate will be realised as the actual value. But in planning the production process, the enterprise would have a mind to whether it will be able to meet that price and still make a profit at the going rate. They can do a calculation of their integral profit along just the lines that Reuten provides us to give us what they would expect to realise on the market. But you never know.

The above turns out to apply only in the instance that all industries have the same composition of capital, but Reuten does not enter in to this question. He has effectively conflated all three volumes of *Capital* into one.

"Socially necessary labour time" is an *ideal* quantity but it is not a *mental* quantity. It is a property of a commodity which is determined by a vast array of social relations relevant to the production and sale of the product. It is an ideal. The expression "socially necessary" encapsulates the idea that the enterprise does not simply do what is average but more or less accurately divines the state of all the multifarious social factors relevant to their business. That is, it is a product of those social relations *themselves*. It is not a *mental* entity, but an *ideal* entity, something different from "average."

2.6.2   Fictitious Capital

"Fictitious capital" is treated by Marx in Volume 3 of *Capital*. Reuten does not mention this idea, and yet, it seems to me, it more than retains its usefulness. The concept arises from the fact that bank credits to enterprises are always *speculative*. Banks, enterprises and governments benefit from issuing as much of this speculative capital as possible. But its reality lies in the extent to which the speculation upon which the credit was made is validated by subsequent production and purchase of goods and eventual repayment of the debt – the extent to which it can be realised. Given the speculative nature of this credit capital it is never possible until later to say definitively to what extent it is fictitious. When the crisis hits, how much of all that capital was fictitious appears. Just as value appears only at the point of sale.

This means that the claim that money is the measure of value has to be qualified – only insofar as money continues to retain its purchasing power. If so much credit is outstanding with no possibility of being repaid, it is surely only a matter of time before the fiction is exposed. I would like to know why Reuten neither included nor refuted the concept in his book.

2.7   *Money as Bank Credits or as Commodities*

According to Reuten: "Money is created by banks" (2019, p. 4). I am persuaded that present-day fully fledged capitalism cannot be comprehended in the absence of an approach to money like this, rather than *simply* money as a commodity like gold. It is outside my life experience to make a judgment about

Reuten's theory in the context of financial discourse. I have always, like Marx, seen banks as "the most effective vehicles of crises and swindle" (*Capital v. 3*, Chapter 36), concerned with the distribution of surplus value already extracted from productive labour. But clearly, capital accumulation begins with a sum of money. M—C—M'. The money-commodity is only the germ cell of the present-day monetary system. I am willing to take Reuten's word for what's going on in the world of financial capital, but I will not expect to understand from Reuten's exposition of anything about how surplus value is extracted from the working class.

This author has not held money, coin or paper, in his hand for more than five years now. Nor do I use cheques.

> There is no fundamental difference between 'bank-issued money notes' and 'bank account money' (or 'bookkeeping money'), the latter being transferred by signature or electronically. There is a tendency for bank-issued money notes to develop into bank account money. This tendency is predicated on, first, cost efficiency. For each of the bank and the enterprises (as well as other agents), the holding of physical money incurs 'carrying costs'. Secondly, the created bank account money stays with the bank so that, on average at least, its lending power increases.
>
> 2019, p. 105

It is true that Marx wrote *Capital* as a critique of political economy, and as such he was obliged to criticise the concepts and theories of the Political Economists, the theoretical capitalists. But not the apologists. I remain of the view that capital does not create value; it is a social relation by means of which a share of the surplus is cornered by those who do not work.

I don't believe that a writer must choose exclusively this or that concept of money. Marx was aware of "bank money" just as he was of paper money even when he talked about the costs of production of gold and so on in Volume 1. There are different life-worlds in capitalist society, and the ethos of present-day Senators and Central Bank managers is very different to that of the worker and petty capitalist who figure in Volume 1 and do not live in the life-world of commercial bankers and National Treasurers. The commodity idea of money is part of the consciousness and practical activity of workers in bourgeois society. Nevertheless, yes, what goes on in the world of hedge funds and so on is central to the management and control of the economy and is always on the scene when there is a crisis of capitalism. How capital moves around from one activity to another has to be grasped. Capital has to be raised before production can begin.

My aim here is different from Reuten's. My aim is to understand the dialectical method of analysis of complex social formations in the tradition of Hegel and Marx, because I wish to apply this method to problems with which I am familiar, not just the political economy of the OECD nations. Consequently, I am content that I must fall silent before Reuten's analysis of the manifestations of capital accumulation in the latter parts of his book. I also accept that the Functionalist approach makes some sense there insofar as these capitalists act as conscious subjects, participating in the design and modification of capitalist governments' economic policies. Functionalism fails however insofar as it claims to enlighten us on the conditions of existence of capitalism.

Since Marx wrote there has been the transition to imperialism marked by two world wars, the Bretton Woods arrangements and their collapse, and the transformation of the labour process by electronic communications. Surely the point is to *continue* Marx's analysis which began from that universal social practice of producing and exchanging commodities, and where necessary add further layers of concretisation whose necessity has only manifested itself in later history. For example, the gold standard *had to* go because it could not encompass the vast expansion in circulating capital required in the post-Keynesian world.

Reuten has effectively *ignored* the significance of Volume 1 of *Capital*, and attempted to go straight to a "cost of production" theory of value, bypassing the contradiction, while relegating the working class to being a part of Nature, free for exploitation.

For the moment I am prepared to accept that the chapters on finance capital are well-informed and I value Reuten's conclusions, in particular his observations about inevitably escalating demands for regulation alongside the impossibility of either compliance or enforcement, and the ever-increasing danger of a failure of too-big-to-fail banks.

3   Outcomes of Reuten's Book: the Capitalist Crisis

At least six important observations come out of Reuten's book, and I have indicated that on the basis of his expertise, I am willing to conditionally accept Reuten's analysis here. However, it is worth observing that although the work of the first three chapters is claimed to ground his conclusions, the outcomes which are significant for the possibility of the collapse or at least a crisis of capitalism are based on *historical observation*. These tendencies emerged, and then Reuten rationalised them. If Reuten had strictly adhered to his synchronic, structural analysis, these tendencies could not have been included in his book.

In each case, the relevant phenomenon is a "tendency," which Reuten defines as:

> A tendency should be distinguished from an empirical 'trend'. A tendency is the generation of a particular form of an entity (e.g. the corporate form of the enterprise) or the particular quantitative expression of an entity or process (e.g. equalisation of inter-sector rates of profit), this generation being predicated on certain forces or compulsions. A tendency may be counteracted by other tendencies, or by other lower-level complexities.
>
> 2019, p. 691

It is not enough to notice that prices are going up every month to declare a *tendency* of prices to rise, one must identify the contradiction which is the ground for rising prices in order to call it a tendency. (See 2019, pp. 594–595 for Reuten's summary).

3.1   *Historical Tendencies towards Large Welfare States*

The capitalist economy cannot provide a decent living for a large proportion of the population and it generates inequalities of wealth. In addition, the modernisation of technique requires that the population has more and more access to information about the lives of others and ever enhances the capacity of people to communicate with each other. As a result the state must take measures to legitimate itself in the eyes of the vast majority of the population. Most significantly, the state must implement a social security system of some kind. This system provides pensions for both the temporarily and the chronically unemployed, children, the sick and injured and the aged.

In addition, the social security system contributes to moderating the business cycle which would otherwise disrupt capital accumulation every few years, and the state is a major buyer for the products of enterprises, realising profit in the process.

On top of this, the state must bear responsibility to ensure that the enterprises have access to an adequate supply of educated, compliant labour capacity (who will be well informed of how the system works, by the way) which presupposes a more or less extensive public education system and public health system.

The net result is that in OECD countries the state now absorbs about 45% of GDP, most of this being allocated to the social security system, and this expense must be recovered through taxation. Most people are blissfully unaware of the "hidden hand" of the state ensuring conditions for capital accumulation. All the wealthy see of the state in their daily lives is the tax deducted from their income, while the majority of the population probably treasure the services provided by the welfare state, but may still resent taxation. Despite tax being collected from the income of the workers as well as the capitalists, the vast majority of tax comes from tax on the wealthy and is transferred to the poor via state services. The need for vast-majority legitimation is put at risk of the wealthy withdrawing their support for the social security system and other public welfare programs.

The on-going off-shoring of production by the developed capitalist countries has proved beneficial for developing countries, but only at the expense of turning whole cities in the old capitalist countries into rust-buckets, threatening the legitimation of the state and placing even heavier demands on the welfare state.

The state budget has increased from 11% in 1870 to about 45% today, and the contradictions which have driven this expansion (and it must be said, successfully *expanded* the conditions for capital accumulation) continue to drive up the proportion of GDP absorbed by the state. All promises by conservative politicians to limit this expansion are broken as they fail to contain the growth of the state budget. Where will this end?

3.2   *Too-Big-to-Fail Banks*

The ongoing perfection of the practice of concentrating capital into fewer and fewer hands, together with the power of the commercial banks and other financial institutions in modern capitalism leads to ever larger banks. It turns out that the larger banks tend to be *more* not less fragile than smaller banks. Smaller banks can be allowed to fail and their capital destroyed, but when larger banks fail the state must step in to save them to avoid a domino effect wiping out capital, and destroying large sections if not all of a nation's economy. The 2008–09 banking crisis drew attention to the fact that the world has already come very close to a situation where, were such a collapse happen again, there would be no state with the resources to prevent the crisis spreading globally and obliterating all financial institutions. There are now *numerous*, fragile, "too-big-to-fail" banks and it seems only a matter of time before an uncontrollable collapse occurs. Money being almost exclusively in the form of bank accounts, this means one day everyone will get up in the morning to find we have no money other than the small change in our pockets.

In addition to this, there are large corporations dealing in communications or energy which are also too-big-to-fail in that were they to fail large sections of economic activity would become impossible. (See 2019, pp. 344–346 and pp. 451–456).

3.3   The Impossibility of Regulating Capitalism

The threat of a failure of a too-big-to-fail bank is aggravated by the tendency which produces ever more complex and complicated regulation affecting every aspect of life under capitalism. "Complex" refers to the infinite interlocking of laws and regulations coming under various responsibilities of the state and various sectors of economic life, all of which inevitably overlap. "Complicated" refers to the language and massive detail of each piece of legislation. It is truly impossible for anyone engaged in even the simplest economic activity to know what rules apply to their activity, let alone actually comply with them. Every large enterprise must employ teams of lawyers trying to keep themselves within the law.

When the state tries to *simplify* regulations it has the perverse effect that simple regulations end up being interpreted in the courts and even more time and expense is entailed in concretising simplistic legislation through litigation. Although the complexity, complication and the sheer mass of regulation defies measurement, there is no doubt that there is a secular tendency to increase, and regulations are almost never repealed. Each new Act adds to the mass of regulation.

The result is that regulation of the activity of capital is becoming more and more impossible. Thousands of lawyers spend their days finding loopholes to allow their clients to evade regulation, while thousands of public servants beaver away trying to plug those loopholes. The rate of technological change increasingly outpaces the capacity of the state to regulate it. In the face of the danger of too-big-to-fail banks – the most impenetrable of all institutions – the rapidly escalating environmental crisis and the complexity of world trade linking together the burgeoning legal frameworks of nations around the world, capitalism seems headed towards its own destruction. (See 2019, p. 479 & pp. 487–488).

3.4   The Imponderable Complexity of Financial Institutions

In 2014 Andrew Haldane (as chief economist at the Bank of England responsible for the stability of the financial sector as a whole) declared to *Der Spiegel*: The balances of the big banks are 'the blackest of black holes'.

2019, p. 461

The business of the largest financial institutions has become impossibly complex, a situation which has become widely known in the wake of the 2008–09 crisis. In the nature of their business, they hold little in actual deposits, have hundreds of interlocking subsidiaries whose activity they may not understand, and the complexity of their "financial products" are understood only by a small number of experts, and are generally opaque to the senior managers of those institutions. If the managers of these institutions don't know what their own firms are doing, what chance is there of the state regulating them? If any of these large banks are heading for collapse, most likely no one will know about it until it has happened and no one will be in a position to prevent such a collapse. Again, it just seems a matter of time before a global banking crisis leaves us all with empty bank accounts and no capacity to get hold of money either from our own bank account or through our employment. The consequences defy imagination. (See 2019, pp. 456–452).

3.5   *Paralysis of World Trade*
Over and above this, the development of international trade, under the imperative of enterprises to maximise profits, has generated a situation where any given product may have passed through the hands of workers in many different countries. This is made possible by aeroplanes and container ships going back and forth across the globe, generating climate-destroying emissions which are unsustainable. If the nations of the world are to meet their commitment to reduce carbon emissions this trade must stop. But, to take Australia as an example, we don't produce motor vehicles anymore and we are utterly dependent on sending raw materials across the world to sustain life. The covid-19 pandemic demonstrated the impact of even a slight disruption of these supply lines and the fragility of this situation. How is a country to restructure its economy so that it produces what it needs in the absence of international trade? Such a transformation of economic life is almost inconceivable, and yet continuation of this system of global trade is incompatible with continued human life of Earth. (See p. 540).

All five of the above crises represent "necessary impossibilities," contradictions which threaten the possibility of continued social life. They all come together in the climate crisis.

3.6   *The Climate Crisis*
In the face of all this, the promises of governments to limit their carbon emissions so as to avoid the collapse of the ecosystem on which human life relies are simply unbelievable.

4   Conclusion to Chapter 2

The work of "practical abstraction" carried out by money, binding every human action into a single system makes political economy a science unlike any other. It is the queen of sciences. So the recent focus on the relation between Hegel's *Logic* and Marx's *Capital* is of great interest. Reuten committed himself to a project of the greatest significance in setting out to write the book on political economy in the tradition of Hegel and Marx, but taking as his subject matter capitalism as it is today in the OECD countries.

There is no doubt that Reuten knows a lot about political economy and I can believe his book remains a good textbook of political economy. However, he has not succeeded in realising the tradition of Marx and Hegel, of systematic dialectic, in the context of today's political economy. I believe Reuten has failed to understand key concepts of this method. However, these misconceptions of the work of Marx and Hegel have not prevented him from writing a significant work on political economy. The same could doubtless be said of many other economists. But if I am to apply the method of Hegel and Marx to other situations, then I cannot use Reuten's book as an exemplar or model.

What I have called "The Outcomes" of the book, the six interlocking crisis tendencies derived from historical observation, is very much valued, and deserve further attention.

Does *Capital* "Mirror" Sections of Hegel's *Logic*?

1   Introduction

Whatever the success of those who claimed to show that the *Grundrisse* was some kind of "mirror" of Hegel's *Logic*, the idea gripped some scholars of Marx to such an extent that they saw the final version of *Capital* as also a "mirror" of the *Logic*, or rather, partially a "mirror" of one or two books of the *Logic*. In preparing the published manuscripts, Marx had dropped explicit references to the *Logic* in order (it is believed) to make the work more accessible, but many believed he had still continued the practice of "translating" the *Logic* into economic terms. Understanding *Capital* therefore entailed identifying *which* section of the *Logic* was being mirrored by *which* sections of *Capital*.

As before, this is not a question to which Hegel scholars have paid attention. It has been Marxists who have been engaged in this debate, and not always with a great familiarity with Hegel's *Logic*.

Capital was a published book and its structure was different to that of the *Grundrisse* manuscripts recovered from his notebooks, so the question of which part of the *Logic* is being "mirrored" in *Capital* had to begin from scratch.

There are four answers to this question according to whether the writer thinks (1) that *Capital* "mirrors" the Essence Logic, (2) that the first Part of Volume 1 of *Capital* mirrors the Logics of Being and Essence and goes no further than this, or (3) that there are echoes of Hegel's *Logic* throughout *Capital* but not of a whole cloth so to speak. Another group finds (4) that *Capital* reflects the Concept Logic, specifically its first part, the Subject, but I will deal with this latter approach at greater length in Chapter 4.

2   Hegel's Use of the *Logic*

Something which is never discussed is whether Hegel himself replicated the *Logic* in other parts of his *Encyclopaedia* where he composed outlines of a range of natural and social sciences.

In general, the Philosophy of Nature, in which Hegel outlines the Physics, Chemistry and Biology of his own times is discounted by everyone outside of specialist Hegel scholars for the reason that what he wrote is closely tied to the relatively primitive state of early 19th century natural science, and apparently much along the lines of the discredited Natural Philosophy. Likewise his study of Psychology (in its broadest sense, i.e., beginning with the formation of a psyche in the lower animals) has received little attention among Marxists, or even among Hegel scholars. Apart from the *Logic*, the only part of the *Encyclopaedia* which Marxists have studied has been the *Philosophy of Right*, an expanded version of the Objective Spirit in the *Encyclopaedia* which Marx studied at the very beginning of the project which culminated in *Capital*. So far as I know, no one, or at least no one familiar with Hegel's work, has claimed any of these sciences to have been given a structure by Hegel which "mirrors" that of the *Logic*.

Doubtless someone somewhere has made such a claim. There are *similarities* to be found here and there; all the subjects treated by Hegel exhibit a triadic structure for instance. But it does beg the question: if Hegel didn't think a scientific treatment of Right (for example) should have the same structure as the *Logic*, why on Earth would someone else, someone critical of Hegel, think that Political Economy should have the same structure as the *Logic*?

The abstraction process effected by market exchange, something unique to the political economy of bourgeois society, can be seen in one way or another as replicating the process of judgment and therefore connected to the *Logic*. I think there is some basis for this claim which also gives rise to metaphors between language and economic value, though neither Marx nor Hegel made this claim. Metaphors have pedagogic value, but limited scientific value.

Both Marx and Hegel have said that "every one is a son of his time; so philosophy also is its time apprehended in thoughts" (Hegel, 1821, Preface). The claim that the political economy of the times "seeps into" a philosopher's thinking, does have a real basis. But whether that can be a basis for Hegel's *Logic* mimicking the logic of the market is something else. Especially when we are dealing with a philosopher of the standing of Hegel. As Chris Arthur says, the scope of the *Logic* is so much wider than any one science such as Economics.

But in any case, capitalism is not a society of simple commodity production, a point on which Chris Arthur has written at length. If value-consciousness was behind how Hegel wrote the *Logic*, was it also behind how he wrote his Physics, his Psychology, his Social Theory and so on? If the domination of value-consciousness is behind the symmetry between the *Logic* and Political Economy, has it been show to be expressed in the other sciences?

Neither Hegel nor Marx ever claimed that political economy or any other science would be a "mirror" of the *Logic*. Hegel's works contain many other possible "models" for the structure of a science, and so far as I know no one in this debate about the *Capital/Logic* relation has examined the structure of the other sciences in Hegel's *Encyclopaedia*.

Nor has anyone in this debate examined the text in which Hegel tells us what he thinks are the appropriate principles for structuring a natural or social science. These principles are to be found in the chapter of the *Logic* entitled "The Idea of the True," and it is never mentioned in the present-day debate. These principles *are* however reflected in all the sciences elaborated by Hegel in the *Encyclopaedia* and some 20th century writers have understood these principles.

A moment's reflection on what Logic is is worthwhile before we proceed further. I assert that Logic has to be the logic *of* something. For example, it could be a propositional logic such as traditional formal logic, a category logic, quantum logic, or an evidentiary logic such as used in the Law, and so on. It seems to me that Hegel intended his Logic to be a logic of enquiry and must therefore make no presuppositions. But at the same time Hegel rightly insists that such a logic must follow the logic of its subject matter. Taking Hegel's two claims together poses interesting questions about how a logic can be *both* the logic of its subject matter *and* a dialectical logic of enquiry. But nowhere do I see any basis in Hegel's writing for the idea of logic as a *model* of some subject matter. I will argue elsewhere that Hegel's *Logic* is the logic of human practice.

The general idea of a philosopher being a child of his time and therefore unconsciously reflecting the economic relations of the time in their logic seems to me to be quite insufficient as a basis for linking directly to value-consciousness the logic of a philosopher of Hegel's standing. Every one of more than 400 conceptual transitions in the *Logic* and as many again in the rest of the *Encyclopaedia* is argued on its own merits by Hegel, and I find the idea that he was blinded by value-consciousness throughout such work implausible. The logic of each step in Hegel's *Logic* needs to be taken seriously on its own merits.

Finally, Hegel took pains to ensure that no content was smuggled into the *Logic* via axioms or the implicit content of whatever concept the *Logic* took as its starting point. Any positive science is based on the opposite stance in that a science must make its beginning from some experience or practical problem. This simple fact, which distinguishes Political Economy and every other science from Logic, is never considered by advocates of Hegel's *Logic* as a "coded political economy."

I shall now examine the work of those writers who have taken one or another part of the *Logic* to be "mirrored" in *Capital*.

2.1   Capital *Mirrors the Essence Logic?*

Tony Smith is a well-known advocate of the idea that *Capital* "mirrors" the Essence Logic. However, Smith cites Arash Abazari as his authority for this claim, so I will first examine what evidence Abazari musters to support the claim in his book *Hegel's Ontology of Power. The structure of social domination in capitalism* (Abazari, 2020). My aim in the review is limited to consideration of his use of Hegel. I shall not further examine the work as it is founded on a fiction.

3   Abazari's Reading of Hegel

Abazari does not believe that Hegel wrote a logic at all: "the logic can be read as an 'encrypted social theory'" (2020, p. 14, note). He further claims that "Hegel's critical theory of capitalism is to be found in his *Science of Logic*," and in a footnote he elaborates:

> A brief note about the structure of the *Science of Logic* is necessary. The *Science of Logic* is a two-volume book, consisting of the "objective logic" and the "subjective logic." The objective logic itself is divided into two parts: the logic of being and the logic of essence. The subjective logic is also called the logic of the Concept. My project is on the logic of essence. For methodological reasons that will become clear later, *I entirely ignore the subjective logic* (except for a brief discussion in the Conclusion). I will also deal with the logic of Being only marginally, namely, insofar as it is necessary for understanding the Logic of Essence.
>
>   2020, footnote, p. 9, my emphasis

and he makes a pertinent and correct point on the relation between the three books of the Logic: Being, Essence and Concept:

> The logic of Being terminates with the category of "absolute indifference" that expresses the unsurpassable conceptual block that is attained within the framework of Being. Hegel's exposition of the logic of Being therefore is intended to *criticise* it.
>
>   2020, p. 22

If you stopped reading the *Science of Logic* with the Logic of Being, aside from the Hegelian language and the sequence by which the categories are arranged, you would be left with little more than the categories of mainstream quantitative science at the level of empirical observation and surveys, winding up with a kind of almanac. It is Hegel's Ontology in the form of an immanent critique of the concept of Being.

The Essence Logic, looking behind what is immediately given and subjecting the "facts" to examination in the light of existing theories, also winds up in an infinite regression of cause-and-effect, action-and-reaction, and so on – "an unsurpassable conceptual block" to use Abazari's apt expression above. Essence is Hegel's *epistemology* in the form of a critique of the traditional concept of Reflection.

The Concept Logic, the book which Abazari decided to "entirely ignore," is the *chief subject matter* of Hegel's *Logic*. This is where Hegel makes his most original contribution. The Concept Logic is a sublation of both Being and Essence, the Logic which transcends traditional Ontology and Epistemology, while retaining them as moments within itself. It is the Logic which grasps that perception is both mediated and immediate.

Thus, by limiting himself to the Essence Logic, Abazari is, despite the Hegelian-looking language, actually stopping at just the point where Hegel's real originality begins. But this is actually irrelevant, because Abazari does not claim to use Hegel's *Logic* as a logic of enquiry, but as an "encrypted social theory."

His claim in relation to methodology is:

> I aim to offer a Marxian interpretation of Hegel's logic *and* a Hegelian interpretation of Marx's critique of political economy. ... my methodological principle is to analyse Hegel's text closely, and to make explicit *only* what is already implicit in the text.
>
> 2020, p. 10

So he claims to read *only* between the lines because Hegel's *encrypted* social theory is "implicit" in Hegel's *Logic*. But this does not absolve him of demonstrating that it is *indeed* implicit there.

He claims to:

> reconstruct the Logic of Essence on the basis of three major categories: *Schein*, which I translate, dependent on context, as "illusion" or "semblance"; "opposition" [*Gegensatz*]; and "totality" [*Totalität*].
>
> 2020, p. 11

However, we wait in vain to find any explanation for the basis on which he ignored Hegel's *own explicit* construction of Essence in terms of Reflection, Appearance and Actuality. (Refer to the 'Outline of Science of Logic', p. 9 above).

"Semblance" and "Opposition" are quite subordinate categories, found along with Identity, Difference, Diversity, Contradiction and Ground in the first phase of Essence (Reflection), and Totality is *not* one of the categories of Essence at all. Indeed, how could it be, because as Hegel shows, the Essence Logic *can never get to the totality*. Like Being, Essence comes up against an "unsurpassable conceptual block," unable to grasp the totality. So already, Abazari has arbitrarily rewritten Essence by copying a few phrases from Hegel's text and arranging them in an order which suits his own purpose.

He goes on:

> for Hegel the "identity" of individuals obtains through the relation of "opposition," and that opposition in its developed form is a relation of domination. The two claims together establish that for Hegel individuals are constituted in and through the relation of domination that obtains between them.
>
> 2020, pp. 11–12

No evidence is given as to how "domination" entered the *Logic* here. It is news to me and I imagine for any Hegel scholar. And

> Hegel's ontology in the Logic of Essence is absolutely relational. That is to say, for Hegel, individuals are not separable from the relations that obtain between them, but are solely derived from those relations. The ontology of absolute relationality commits Hegel to conceiving of the totality of relations as prior to individuals, as that which constitutes individuals.
>
> 2020, p. 12

Ontology is defined as the study of Being, the preceding phase of the Logic. But Abazari sees in the Logic of Essence an *ontology* of his own, and the beings in question turn out to be not logical categories, but individual persons and "absolute relationality," presumably referring to social relations between persons. Nowhere does Abazari explain the basis on which what Hegel presented as logical concepts and the relations between them can be taken to be individual persons and the relations between them. And nor is there any explanation given for why Hegel encrypted his social theory while at the same time presenting his social theory in the *Philosophy of Right* (which is basically a reform agenda advocating a constitutional monarchy), in which he had already said:

> The scientific method by which the conception [of freedom] is self-evolved, and its phases self-developed and self-produced ... The true process is found in the logic, and here is presupposed.
>
> HEGEL, 1821, §31

Hegel *did have* a social theory, and censorship notwithstanding, he was able to publish it. He made it clear that the *Logic* is the *scientific method* (and not the "philosophical foundation," 2020, p. 6). Hegel took the *Philosophy of Right*, to be about Freedom, actualised as Right, not "power" or "domination" or "recognition." Hegel presented the *Logic* as the first Book of the *Encyclopaedia of the Philosophical Sciences*, and then went on to implement this method in outline based on the existing body of science, first in the natural sciences and then in the human sciences. The only place "individuals" (*i.e.* persons) appear in his works is in the human sciences. The Logic contains *logical* concepts. Granted it is not as simple as that. Hegel's *Logic* is evidently more than just logic in the normal sense, but it is still logic, a logic of enquiry.

Over and above this Abazari misrepresents many of the Hegelian categories in matters of detail, but in the light of the above, this is hardly surprising, since he has bent Hegel's meaning to match his own agenda. I will spend no further time on reviewing Abazari. How the *Logic*, let alone which part, can be used for social theory remains an outstanding question.

4 Tony Smith on *Capital* and the Essence Logic

Tony Smith has written a great deal on this question since the 1980s, and has responded to numerous critiques, but I will just focus on his (2014) contribution to the volume he edited with Fred Moseley, *Marx's Capital and Hegel's Logic*. It is entitled "Hegel, Marx and the Comprehension of Capitalism."

Smith says that he accepts that Marx took himself to be basing the structure of *Capital* on his understanding of Hegel's *Logic*, and in particular he is aware that Marx took capital to be a "Subject" (the first chapter of the Concept Logic). But Smith tells us that we should "put aside" (2014, p. 25) Marx's own view of what he was doing because the "the concept of capital does not fit what Hegel referred to as the Logic of the Concept" (2014, p. 29). This claim, however, rests on Smith's own misunderstanding of the relevant concepts of the *Logic*.

None of the concepts of the *Logic* can be understood without first accepting the intention of the *Logic* as a logic of enquiry, and understanding the overall structure of the *Logic* by means of which Hegel fulfils this central intent. In the opening section of his contribution, Smith correctly draws attention to the mistake of interpreting Hegel as some kind of Deist with the Absolute Idea playing the role of God. However, remnants of this mistake remain in his own "methodological" interpretation of Hegel's *Logic*.

4.1 Preamble on the Structure of the Logic

Hegel's *Logic* is a logic of enquiry. A logic is not a model. A logic is not a post facto representation of a completed, complex object, but a *logic of enquiry* which unfolds from the facts of a subject matter and adapts to the logic of its subject matter, which could be logic, political economy, biology or some other science. In Hegel's words:

> all that is needed to ensure that the beginning remains immanent in its scientific development is to consider, or rather, ridding oneself of all other reflections and opinions whatever, simply to take up, *what is there before us.*
>
> HEGEL, 1816, p. 68

Having made a beginning, science must "lead towards a reproduction of the concrete by way of thought" (Marx, 1973/1858), that is, a concrete concept of the subject matter. There is nothing idealist about this "reproduction of the concrete by way of thought." Marx did not *end* with this characterisation of his own project. He said that "[t]he real subject retains its autonomous existence outside the head just as before; namely as long as the head's conduct is *merely speculative*, merely theoretical" though "in the theoretical method, too, the subject, society, must always be kept in mind as the presupposition" (Marx, 1973/1858, p. 102). Marx was a revolutionary; his method was agitation and intervention in popular struggles, not merely "speculative." But the "theoretical method" offered by Hegel, was "the presupposition." But as Marx wrote in *Theses on Feuerbach* (1845) – the *point* is to change it.

How does Hegel propose that such a "theoretical method" should "reproduce the concrete"? He does not, as is frequently supposed, "derive" the world as it is from a presuppositionless concept like Being. Hegel did not contradict Kant's observation that "all our knowledge begins with experience" (Kant, 1787). But he recommended the researcher apply the method of the *Logic* to each of the myriad of sciences which together make up human knowledge. This he demonstrated in outline in the *Encyclopaedia*. But note that none of the sciences outlined in the *Encyclopaedia* have the same structure as the *Logic*. Logic is just one very peculiar science. Any of the sciences of "nature or spirit" takes its beginning from what Hegel calls "externality," specifically the field of practice which provides the science with its content. The *Logic*, on the other hand, is abstracted entirely from "externality," *i.e.*, from all empirical and practical content. In this sense, Logic is obviously something different from Physics or Psychology or Law, or Political Economy.

So, how then does Hegel suggest that a philosopher should proceed in forming a reproduction of the concrete in thought, a concrete concept of the subject matter? First, Hegel takes from each of the sciences, "the concrete in thought," the unit from which to make its beginning. This unit is taken from practical experience and the existing science and represents the simplest immediately given individual form of the subject matter in the given science, a unit which can be grasped independently of the science, without yet a knowledge of the universal and particulars of the science which is built upon it. Identifying this unit is the first task which confronts the researcher in investigating a field of practice.

Hegel suggests that we proceed one science at a time (The age of encyclopaedic individuals ended with Hegel. Henceforth, each science would be taken up separately by different people). Any one science he saw as one, initially abstract, concept which concretises itself and successively merges with other concepts – "abstract determinations leading towards a reproduction of the concrete by way of thought" (Marx, 1973/1858). The Concept Logic represents the trajectory of *just one* of these concepts. The initial, abstract concept which is definitive of that *one* science (or form of practice) is what Hegel calls the "Subject" in the *Logic*.

The first two books of the *Logic*, Being and Essence, are the logic of the *genesis* of a Subject (a science, or some form of practice), and the third book of the *Logic*, the Concept Logic, reflects the *development* of the Subject itself once its founding concept is established. The development of the Subject takes place both "internally" and "externally." The internal development of the Subject is described by the three-way interaction of Universal, Particular and Individual moments of the concept, in which an initially abstract conception takes on innumerable nuances, applications, specialised principles, etc., drawing into its scope divers concrete individual instances. This internal development of the Subject takes place simultaneously with the external development, namely the formation of successively deeper relations with *all the other concepts or forms of practice*, together called the "Object." The third and final part of the development, the Idea, represents the Subject merged with the Object – all the other concepts or forms of practice, changing and changed by each other, and developing together. It is important to see that these various phases (including those in Being and Essence) do not unfold in *temporal succession*, one after the other, though they do develop thanks to what Fred Moseley has called "successive determination." The seeming movement plays out for the reader like waves endlessly washing over one another, or like individual people whose lives are both products of the world they live in and change the world. It is not like a train travelling down a track, one station after another, to its final destination, as in Formal Logic, but nor is it a static *structure*. It is a logic of successive determination.

So "Subject" does not at all mean some God-like agent building the world. It is just *one* science (or one social movement, form of practice, new technique, business, one person, one branch of production, ...), but one alongside, before and after innumerable *other* subjects ... such as *capital*. Think of Marx's apt observation: "There is in every social formation a particular branch of production which determines the position and importance of all the others, and the relations obtaining in this branch accordingly determine the relations of all other branches as well." (Marx, 1859).

Once you understand this structure of Hegel's *Logic* then it is possible to make well-founded judgments about what this or that concept in the Logic "is like," "reminds you of", or is "isomorphic or homologous with" etc. But it is best of all to just take the *Logic* at its word, as the logic of forms of practice, reflected in the relevant logic of enquiry.

Nothing in the above synopsis is an "interpretation" of Hegel's *Logic*. Admittedly, I have popularised the *Logic* in my explanation and have avoided, so far as possible, Hegel's obscure, idealistic language and avoided theistic connotations. But Hegel called it a "logic," albeit a logic which is to be governed by its subject matter, and he meant it and it should be read as such. There is no basis for taking the *Logic* as a "model."

Many Hegel scholars, including Walter Kaufman, Charles Taylor, Robert Pippin and even Robert Brandom agree that the real subject matter of Hegel *Logic* is human activity. Marxists are not alone in this belief. However, none have been able to go beyond this generalisation as I do. Humans may be irrational beings, but everything they do passes through their minds; we do things for reasons, however irrational those reasons. Thought exists only as an aspect abstracted from the human activity of which it is a part.

4.2   *Mixing Up Absolute Idea, Thought, Spirit and Subject*
I will now briefly review a couple of key concepts of Hegel's *Logic* which make it possible to see how Smith misunderstands them.

4.2.1   The Subject

> In [Marx's] view the structure of capital is precisely isomorphic with the structure of Hegel's Absolute.
>
> 2014, p. 23

Marx never made any such claim. Two points. Marx's aim is to create a concrete concept (i.e., a science) of capital, so the Hegelian concept at issue is the Subject, not "the Absolute." In any case, "Absolute" is ambiguous: which Absolute? Hegel applies "Absolute" to any category which in the given logical context, is relatively perfect, complete or self-sufficient. Smith says:

> Marx's claim, in brief, is that capital must be comprehended as an absolute 'Subject' in the Hegelian sense of the term.
>
> 2014, p. 24

This recalls Postone's (1993) claim that Marx takes capital to be an "identical Subject-Object." But this is false, too. Marx aimed to analyse capital *as it was*, not some imagined future, all-embracing 'Absolute capital'. More precisely, Marx aimed to *abstract capital* from its intersection with the various *other* practices summed up in Hegel's concept of the Object, and which together with the Object made the Idea, or Life. But the conception of "Absolute capital," capital which exists without the support of any *other* practices such as production, the state, the family ... is a fantasy.

Secondly, the claim of *isomorphism*, capital having the same form or shape, so to speak, as the *Logic* or some part of it, is absurd and no one has demonstrated this isomorphism. In any case, such structural similarity is the most superficial view possible of the relation between the *Capital* and the *Logic*. It is the *logic of capital* which Marx was interested in.

To make sense of the *Logic* in respect to one particular activity, in this case *capital*, it is important to understand "concepts" as forms of human practice (activities), just as Marx suggested in *Theses on Feuerbach*,

> 1. The main defect of all hitherto-existing materialism – that of Feuerbach included – is that the Object [*der Gegenstand*], actuality, sensuousness, are conceived only in the form of the object [*Objekts*], or of contemplation, but not as human sensuous activity, practice, not subjectively. Hence it happened that the active side, in opposition to materialism, was developed by Idealism.
>
> MARX, 1845

And in Hegel's words:

> Philosophy has to do with ideas or realised thoughts, and hence not with what we have been accustomed to call mere conceptions [*abstrakte Verstandesbestimmungen*].
>
> HEGEL, 1821, §1n

So in this very general sense, "capital" has the same structure as *any* concept, insofar as it is a concept and that concept is grasped scientifically. The Concept Logic is a logic of concepts. *Any* science could be studied in this way, as a particular realisation of the Concept Logic. What is special about capital is, among other things, that capital is a form of human activity that acts on people *as if* it were an alien force of Nature, a quasi-natural force, seemingly independent of the intentions, consciousness or actions of any individual, but is in fact nothing other than social relations between people. All sciences, social movements, institutions or whatever have this character to a greater or lesser degree, but this is particularly striking in relation to capital.

Smith expresses this important aspect of the Concept Logic when he says: "capital is a universal *distinct* from its moments, while being simultaneously *continuous* and *identical* with these moments" (2014, p. 23). Individual companies, particular industries and regulations come and go, but through every bankruptcy and every takeover, every disaster and every discovery, capital continues unabated according to its own logic. Any such genuinely fundamental concept, be it capital, science, religion, evolution, war, or whatever, exhibits this character. But Science is also a practice and it has its own logic.

The error of seeing in this approach an Idealism originates to some extent from Hegel's idealistic presentation, but generally it arises as much from the readers' own idealism in presuming that "concept" refers to some "abstract determination of the understanding," or some *mental* entity. This subjective idealism is then imputed to Hegel. Hegel was a monist, and his language makes it very easy to interpret the subject matter of the Logic to be thinking. But it makes much more sense in our times to see that the real subject of Hegel's *Logic* was always human practice, except that Hegel chose to present only the ideal side of human activity (the "shadows" as Marx put it), even though Hegel never doubted that:

> Consciousness is spirit as a concrete knowing, a knowing too, in which externality is involved; but the development of this object, like the development of all natural and spiritual life, rests solely on the nature of the pure essentialities which constitute the content of logic.
>
> HEGEL 1816, Preface

Being true to Hegel's conception of the sciences, the science of capital begins with the concept of *capital in general*, what Hegel calls the Universal moment of the Subject, and proceeds from there to particular formations of capital and their interrelations. Hegel tells us to make a beginning from the Universal.

> The first requisite for this is ... that the beginning be made with the sub-
> ject matter in the form of a *universal*.
>
> HEGEL, 1816, p. 801

The logic of the *genesis* of the Subject is treated in the first two books of the
Logic: Being and Essence. But the genesis of capital out of pre-capitalist or
early capitalist formations and the genesis of the theoretical expressions of
capital are not part of the science of capital, and are largely not included in
Capital, but are treated by Marx elsewhere.

Smith however rejects the idea that *Capital* bears any relation to the Concept
Logic, and does so in the face of Marx himself seeing capital as a subject, albeit
an "automatic subject."[1]

> Just as in general when examining any historical or social science, so also
> in the case of the development of economic categories is it always nec-
> essary to remember that the subject, in this context *contemporary bour-
> geois society*, is presupposed both in reality and in the mind.
>
> MARX, 1859

4.2.2   Thought and Geist

Smith chose not to take "thought" in the sense quoted above – as realised
thoughts, i.e., practices; rather Smith takes thoughts to be "abstract determinations of the understanding." So Smith argued against "the *Logic* as the
unfolding of a reified and all-powerful Absolute Thought." He suggested that
"'absolute thought' refers instead to *anyone's* thinking in so far as it 'cognises
the immanent soul of [the] material ...'" (2014, p. 25, citing Marx) and alluding to "Hegel's inexcusably idiosyncratic way of discussing my thinking, the
thinking of any 'I' and the thoughts that are products of this activity." Smith
had already noted that the younger Marx, as a part of his struggle against the
Young Hegelians, was rhetorically inclined to such condemnations of Hegel
and never recanted these views. However, having made this point, he continues to cite Marx in order to impute frankly absurd beliefs to Hegel.

But what is distinctive about Hegel's philosophy is that he was a *monist*. He
did not set out from a dichotomy between matter and mind. This fact should
alert any attentive reader of the *Logic* to the ascription of mystical ideas to
Hegel. Anyone who objects to or ignores this monism will have to be content
with Kant, because dualism can take you no further. When Hegel writes about

---

1   *"ein automatisches Subjekt,"* (1983/1867, *Das Kapital, b. 1,* k. IV). This expression was lost in
    some English translations.

"thought" he is *not* talking about subjective thought-forms. Likewise, *Geist*, as in the *Zeitgeist* or "spirit of the times," does *not* mean some supernatural ethereal entity ruling human life, but rather the *totality* of human activity *itself*, the institutions, practices, technology and customs which condition what can and can't be done. *Geist* is grasped through concepts (German *Begriffe*, from *begreifen*, to grasp). How else? Marx largely resolved the problem of taking up Hegel's monism without the idealistic baggage in *Theses on Feuerbach* in which he says: "All mysteries which lead theory to mysticism find their rational solution in human practice and in the comprehension of this practice" (Marx, 1845).

This is not to deny that there remain important methodological (not to say political) differences between Marx and Hegel on the question of the relation between consciousness and behaviour. But as I argued in my chapter, "What is the Difference Between Hegel and Marx?" (Blunden, 2021), six different dimensions can be identified along which the materialist/idealist difference can be rendered, and Marx counts as an Idealist along at least two of those six dimensions. The difference is by no means cut and dry.

4.3   *Mixing Up Universal, Subject and Being*

Smith gives a one-paragraph summary of the structure of *Capital*:

> the movement from capital in general (understood as the theory of the production and circulation of total social capital), through many capitals (the 'redistribution' of total social capital within and across different sectors of capital), to bank-capital (the empirically existing form of capital as such) corresponds to the moments of universality, particularity and singularity examined in the chapter of the *Logic* titled 'The Concept'.
>
> 2014, p. 38

Smith here more or less accurately represents Marx's position, as I see it. Marx did take bank-capital to be the Individual (or Singular) moment of capital at one point in the *Grundrisse* and finance capital does occupy the last part of Volume 3. But in Part v of Volume 3 of *Capital*, where bank-capital is dealt with, Marx applies the word "individual" to individual shareholders or individual capitals (firms). I believe that Marx was mistaken in taking bank-capital as the Individual moment, but in any case, it plays a subordinate role in *Capital*. Smith is correct on the Universal and Particular moments.

Having just plausibly and clearly outlined the resemblance of the structure of *Capital* to the Subject in the Concept Logic, Smith goes on to compare *Capital* instead to the *entire Logic*:

At the beginning of a Hegelian systematic ordering [of logical categories in the *Logic*] the 'universality' we find is an empty determination, abstract universality* [Being]. At the conclusion of the theory we attain a comprehension of concrete universality [The Idea], that is, a universal whose determinations are fully developed and explicit.* Marx's notion of 'capital in general' is not homologous with either of these notions of universality. 'Capital in general' is not an empty abstraction. Nor is it transcended as Marx's theory advances the way an immediate (simple) form of abstract universality is transcended in Hegel's methodological framework ... On the other hand, 'capital in general' does not correspond to the Hegelian notion of concrete universality either. The latter *includes* all essential determinations of the relevant region, while the level of capital in general *abstracts* from all essential determinations of capital but not directly relevant to the production and circulation of total surplus value.

2014, pp. 38–39

What is the point of comparing *Capital*, which he has *just shown* to be comparable to the first part of the *Concept Logic* (the Subject), with the *whole* of the *Logic*? Political Economy is not Logic. Capital is a Subject, not The Absolute Idea.

In a footnote to 'universality' at the end of the first sentence cited above (*) he says: "Hegel describes 'Being', the first category of the *Logic* in these terms." (fn p. 38). But 'Being', the first category of the *Logic*, is *not* 'universality', which is the first category of the Concept Logic, 520 pages after 'Being'. *Logic* begins from such an "empty concept" because Logic has no presuppositions, but this is not the case with any of the natural or social sciences which always begin from some natural fact or problem.

A footnote to the second sentence (*), tells us that what is being referred to here is the Absolute Idea. However, Marx deals only with the moments of the Subject, capital, and does not deal with the Object or the Idea, falling far short of the Absolute Idea. His exposition of capital even stopped short of elaborating the Individual moment of Subjectivity (in my view, individual capitalist companies). If Marx had gone on to explore the interaction of capital with the Object (state, family, science, technique, the environment, religion, etc.), and developed a finished theory of capitalist *societies as a whole* in the light of the interaction of capital with the multiplicity of other projects, then he would have to go so far as the Idea in Hegel's terminology. Marx wisely left that task to "posterity, who will be more intelligent than us" (Trotsky, 1936). It was however the kind of task Hegel undertook in his *Encyclopaedia*, and such "systems of everything" were thoroughly discredited by the time Marx wrote *Capital*.

Smith contrasts the "grand sweep of Marx's theory" with "a particular chapter in Hegel's work" (2014, p. 38). But Marx's life's work on *Capital* was focussed on one Subject, viz., capital, elaborating a general theory for just *one* science (or one practice, …) abstracted from its cultural and economic surroundings and its historical development. The Subject is one chapter out of all Hegel's works which were *literally* encyclopaedic in scope. Marx did not set out to write a replacement for the *Encyclopaedia of the Philosophical Sciences*, but to bequeath to the world *the paradigm of just one science*, the science of capital. This is how Science has mostly developed since Hegel died. A single writer writes a paradigmatic study of one phenomenon, and the history of science unfolds through the mutual interaction between these paradigms, the development of technology and social life. Much as he would have liked to have written a book on the state and other topics, he had only one lifetime to write *Capital*, whereas Hegel skipped over the topic in a few paragraphs in the *Philosophy of Right* so as to cover all the sciences in his *Encyclopaedia*.

"Putting aside" (2014, p. 25) Marx's well-founded use of the Concept Logic as the basis for the structure of *Capital* by conflating two sections of the Subject with the entire *Logic*, Smith went on to argue instead for a homology of *Capital* with the Essence Logic.

4.4　　*The Claim That* Capital *Is an Essence Logic*

It can be useful to understand the logic of enquiry (which is how Hegel intended it to be read), in terms of how one new fact or observation "ripples" through an existing science or system of belief eventually modifying its central concept. The Logic of Being begins from such a hypothetical new observation, as yet uninterpreted.

At first this new observation just *is*. *What* it is is still indeterminate – a sharp drop in GDP, an unexpected vote for a fringe candidate, a sharp rise in sea temperature, or maybe a global financial crisis, … This is Being, the empty concept from which the enquiry begins, without prejudice, so to speak. First, there is an *analysis* of the new observation, what's distinctive and makes it stand out from the background, and concludes with the concept of One, i.e., that the new observation is One, of which there are presumed to be many if we are to make sense of this one new observation. There follows a *synthetic* conceptual process which concludes with Measure, effectively the concept of a kind of 'almanac' of such observations, like, for example, the government's statistical report on the economy in the past year, of which economists have to make sense with their theories. This 'almanac' would be an exemplar of the category of Real Measure, completes the first book of the *Logic*, Being.

Next comes the Logic of Essence in which past knowledge has to modify itself and develop in response to the new data. No analysis can begin without data which confirms at least that *something* is happening.

The Logic of Essence outlines the concepts which arise as the past body of knowledge responds to the new fact trying to make sense of it. So the first moment of the Essence Logic is called "Reflection." The Essence Logic is unable to complete this process aimed at characterising the new situation "as a whole," or "in a nutshell." It gets to the brink of that moment, but the leap to a new concept marks the beginning of the third book of the *Logic*, the Concept Logic.

Let's look at how Smith finds a "model" for capital in the Essence Logic.

4.4.1   Smith's Reason for Choosing Essence as the "Model" for Capital

Smith sets up his claim for the similarity of *Capital* and Hegel's Essence Logic by arguing:

> Marx's theory begins where the Doctrine of Being ends. Hegel starts with the pure simplicity and utter emptiness of a category enabling only an affirmation of being. Marx begins with the simplicity of the 'commodity' [why?] in generalised commodity production, rent in two by the massive gulf separating (the nonetheless inseparably conjoined) dimensions of use-value and exchange-value.
>
> 2014, pp. 30–31

But the commodity is emphatically *not* an empty category! Its content is human labour. Smith continues:

> Hegel then considers attempts to categorise a supposedly separate something in terms of what it is in itself, apart from its relationship to what is 'other', with the incoherence of all such attempts a result. Marx, in contrast, begins his critique of political economy with a social world in which a) no separate commodity can be adequately comprehended in itself apart from its relations to other commodities, and b) no separate act of producing commodities can be adequately comprehended apart from its relations to other acts within a division of labour.
>
> 2014, p. 31

The footnote indicates that this is Smith's gloss of the first few Chapters of *Capital*, which, given that Smith claims that *Capital* reflects the Essence Logic, is to be compared to what appears to be Smith's gloss of the first moment of Reflection in Hegel's Essence Logic, but a moment ago he was comparing it to Being. Reflection, it should be noted arises from reflection on the last category of the Logic of Being, namely, Real Measure, which is not really an "empty concept" but in the *Logic* it *is* a formal concept. (And incidentally, I cannot relate Smith's gloss of this Chapter of the *Logic* to *anything* in the *Logic*).

This point needs to be emphasised because it reflects a widespread misconception. The Logic begins from Being, an "empty concept," yes. It is important that the beginning of Logic imports *no unstated presuppositions* through its starting point. However, this is *not the case* for any of the natural and social sciences. Each of these positive sciences has some definite subject matter, and makes its beginning from some "germ cell" which has its origins in observation. The starting point for any science *other than Logic* is some simple, "universal individual," which in the case of political economy is the product of human labour. The commodity is not of course an "empty" concept, but on the contrary is the unit in which all the wealth of modern society appears. So all attempts to find the starting point for some science in one of the concepts of the *Logic* is vain and mistaken. *Economics is not Logic.*

Far from resulting in incoherence, Reflection leads to the Ground of the Contradiction generated by the new data. Smith is at least correct when he says "Marx, in contrast," if little else.

Smith bases his claim for locating *Capital* at this point, corresponding to the beginning of Essence, on the apparent *similarity* of the Essence Logic and *Capital*:

> Essence categories ... define cognitive frameworks that allow truths about more concrete and complex states of affairs to be articulated. The determinations of the Doctrine of Essence come in pairs neither of which can be considered apart from the other ... truths articulated within explanatory frameworks relating an essence and its appearance, a cause and its effects, a substance and its accidents, and so on.
>
> 2014, p. 31

It is true that Essence displays this "two-ness," whereas in Being, as each concept is taken up and critiqued in a series, it gives rise to a new concept which shows the previous concept to be *untrue* (one-ness), classically illustrated by how Being is shown to be Nothing! The concepts of Being come in a serial form like this. By contrast, in Essence, each successive pair of concepts uncovers a deeper duality which includes, but pushes into the background, so to speak, the former pair of concepts without abolishing it, everything is relative. The Concept Logic is then characterised by "three-ness," in which each new triplet *develops* and concretises the former rather than supplanting it.

The way Essence works is illustrated in the initial *analysis* which begins with Identity (reflecting what the new perception *is* (Identity), based on the existing ontology). Identity is shown to *include* Difference (something absolutely identical to itself cannot be), and the resulting Diversity is *essential difference*, the unity of likeness and unlikeness. Hegel repeats this process, sharpening the oppositions till arriving at *Contradiction* and then revealing *Ground*. That is to say, an initial determination of what it is that is *truly* new (distinctive) in the new perception and the grounds of that contradiction. But this is only the beginning of the process of enquiry into a new fact. The two phases of Essence which follow Reflection are first Appearance (the dialectic of Form and Content) and then Actuality (the dialectic of Cause and Effect). Essence is a *continual process* of going behind the surface to find the ground of the contradiction beneath, but this process is *never ending*. This of course poses a problem for using the Essence Logic as the model for a science.

The Essence Logic is a journey. It never reaches the "essence" of the matter. It has the effect, as Smith says, of delving ever more deeply, but finds itself in an *infinite regress*. The regression is terminated with a leap to the Concept Logic.

For example, when a new phenomenon is investigated by seeking the causes of things, we find that each cause is also an effect, the effect of some other cause, which in turn is the effect of a deeper cause, and so on *indefinitely*. This can be overcome only by the determination of Reciprocity in which, say, crime and poverty are found to be causes of each other – crime and poverty are 'two sides of the same coin'. But having arrived at this insight, no 'solution' is found, the basis for that unity still remains to be uncovered, encapsulated in some new *concept*. The dialectics of Chance and Necessary, Possibility and Real Possibility represent efforts to formulate such a conception. But this conception (e.g. capital) is *not* part of Essence. The leap to the simple concept which unites Chance and Necessity, Cause and Effect, etc., brings a new abstract concept which characterises the whole of the reality and which reveals the path to a theoretical explanation (and/or remedy) which can represent the new facts. This is the first concept of the Concept Logic, the Subject, which Smith wrongly identified as an "empty concept." It is far from empty.

Now, I can see why the Essence Logic is appealing. It is, as Smith notes, made up of pairs of opposite determinations. Appearance, the second division of Essence, is the explicitly contradictory relation of Form and Content, of an appearance and what appears; it is not a synonym for "surface," but the unity of an appearance and what appears which leads to a deeper contradiction.

Despite sounding very Hegelian, "essence and appearance" is not, as Smith believes, one of these pairs of concepts. Essence is, in fact, a logical representation of the path of immanent critique of an *existing theory* which was the basis on which observations were collected, and the conflict between the new observations and the existing body of knowledge generate the critique represented by the Logic of Essence. Marx's extended enquiry into the established theories of surplus value, which underlay his formulation of *Capital*, could be taken as a realisation of the Essence Logic. If the Essence Logic is a "model" of anything it is a model of that immanent critique of political economy. *Capital*, on the other hand, is the *reconstruction* of political economy based on the *outcomes* of that *immanent critique*, as illustrated by Marx (1973/1858, p. 100) in "Method of Political Economy" in the *Grundrisse*.

4.5   *The Misconception of the Concept Logic*

Smith sees Hegel's Concept Logic as representing some kind of utopian political-economic order. Smith correctly notes that Hegel attempted to establish a strong normative justification for the system of right set out in the *Philosophy of Right* through a process of mediation which resembles the series of Syllogisms laid out in the third section of the Subject and in which Universal, Particular and Individual moments are combined in a series of syllogisms. Hegel believed that a state needed to gain legitimation and this is achieved by means of layers of collegial consultation. Whether or not Hegel is credited for this insight, it is one widely recognised in bourgeois democracies today.

But in claiming that this "strong normative justification" applies to "the modern socio-political order," Smith overlooks the point that the Germany in which Hegel lived at the time the *Philosophy of Right* was published was an *absolute* monarchy. Hegel was promoting a vision of *constitutional* monarchy in which the actual power of the monarch was reduced to the traditional role of head of the army with a purely symbolic role in internal affairs. Meanwhile, universal suffrage of the kind which is the almost universal political basis for capitalism today was transcended in Hegel's vision by a collegial system of regulation and consultation based in each industry. Whether you approve of this system or not, it was based on a critique of the existing order while striving to avoid utopianism, by calling upon norms which had some basis in the past or present. But it was not a justification of the status quo. It was an immanent critique of the existing system of custom and law which accepted that social and political life was "rational," i.e., intelligible, and open to scientific analysis. One of the many criticisms one could make of the *Philosophy of Right* is that Hegel's critique of value and his conception of capital and wage labour are inadequate, mainly because Hegel was merely *appropriating* the work of contemporary Political Economists. Nonetheless, he did see the inhumanity of factory labour, the right of workers to own their own tools, the inherent tendency of capital towards inequality and inhumanity and the inadequacy of the only solutions he could see, viz., a welfare state, philanthropy or colonial expansion, all of which he rejected. He was writing in economically backward Germany at a time when an organised workers' movement had yet to show its face even in Britain where it still existed underground. Of course, this was not the situation in 1867 when Marx wrote *Capital*.

Smith goes on to ask:

> whether Hegel unintentionally contributed to the understanding of capitalism by developing a Logic of the Concept precisely homologous with the 'logic of capital'. This would be the case if it were possible rationally to reconstruct a social order of generalised commodity exchange as a system of syllogisms mediating universality, particularity and singularity along the requisite lines once capital has been made visible. This cannot be done.
>
> 2014, p. 28

> In the relevant sense ... the concept of capital does not fit what Hegel referred to as the Logic of the Concept.
>
> 2014, p. 29

> Capitalism does not institute the sort of harmonious reconciliation of universality, particularity and singularity required to instantiate the Logic of the Concept in the socio-political realm. Capitalism therefore lacks rationality in Hegel's strongly normative sense of the term. It could even be said that Hegel's Logic of the Concept provides a categorical framework within which capital can be *subjected to critique*, although Hegel himself, lacking an adequate concept of capital, failed to recognise this.
>
> 2014, p. 35

There is merit in suggesting that the *Logic* provides a more useful starting point for a critique of capitalism than the *Philosophy of Right*, but how? The *Logic* is not a model political system. It is a Logic.

In the Concept Logic, a series of ten syllogisms are subjected to critique in the section called "Syllogism," and *all* of them are shown to be deficient, and even the last one still fails to quite grasp the concept as a true concept. These fallacious syllogisms do, however, reflect real, human actions in this imperfect world in which people often act on spurious reasons, but reasons nonetheless.

The Logic of the Syllogism is by no means "harmonious," it is agonistic. Anyone involved in leading or criticising organisations (unions, businesses, scientific bodies, states ...) would be well-advised to study this section of the Logic and how Hegel utilised it in the *Philosophy of Right*.

Secondly, Hegel is not alone in disclosing the strong normative power of the relations described in the *Philosophy of Right*. He was pointing to the normative power of many relationships which did exist or were marginalised in the absolute monarchy. Likewise, Marx showed for example, how the universal exchange of commodities underpins a powerful norm expressed in the universal moral equality of human beings, as against feudalism and ancient society, in this way laying a precondition for Socialism. But in Volume 3, the uniform rate of profit realises instead the norm of equality of capital irrespective of its human owner. This expressed in sharp relief the class basis of capitalism. These norms are the sine qua non of capitalism. *Capital* is as much a work of Moral Philosophy as of Economics, just as the *Philosophy of Right* is as much a work of Social Science as it is a work of Moral Philosophy. Both writers recognise the unity of Ethics and Economics. But in 1821, this unity had not yet manifested itself. Smith is wrong to claim (2014, p. 39) that "a normative progression ... of Hegel's affirmative systematic dialectic is thoroughly absent in Marx's critical dialectic." And he is not quite right in saying that "the contradictions of Essence Logic are *overcome* in the advance to the Logic of the Concept. In the Essence Logic" (p. 34). The contradictions are made comprehensible but not abolished, merely placed in a context.

The Concept Logic could be said to "resolve" the infinite regression in which the Essence Logic finds itself by the discovery of the abstract concept which captures the field of activity in a nutshell, but this does not result in any "harmoniousness."

4.6   *Affirmative or Critical Dialectic*

There can be no doubt that there are important differences between the dialectic of the Professor of Logic who advocated for a constitutional monarchy and that of the communist revolutionary who wanted the overthrow of the state. But the claim of a contrast between "Hegel's affirmative systematic dialectic" and Marx's "critical dialectic" are exaggerated. To understand the value of Hegel's *Logic* it is important to understand how it is *simultaneously critical and productive*. Its aim is both to make intelligible what exists and bring out the contradictions which point beyond what is.

In writing his *Encyclopaedia*, Hegel simply *appropriated* the existing natural and social sciences, rearranging them in way which brought out their dialectical progression. He did not actually engage in research in the natural and human sciences covered in the *Encyclopaedia*, except for the *Logic*. Generally, only in logic and politics did he have strong and independent views. Marx, on the other hand, did actual research on political economy, applying the *Logic* to economic data, and critically engaging with existing political economy, in a way which Hegel had not.

It was Kant who introduced the word "critical" to philosophy, and the series of philosophers who followed Kant and culminated in Hegel based themselves on critique. One of Hegel's most important contributions was to develop a dialectic which did not just merely tear down concepts, as had the ancient Sceptics, but was *productive*. Every new concept produced in the *Logic* appears thanks to criticism of the foregoing concept, which is taken to its limit and transcended. This is the meaning of "sublation." There are countless examples of this as every transition in the *Logic* is a sublation, but for example:

> The negation of negation is not a neutralisation: the infinite is the affirmative.
>
> 1831, §95

Marx's dialectic was also both critical and affirmative – think of the hymn of praise to capitalism with which the *Communist Manifesto* begins! No, the difference is that while both agreed that social practice is intelligible, in the absence of his own original scientific research, Hegel relied on the logical appropriation of the work of others, while Marx criticised others' in the light of social practice and original research and intervention.

4.7   *Failure to Understand Dynamics of the Logic*

I believe that Smith's failure to understand the significance of the various concepts of the *Logic* derives mainly from a failure to understand the overall dynamics and structure of the *Logic* as a critical, immanent logic of enquiry, and as such, an invaluable weapon for *every* revolutionary or social critic. The obscurity of Hegel's exposition and terminology, makes all the concepts of the *Logic* open to misconstrual.

In a monist philosophy, whether that of Hegel or of Marx, concepts can be seen as *forms of human activity*. Consequently, a work of logic *is* open to a fruitful interpretation as the logic of all forms of social practice. But the concepts of the *Logic* must be properly grasped as logical terms before we can understand how they can be realised as in terms of social action.

I wonder, when Smith says:

> But when sociality takes the historically specific form of *dissociated* soci-
> ality these social relations are mediated through relations among things
> (commodities, money).
>
> 2014, p. 30

is he aware that Hegel determined that human actions are *always* mediated
by things? See Hegel (1816, p. 821, The Syllogism of Action). It is not this which
concerns Marx, but the fetishism which is engendered by capitalism and the
alienation which results from the fact that the products of workers' labour
become the property of an *alien class*. A commodity is not something which
is characterised by its physical or chemical properties, but rather by its *social*
properties, i.e., as mediating a form of human activity. Marx of course takes
as his starting point not a thought-form (such as the concepts of Political
Economy), but the form of practice in which the thought-form is realised; but
both are aspects of a concept.

Hegel's *Logic* is unlike any previous logic. When reading it, one gets a distinct feeling of movement and time. This is illusory of course; the *Logic* deals
in ideals, not material objects which can move through space. The aspects of
the *Logic* which create this feeling of movement are the transitions from one
concept to a "new" concept. These transitions are driven by contradictions
(as Zeno discovered, movement is "existing contradiction") and what Fred
Moseley aptly called "successive determination." These ideas are captured by
the concept of "sublation," (*aufhebung*) which is descriptive of every transition
in the *Logic*. Any attempt to render the *Logic* into some kind of system or structure fails, because of this constant restlessness which characterises the *Logic*.

Smith is right, however, to note that abstract labour is a distinctive feature of
capital, a feature which makes capital particularly suitable for a "model" based
on logic. Values appear to individuals as objective properties of commodities
formed by means of "practical abstraction." Exchange of commodities renders
the relation between qualitatively different actions to the single dimension of
value. Value expresses a totalisation of social relations in much the same way
as when a person makes a judgment and acts. The *Logic* is based on such judgments. The logic of value is thus a special case of the logic of judgment. It is
not a simple matter, but this shared starting point does provide a basis for a
particularly strong similarity between commodity exchange and the *Logic*.

Where Hegel touched on value, not of course in the *Logic*, but in the
Philosophy of Right, he treated value superficially and failed to see the con-
tradictions inherent in value. But this tells us nothing about the relation of
Capital and the *Logic*.

4.8   *Conclusion*

In the light of Marx's claim indicating that capital is an "automatic subject" and *Capital* having a structural resemblance to the Subject in Hegel's *Logic*, the thesis that *Capital* follows the Logic of Essence, based on a superficial reading of the Essence Logic and the *Logic* is untenable. The process of "looking behind the surface of things," which is seen in the Essence Logic, is likened to the series of different forms of value found in *Capital*. But the Essence Logic is the *becoming* of a new concept or practice and a logic of enquiry which never quite reaches a concept of its subject matter.

5   Chris Arthur: *Capital* Mirrors the Logics of Being and Essence?

While efforts to link the *Grundrisse* to Hegel's *Logic* relied on philology – that is, linking terms and phrases in Marx's text to similar or identical terms in the *Logic* – this was no longer possible in the case of *Capital*. Here parallels tend to rely simply on broad generalisations about the type of logic being used.

Chris Arthur goes further than this. Arthur traces the concepts of Part I of *Capital* Volume 1 (i.e., the first 3 or 4 chapters) in which he claims commodities exhibit the logic of Being, money exhibits the logic of Essence up to the first concept of the logic of the Concept. However, he argues for this relationship on the basis of logical analyses of the economic entities themselves, as described in *Capital*, rather than simply linking or likening the concepts to terms in Hegel's *Science of Logic*. This implies a real basis for the dialectic in the practices of the capitalist economy itself, rather than just seeing the dialectic as located in logic as such. According to Arthur, as well as others in this discourse, this relation is specific to the social relations of capital. However, Arthur observes that value is a much narrower domain of relations as compared to Nature and human activity as a whole. As Arthur notes, the *Science of Logic* was written for the *Encyclopaedia* so it had a much richer array of concepts than are exhibited in the development of value. So, only *some* of the concepts of the *Logic* are traceable in *Capital*. Consequently, Arthur proposes a *partial* homology between the *Logic* and *Capital* which extends only for the first few chapters.

The key feature of capital is that it is a real, self-reproducing *concrete whole*. This implies that the various categories representing partial aspects of capital are determined by the whole, not the other way around, and in particular, that the whole creates and recreates the necessary conditions for its own existence.

5.1   *Historical Dialectic and Systematic Dialectic*

According to Arthur, earlier Marxists had understood a *historical dialectic* to be manifested in history, while a systematic work like *Capital* differed from this 'historical dialectic' by being "nothing else but the historical method, only stripped of history's fortuities" (Engels, 1859).

Arthur says:

> I draw a distinction between systematic dialectic (which is a method of exhibiting the inner articulation of a given whole) and historical dialectic (which is a method of exhibiting the inner connection between stages of development of a temporal process).
>
> ARTHUR, 2011

This dichotomy may have some relevance to the history of Marxism, but in relation to Hegel, there is no such dichotomy. Hegel's claim is that history is intelligible. Is anyone denying this? The only instance where Hegel claims something like an "historical dialectic" is in the history of philosophy.

> To the historian of philosophy it belongs to point out more precisely how far the gradual evolution of his theme coincides with, or swerves from, the dialectical unfolding of the pure logical Idea.
>
> HEGEL, 1831, §86n

The broad classification of epochs in the last section of the *Philosophy of Right* on World History, goes no further than any treatment of history on the grand scale. He does not analyse current events in terms of fulfilling an "historical dialectic" or Destiny. And who does *not* recognise the existence of epochs in long-duration history? Some remarks in Hegel's systematic study of the State make this clear:

> But if we ask what is or has been the historical origin of the state ... all these questions are no concern of the Idea of the State.
>
> HEGEL, 1821, §258n

However,

> The state is an organism, i.e. the development of the Idea to the articulation of its differences. Thus these different sides of the state are its various powers with their functions and spheres of action, by means of which the

universal continually engenders itself in a necessary way; in this process it maintains its identity since it is presupposed even in its own production. This organism is the constitution of the state; it is produced perpetually by the state, while it is through it that the state maintains itself.

HEGEL, 1821, §269ad

In the latter excerpt Hegel is (1) claiming that a state creates the conditions necessary for its own existence (the key claim also for capital) and (2) the state transforms pre-existing institutions into organs of itself and this will be exhibited in the history of a state. It follows from this that the *logical* order of consideration of these institutions is the *reverse* of the *historical* order, a point also echoed by Marx.

where agriculture predominates, as in antiquity and the feudal period, even industry, its organisation and the forms of property corresponding thereto, have more or less the character of landed property. ... The reverse is the case in bourgeois society. Agriculture to an increasing extent becomes merely a branch of industry and is completely dominated by capital. ... Capital is the economic power that dominates everything in bourgeois society. It must form both the point of departure and the conclusion, and must be analysed before landed property.

After each has been considered separately, their interconnection must be examined.

MARX, 1973/1858, p. 44

and

It would therefore be inexpedient and wrong to present the economic categories successively in the order in which they played the determining role in history. Their order of succession is determined rather by their mutual relation in modern bourgeois society, and this is quite the reverse of what appears to be their natural relation or corresponds to the sequence of historical development. The point at issue is not the place the economic relations took relative to each other in the succession of various forms of society in the course of history; even less is it their sequence 'in the Idea' ..., but their position within modern bourgeois society.

loc. cit.

As Arthur acknowledges, the *Science of Logic* and *Philosophy of Right* are Hegel's models for the systematic dialectic developed by Marx in *Capital* and both writers make the same points about organic wholes and reversal of the historical sequence.

The point for Hegel is that history is *intelligible* (this is the meaning of "rational"), and it does not follow that history unfolds in a "logical" sequence. All real processes of development, both natural and human, entail the intersection of a vast array of mutually independent processes each of which is initially external to one another. A systematic concrete whole is an *outcome* not a pre-condition of historical development, which is necessarily affected by contingency, accident and human fallibility.

On the other hand, a single form of practice or a social movement, abstracted from other processes of development, once initiated, does unfold in a sequence which is essentially logical, despite the presence of some degree of accident and contingency. Arthur and others correctly locate the source of the logical character of capital in the fact that it is a concrete whole which creates and fosters all the subordinate relations which constitute it (as in other instances of concrete wholes). However, Arthur's explanation of how it is that Hegel's *Logic* describes the logic of a concrete whole is just that "his logic of categories is well suited to a theory of *forms*," such as the value-form. On the other hand, the *content* of the value-form, namely labour, can be understood only if we "enter the hidden abode of production" (alluding to Marx, *Capital*, chapter VI, v. 1).

Is production such a hidden abode though? Production is, after all, nothing but the practice of moulding Nature to human requirements, and is consequently a *rational* and *intelligible* process in which the worker "opposes himself to Nature as one of her own forces" (*Capital*, VI, Ch. 7). Indeed, it is noted by many commentators that since the beginning of industrialisation and full-blown capitalism Science has become intimately connected to the development of capital. Science is itself such an organic whole, eminently susceptible to Hegelian logic, as Hegel himself was at pains to demonstrate. So to the extent that Science becomes integrated in production, production is itself a complex whole. Surely, this is what is implied in Marx's dictum: "the material transformation of the economic conditions of production, [...] can be determined with the precision of natural science" (1859). Unlike many aspects of human practice, scientific and technical discovery is a reasonably *irreversible* process; it is hard to forget a useful technological innovation. Quickly or slowly, knowledge of Nature tends to accumulate and this lends a directionality to history. Nonetheless, production is a different sphere of human practice from economy. The course of human freedom turns out to be more complex than the unfolding of one systematic whole.

The point is that the development of a concrete whole and the logic of the relation *between* complex wholes is captured in Hegel's Concept Logic, not the Essence Logic or the Logic of Being. To be a complex whole is to exist in relative independence of other processes. Initially, a complex whole relates to other processes externally, but with the passage of time complex wholes interpenetrate, modify and ultimately merge with one another. In the course of their development, however, systematic wholes reproduce the conditions for their own existence, modifying their surroundings, and become more stable. This is a feature of the *Concept Logic*.

5.2   *The Logic of Being and Value*

In Arthur (2015) and somewhat more extensively in Arthur (2011), Arthur identifies in Chapter 1 of *Capital* the following concepts from the Logic of Being: Determinate Being, being-for-itself, genuine infinity, being-for-self, attraction, quantity, quantum, pure quantity, unit, number, magnitude, measure, ratio, series of specific measures, up to real measure, which is the final section of Being, but which Arthur thinks should belong to the Logic of Essence. He claims that "we can speak of value as the essence of the commodity." As *Capital* moves to money, this leads through the Hegelian categories of reflection, semblance, external reflection, appearance, the first intelligible world, the second intelligible world, reflected and immediate totalities, essential relation, and actuality with possibility, contingency, necessity and activity.

All this is how Marx traces what you could call the spontaneous evolution of money and value from commodity exchange.

Arthur does not follow the logic of the Concept beyond what he sees as its first appearance in Chapter IV of Volume 1, and his claim that capital exhibits the Logic of the Concept is only ever stated in very general terms, and is unsubstantiated, I think. This shows quite a considerable degree of correspondence to the main concepts of the first two books of the *Logic*. Before wage labour, profit or surplus value have even appeared in *Capital*.

Arthur (2011) has been at pains to point out that there has never been in history any such thing as "pure commodity production." Commodity exchange is a necessary pre-condition for the historical emergence of capital and is (according to Marx) also its *logical* premise. In the past commodity exchange has always played a subordinate and marginal role in social formations governed by other principles, whereas in capitalist society the commodity relation has become the dominant and all-pervasive relation. A society of "pure commodity exchange" turns out to be incompatible with capitalist exploitation of wage labour because capital presupposes producers who lack means of production. The logical and historical sequences are inverted in the case of complex wholes: the historical progression from commercial capital, landed capital to industrial capital is inverted in the hierarchy of domination. What was marginal in the beginning becomes dominant in the end, and what was dominant in the beginning becomes marginal at the end.

Arthur says that:

> The effort is to deploy a systematic dialectic in order to articulate the relations of a given social order, namely capitalism, as opposed to a historical dialectic studying the rise and fall of social systems.
>
> ARTHUR, 2011

This is not quite true. The *point* (for revolutionaries, in any case) of disclosing the inner workings of capitalism is to disclose *contradictions*. By contradictions I mean, to use Geert Reuten's apt expression, a defect or impediment to the continuity of social life (the ultimate pre-condition for capital), which arises from and is necessary to the existing systematic relations, impossible situations. Such impossible situations have arisen in the past history of capitalism and as a result changes were made to capitalist institutions to overcome the contradiction. When contradictions arise conflict necessarily moves to the political realm where opportunities for the advance of socialist objectives may be pursued. Systematic dialectic is therefore important in understanding the historical development of the system and for working for the overthrow of the bourgeois order. But it is hard to imagine a political economist being able to identify such a contradiction, such an impossible situation, unless and until that contradiction is *manifested* in a social crisis. And these crises occur in *historical* sequence: "The real subject retains its autonomous existence outside the head just as before ... the subject, society, must always be kept in mind as the presupposition" (Marx, 1973/1858, pp. 101–102). The historical sequence of the *crises* which bring about social transformations is how the Subject makes itself known to us, shaping itself through the working out of these impossible situations.

Value-form theory is invariably linked to study of the *Capital-Logic* relation. The thesis of this theory is that "the peculiar form of commodity-exchange that is theorised [is] the prime determinant of the economy rather than the content regulated by it" (Arthur, 2011). That is, the ubiquity of the practice of commodity exchange overrides in significance, for example, *which* services, manufactured goods or raw materials are exchanged. It also implies that the development of the forces of production, which is affected by a logic internal to the production process itself, is secondary in its determination of the development of social relations to the demands of the value-form of the products. I think it is necessary to recognise that this is a *relative truth*. For example, the extreme concentration of retail trade in the hands of Amazon is conditional upon the production of semiconductors and the political conditions necessary for and created by the internet. There is little room for the corner shop in the age of the internet. I am of the view that the basic facts of the exploitation of wage labour by capital as described in *Capital* remain unaffected by the immense changes which have taken place in the production process in recent decades. However, these changes in the labour process do have a profound impact on cultural and political life and the conditions in which "impossible situations" are played out.

In addressing the question of why it is that Hegel's logic has an affinity with the 'logic' of commodity exchange, Arthur mentions two important points. (1) Because commodity exchange forces the same *form* on to every product and the relations between entities having the same form is particularly suited to logical analysis. (2) The human bearers of the structure of capital are reduced to being *personifications* of its categories, and consequently, the human will invests the categories with the self-acting forms found in Hegel's *Logic*. He says that "they cannot be forms of *thought* as they are in Hegel" (Arthur, 2011). But Hegel did not understand "thought" in this way, as subjective fancy, 'mere conceptions'. He was concerned only with "realised thought," or, "thought insofar as it is true," practice in other words.

In Hegel's *Philosophy of Right*, which includes political economy, Hegel says the categories are forms of the *Will*. More generally, the categories of the *Logic* are categories arising from enquiry into forms of *human practice*, as Marx himself advised in *Theses on Feuerbach*. As Hegel says in the Preface to the *Philosophy of Right*:

> Philosophy has to do with ideas or *realised thoughts*, and hence not with what we have been accustomed to call mere conceptions (*bloße abstrakte Verstandesbestimmung*). It has indeed to exhibit the one-sidedness and untruth of these mere conceptions, and to show that, while that which commonly bears the name "conception," is only an abstract product of the understanding, the true conception alone has reality and gives this reality to itself.
>
> HEGEL, 1821, §1

That is, the subject matter of Hegel's philosophy has to do with human *practices*, institutions and products, and this is what Hegel means by "thoughts."

Arthur says that the categories of capital are instances of universals, namely, value. The formation of categories through the ubiquity of the exchange relation is an instance of what Arthur aptly calls "practical abstraction." Practical abstraction is the general basis for social processes exhibiting logical relations. Value manifests practical abstraction in an exemplary way, but the process in general is not limited to value relations.

Arthur says, correctly, that "capital has in part an ideality" (2011). This is the reason that Hegel's logic is applicable to capital. But isn't this property of "ideality" which is exhibited by value also common to all the significant features of the social world? If it is ideality which makes capital amenable to analysis by Hegel's *Logic*, think of everything else which has this property of "ideality." Now it is true that because money provides an immediate material expression of value, the reality of value is more striking than is, for example, the principle manifested in an institution or social movement. But that only means that *Capital* provides us with an archetype for the use of Hegel's logic freed of its Idealist form. When Arthur notes: "But capital as an ideal totality cannot account for what is in excess of its concept of itself, the concrete richness of social labour, not to mention that of Nature," this is true also, and perhaps to a greater degree than in reference to other artefacts and institutions. But the idea that "abstraction is out there" is by no means unique to capital. It is present in fact in all human practices. We all act for reasons, after all.

Arthur makes a nice observation about the use of Hegel's logic to understand social processes:

> The difficulty capital has in practice in achieving its hegemony over the material sphere of production has some analogy with the philosophical problem Hegel has in making this turn from logic to reality; for in both cases pure form has to show itself active in a variety of contingent circumstances.
>
> ARTHUR, 2011

Arthur argues that:

> while I believe capital is an Hegelian Idea, I also admit that in the last analysis, it is not unreasonable to characterise capitalist society as a structure of essence, along the lines of the middle part of Hegel's

logic, that characterised by antitheses, and that it cannot achieve the self-transparent unity of the Concept.

op. cit.

But Arthur overlooks the fact that in the Logic of the Concept, the *Subject* (e.g. capital) enters into relations with other subjects (e.g. the State, Science, the Labour movement, production, etc.) to constitute the Idea.

The Logic of Essence, however, makes some sense as a representation of the logic of *emergence* of capital (or any other subject) towards being a subject in its own right. The claim that capital *is* the logic of essence, based on the Content-Form relation exhibited in the commodity-money relation is far too shallow.

The *Encyclopaedia* manifests dozens of different processes each of them manifesting complex wholes. As Hegel says, "Philosophy is a circle of circles" (1831, §15), the greatest of which, surely, is that of the human labour process, from humanity's interactions with Nature up to art and philosophy, continuously undermining and creating revolutions in the social relations of production.

Finally, Arthur correctly notes the importance for this project of one passage in the *Science of Logic*:

> Let us look at how the logic is related to the real world. What is striking is that this is thematised by Hegel in the part preceding the Absolute Idea, namely Cognition. Here there is a discussion of how, in theory and in practice, the Idea both discovers, and creates, itself in what seems other than it. ... *Cognition is surely the hinge of the logical and the real.*
>
> ARTHUR, 2011, my emphasis

I agree! And the resources for an interpretation of the part played by Hegel's logic in Marx's *Capital* should *begin* with "The Idea of Cognition," the second last chapter of the *Logic*, especially the section titled "The Idea of the True." This is the logic which Hegel used in composing the *Encyclopaedia*. One thing this tells us is that *Capital* cannot be comprehended in terms of the unfolding of a *single principle*, but on the contrary we should expect to find in *Capital* several foundational principles.

5.3   Summary

Altogether, I think Arthur's claim is well made, that is, that there is a likeness between Marx's discourse on the commodity relation as a form of value and the Logic of Being. This likeness becomes less and less convincing as he goes on through the third and fourth chapters of *Capital*. But I also know from following Meaney and Uchida in particular how much such likenesses are in the eye of the beholder. Of course, the objective social process under which diverse labour products gain for themselves a value will inevitably reflect Hegel's treatment of Quantity in the Logic of Being. Arthur is right to point out that a Logic composed for the entire diversity of human practices will not be exhausted by the economic value relation. However, I think we can conclude from Arthur's careful analysis that if there is such a parallel it does not go further than the first three or four chapters of *Capital*, and that leaves 110 chapters across the three volumes of *Capital* still unaccounted for.

However, a fundamental problem remains with identifying the early chapters of *Capital* with the early sections of the *Logic*, and it is the problem raised by Terrell Carver back in 1976 at the beginning of this discourse. Hegel wrote a logic, and took care that no presuppositions were surreptitiously imported into the *Logic*. How do logical relations become transformed into objective social processes? The *Logic* is the logic of a cognitive process without presuppositions; how does it come to govern a social process, and in particular one which begins with the products of human labour? Further, what is left of the analysis of social relations of capital if your analysis of *Capital* ends before you get to wage-labour, labour-power, surplus value and profit?

6   *Capital* Mirrors Various Parts of the *Logic*?

In his contribution to the volume "*Marx's Capital and Hegel's Logic*, A Reexamination," Igor Hanzel makes a study of the logic which Marx uses in Volume 1 of *Capital*, entitled "The Circular Course of Our Representation." Each concept Marx takes up – exchange-value, wage, profit, price – he analyses using the "circular" logic exhibited by Hegel in the *Logic*. This is what Hegel was talking about when he described philosophy as a "circle of circles" (Hegel, 1831, §15).

Hanzel describes this logic in the following terms: something *appears*, cognition discovers the *ground* of this appearance, a ground which contains more than the appearance, and the appearance is then reconstructed in thought on the basis of a comprehension of the ground.

As Hanzel explains, this is the same movement of science in which Copernicus and Galileo discovered that the heavens were not merely points of light in the sky, but orbs like the Earth. The movement of these orbs through space and the laws of that movement (and the ground for those laws ...) had to be discovered and explained so that the appearance of their movement as seen from Earth could be explained. Thus, cognition returns to its starting point in what is given in perception, Being. Hanzel claims that this is a movement which Hegel describes in the moments of Reflection in the Essence Logic

(Hanzel, 2014, p. 229), but this is not quite true; the circle is not completed without the Concept Logic which reconstructs the whole in the light of each new distinctive observation.

Hanzel examines the German words used for the categories entailed here. *Schein*, usually translated as "illusory being" or "semblance," contains nothing other than what is given in Being. Hanzel makes the interesting observation that *Schein* is a mass noun, not a countable noun, and has no plural form. This highlights the essentially indeterminate character of *Schein*.

Hanzel points out that *Erscheinung* (a countable noun), usually translated as "appearance," is ambiguous. But "appearance" is ambiguous in English as well, and in just the same way. Hanzel proposes to translate *Erscheinung* as "appearance" where it indicates what is to be explained through its *Grund* (ground), and "manifestation" as the phenomenon once explained from its ground. "Appearance" has the same ambiguity in English, and Hegel's use of *Erscheinung* (Appearance) is intentionally "ambiguous," or "double-barrelled" to use John Dewey's apt expression. That is, Appearance is the phase of cognition in which what appears is taken to be the form *of something else*. The concept of "appearance" implies a reference to something else which the appearance is the appearance *of.* It is a relation. This contradiction is *implicit* in the concept of "appearance." To use two different words, each of them supposedly lacking in internal contradiction, in place of the word with the implicit contradiction obscures Hegel's method and destroys the "movement."

Likewise, in my view, Hanzel, like everyone else in this discourse, misunderstands the Hegelian term, Essence (*Wesen*), as the *final outcome* of going behind appearances, in the sense of when we say "the essence of matter is such and such." But by Essence, Hegel meant the *whole process* of going behind what is given, and it is an *endless* process. It is one thing to say that price is the manifestation of value, but that does not explain the value of a specific item at a specific time, that would in fact entail a truly infinite enquiry into the entirety of social conditions and even the history behind that moment.

At key moments in the movement of cognition the thinker is able to capture what is given in a nutshell, so to speak, and this is the Concept, *Begriff*, not ground (*Grund*), which is merely one of the stages towards the Concept which itself turns out to be inadequate. The Logic of Essence is continued after the phase of Appearance (the dialectic of Form and Content) via Actuality (the dialectic of Cause and Effect, Possibility and Necessity). Ultimately, the concept is concretised by *successive* such insights which go beyond the process of Essence, beyond looking behind appearances, and forming a concept which captures the process in a nutshell. Successive such insights merge and modify one another as described in the Logic of the Concept to reproduce concrete reality in thought. Over time, a Concept will be replaced by others in the light for further information and further reflection.

There is an element of truth in rendering Volume I of *Capital* in terms merely of the dialectic of Appearance. But there is a lot more to *Capital* than these insights and a lot more to the *Logic* as well.

This conception of Hegel's Logic as encapsulated by the idea of going behind the appearance to reveal it as the manifestation of "essence" (substituting the word "essence" for "concept") is an impoverished representation of the Logic and an impoverished reading of *Capital*. As Hanzel says, Copernicus not only defended this idea but *exhausted* its content. There is more to science than this one insight.

I think Hanzel is right though to see Marx's use of Hegelian logic as manifested *multiple times* in the course of Volume I of *Capital* in how he dealt with each of the key insights and concepts, rather than looking for an image of the *Logic* in the overall trajectory of *Capital*. The analysis of the commodity form of value is surely not the only insight in *Capital*.

Hanzel's (2014, p. 235) reflections on "capital as subject" are interesting. He cites Marx (1983/1867, *Das Kapital, b. 1*, k. IV) observing that value is an *automatic subject*: "in truth ... value becomes the subject of a process in which ... it valorises itself" ... "a self-moving substance" ... "as such capital." But Hanzel claims that Marx is using the idea here in the sense of an *appearance* of capital being an independent subject. This has to be the case because in this chapter of Volume 1 Marx is just introducing the concept of capital; the task of revealing its real dynamics still lies far ahead. Self-valorisation is an appearance, not real ground, because capital is *appropriating* value produced by the exercise of wage-labour. But appearances are real, too.

Hanzel's interpretation of the *circular logic* exhibited in each concept cannot be extended to the Logic of Being which Chris Arthur has connected to the first chapter of *Capital*. There is some sense of this idea in the Logic of Essence, but it is fully exhibited only in the Concept Logic, in which a Subject is characterised by recreating the conditions of its own existence.

But then Hanzel asks whether Marx's idea of capital corresponds to the Subject in the *Science of Logic*. "The ground of capital as a type of social relation," he says, concluding from this that Marx is *not* using subject-substance or the concept of Subject in the Concept Logic in his observation about an "automatic subject" but rather from the Objective Logic, i.e., the Essence Logic.

But he goes on:

> "Still, certain categories of Hegel's Subjective [i.e., Concept] Logic can also be realistically reinterpreted. They could be viewed as corresponding to categories involved in the creation of thought projects of the future

transformation of the (natural and social) world." ... [as in] Hegel's concepts in Teleology. ... "certain categories of the Subjective [i.e., Concept]
Logic could also be realistically interpreted, that is, interpreted in such a
way as to grasp in categories the structure of human practical action in
transforming the world. Here I mean especially Hegel's cluster *Life* with
its subcluster: *the living individual, the life process* and *the genus*."

  2014, p. 239

Hanzel here suggests that the concepts found in the third section of the
Concept Logic, the Idea, could be utilised to understand social movements. But
surely this can only be the case if the *entirety* of the Concept Logic is realised in
social life. But Hanzel rejects the idea of the category of Subject being relevant,
because "capital is a social relation"! But so are social movements, so are all
the institutions of modern society, all the enduring products of social practice.
This is also behind Marx's use of the term "automatic subject," albeit somewhat
in passing.

Hanzel wants to limit this application to *intentional* movements, as opposed
to, for example, movements manifested by economic institutions and political
tendencies. I think he is mistaken here. While Structuralism is mistaken in ruling the Subject out of social science altogether, limiting the Idea to *intentional*
subjects is a mistake which obscures the genius of Hegel's *Logic*. Even social
movements are not manifestations of a single will, but rather the combined
process of many like or even antagonistic wills. Isn't it possible that social processes such as these could also be grasped with the concepts of the Concept
Logic?

Altogether, Hanzel offers a bewildering array of angles on the *Logic/Capital*
relation, and his article is fruitful in the way he has brought out the richness of
the relation. Hanzel has indicated the folly of trying to represent *Capital* as a
"mirroring" of just one or another section of the *Logic*.

7 Conclusion to Chapter 3

I conclude from this examination of Abazari, Smith, Arthur and Hanzel, that
the writers have proven that the echoes of Hegel's *Logic* identified in *Capital*
are real and not simply in the eye of the beholder, but there is no direct relation between any part of *Capital* and either the Logic of Being or the Essence
Logic. In order to "prove" such relations writers have had to bend Hegel's concepts to fit their own vision. And in the process of abstracting this likeness, the
content of social relations of capital has been omitted by reducing *Capital* to

a Logic. Nevertheless, Hegel's presence is clear throughout the early chapters of *Capital*.

None of the writers treated so far have been able to extend their perceived homologies beyond the first four chapters of *Capital*. This means that my project of finding out how Marx and Hegel shared some insight into how to understand social problems and processes remains unfulfilled because we know that the "society of pure commodity exchange" suggested by the first chapters of *Capital* is counterfactual and is itself only the first stage in the logical reconstruction of bourgeois society. The crucial steps in Marx's analysis of capital come later, *after* the analysis of the commodity relation in Part I of Volume 1 of *Capital*.

In any case, no one explained satisfactorily to my mind how it came to be that a *logic* describes objective *social* processes such as exhibited by value.

CHAPTER 4

Fred Moseley's Analysis of *Capital* and the Concept Logic

1   Introduction

Fred Moseley's contribution to this debate is unique in finding a basis in Hegel's *Logic* for the structure of the *whole* of the three volumes of *Capital*. Within this Moseley explains the unique problem which is solved by Volume 1 of *Capital* and resolves a number of difficult problems presented in trying to understand *Capital*. Further, Moseley sees the Concept Logic as the key part of the *Logic* needed to understand *Capital*, recognising that for Marx and Hegel, the first task is to establish a *concept* of the subject matter in general.

Moseley shows that Volume 1 of *Capital* determines the total amount of surplus value appropriated by the capitalist class from the working class on the basis of a concept of value whose substance is "socially necessary labour time." In Volume 3, however, Moseley shows how Marx allows that under the rule of capital products are exchanged on the basis of costs of production, not their value. Socially necessary labour time does not determine the exchange value of the products of capital. The result is that surplus value appropriated from the working class is shared between capitalists in proportion to their total capital such that the rate of profit is equalised.

In *Money and Totality* (2016), Fred Moseley deals with a relatively small number of issues in Marx's *Capital* and its relation to Hegel's *Logic*, but the issues Moseley touches on include the most important and controversial aspects of Marx's approach. He examines these issues with precision and thoroughness. I shall also briefly refer to Moseley's chapter in *Marx's Capital and Hegel's Logic* (2014).

Moseley has identified in Marx's manuscripts four successive drafts of *Capital*, which, taken together with numerous partial drafts and Marx's correspondence with Engels, enable him to trace the gradual evolution of Marx's ideas until they reached their final form in 1867.

Moseley's aim is to elucidate key aspects of Marx's thinking and he has done so in such a way that his conclusions are really beyond doubt. There is just one case where Moseley finds that Marx "misspoke" in *Capital* and a couple of occasions where he claims that a word was chosen at the pleading of Engels in the interests of popularising his ideas but which have proven to obscure rather than elucidate Marx's meaning. Otherwise, Moseley simply represents Marx's meaning and intention as written in the three volumes of *Capital*. He makes no effort in this book to consider how Marx's *Capital* could be updated for our own times – he leaves such thinking to others, nor does he criticise or cast doubt upon anything Marx wrote (other than the couple of minor errors or what he claims are minor errors by Engels in his editing of Volume 3), or try to extend *Capital* beyond its scope as Marx left it. These few minor "corrections" are the exception that proves the rule such that we are left in no doubt about Marx's intentions, insofar as that is humanly possible.

One of Moseley's achievements is to refute the claims of "value theorists" that there are two distinct "measures of value" throughout *Capital*, one in monetary prices and the other value measured in socially necessary hours of labour, and that Marx failed to reconcile values with prices. And Moseley does this without simply abolishing the concept of abstract labour as the substance of value, as Reuten has done.

2   Volume 1 and the Total Surplus Value

Moseley makes it clear that the first assumption under which Marx's analysis is carried out is this:

> Marx's theory in all three volumes of *Capital* is about a *single system*, the actual capitalist economy, which is assumed to be in long-run equilibrium.
>
> 2016, p. 6

Moseley's most important finding is that the objective of Volume 1 is to determine the *origin* of surplus value in the exploitation of workers' unpaid labour time, and the *total* quantity of surplus value appropriated from the working class by capitalists across a whole economy.

> Marx's theory is structured according to *two main levels of abstraction*: the *production* of surplus-value and the *distribution* of surplus-value, and the production of surplus-value is theorised prior to the distribution of surplus-value, which means that the *total surplus-value* in the economy as a whole *is determined* [in Volume 1], *logically, prior* to its division into individual parts [in Volumes 2 & 3];
>
> 2016, p. 3

To determine the total surplus value appropriated by capital presupposes a concept of value. Marx's concept of value is based on labour time, but it is not "measured" as such; rather value 'measures itself' through the exchange process. However, the determination of the total surplus value has profound significance both ethically and in terms of understanding the vast economic infrastructure built on this total quantity of value, and analysed in later volumes. Capital is understood to be a single entity which nonetheless appears as distinct units of capital. Using the terminology of Hegel's Concept Logic, the universal moment of capital, capital in general, is represented as these multiple individual units and quantified by the total capital of all of such units.

It makes no difference at this first stage of the analysis, then, how much surplus value is appropriated by each individual capital, so long as the *total* remains valid. Quantitatively, the effect is that Marx is treating the entire economy as a single capital, with each unit taken as "average" and indifferent to the distribution of capital, labour and surplus value between the individual units of capital.

Moseley cites the *Grundrisse*:

> To the extent that we are considering it here, as a relation distinct from that of value and money, capital is *capital in general*, i.e. the incarnation of the qualities which distinguish value as capital from value as pure value or as money. Value, money, circulation etc., prices, etc. are presupposed, as is labour etc. But we are still concerned neither with a *particular* form of capital, nor with an *individual* capital as distinct from other individual capitals etc. We are present at the process of its becoming. This dialectical process of its becoming is only the ideal expression of the real movement through which capital comes into being. The later relations are to be regarded as developments coming out of this germ.
>
> MARX, 1973/1858, p. 310

This claim, which Moseley documents meticulously, *seems* at odds with Marx's exposition which refers throughout Volumes 1 and 2, to *single units* of capital, each with its expenditure on constant capital (machinery, materials, etc.), variable capital (wages) and the increase in the money invested by that capital once the product is sold. From this a quantum of surplus value is calculated by simple subtraction (total price of the product minus money outlaid on wages, materials and fixed capital), a rate of surplus value determined by the proportion of surplus value to the variable capital invested and a rate of profit by the proportion of the surplus value to the total capital invested. Both rates are calculated with respect to each individual unit of capital. It is a matter of indifference whether the rate of surplus value or the rate of profit determined from each unit of capital varies from one particular sector of the economy to another, or is uniform. What matters is *only the total*, and Marx makes no claim that the rate of surplus value, the rate of profit, or the composition of each capital (ratio of constant to variable capital) is uniform or not.

Note also in the quote from the *Grundrisse*, the reference to the "germ" out of which (logically) later forms of capital will grow. That is, the unit of capital as first conceived in the exposition of must be seen as a "germ cell" or "embryo." This is just like the commodity was the "economic cell-form" of value mentioned by Marx in the 1867 Preface to *Capital*.

This viewpoint is quantitatively equivalent to considering the economy as one unit of capital, except that by its very nature, capital exists in numerous, competing units, not a whole single entity. Moseley cannot tell us why then Marx posed the issue in Volume 1 solely in terms of *single units* of capital and not in terms of an entire economy, but he does show that this is indeed what Marx did. Moseley correctly insists that Marx's interest in Volume 1 is the total surplus and the proportion of that surplus value to the total capital invested in workers' means of subsistence, and that this constitutes beginning with the *Universal* (Moseley, 2015), in Hegel's terms. In adopting this approach, Marx is following Hegel's example perfectly. But how is it that he deals throughout Volume 1 with single units of capital, thus *appearing* to begin, not from the Universal, but from the Individual? I will return to this issue later, when I deal with Moseley's claim about the relation of the structure of *Capital* and the structure of Hegel's *Logic*.

Because it is the *total* values which are to be determined here, in Volume 1, there is no problem in treating all the factors as *averages*, since "average" simply means dividing the given total by the number of units. It does not matter that the "average" as such forms no part of the motivation of any of the parties involved, and has no material representation in the economy as such, but is simply derived analytically from the total.

If one were to keep one's focus on the single firms, and, as Marx appears to invite us to, take the surplus labour time measured against the variable capital invested to determine a rate of surplus value for that firm, and against the total of constant and variable capital invested to determine the rate of profit for that firm, then we would find that the rate of profit and rate of surplus value vary from one firm to the next with no consistent proportion between them. If all workers are taken to be equally industrious and buying their means of subsistence from the same market, and capitalists are taken to be paying for labour power at its value and applying the socially necessary technology, then it would seem that the rate of surplus value would tend to be uniform economy-wide across all units of capital, while the rate of profit would vary according to the composition of each unit of capital. But empirically this is not the case, as there is a strong empirical tendency towards the equalisation of the rate of profit across the capitalist economy.

This is the root of the claim by value theorists that Marx has failed to solve the "transformation problem." Moseley resolves this paradox which has emerged at this stage by examining the distinction between commodities produced by capital and simple commodities sold at their value by their producer. But in Volume 1 Marx has not taken account of the capital market and its effect on the distribution of surplus value between capitalists.

3   Value and Price in Volume 1

Prices for one and the same product may vary from one moment to the next to the extent that transitory and incidental factors impact on the price realised upon sale. In these circumstances, it is common to take "price" as the actual and "value" as the average, eliminating "statistical noise." However, if the assumption underlying the analysis is that of long-run equilibrium, this distinction is redundant. In keeping with this assumption, Moseley insists that in Volume 1, quantitatively, *value is* (average) *price*. Price can be distinguished from value in the sense that one can talk of value as a hypothetical or expected price, but once a commodity is sold, its *value has been realised as its price*, and value is a matter of speculation until the commodity is sold. No further distinction is possible. Price is value, or more precisely, *price is the appearance of value*, and like any appearance, is relatively unstable. Although the value of a commodity is not known until the value appears in the form of the price realised, it is value which determines price not the other way around. Just like the colour of an object is determined by material properties of the object, but it *appears* only when light is shed upon its surface.

The quantity of labour "embodied" in the commodity is a matter of concern when setting up the production process, but it is a matter of indifference to both buyer and seller once it comes to the point of sale. When a capitalist buys an input from another capitalist, the market will tend to drive the price of that input down to its cost of production, including the cost of borrowing, and has nothing to do with its value. The past history of the product and the amount of "embodied labour" is of no account to capitalists. If a capitalist is buying labour-power from a worker, then he will pay a wage which also represents its cost of production, which will be equal to its value. When he is buying input from a fellow capitalist, then the situation is different because profit is involved.

We know the *total* labour time embodied in commodities, being simply the total hours of labour expended by the entire working class employed by capital on a given quantity of any given product. All deviations between the actual labour time expended by a given unit of capital and the average is accounted for by the qualification "socially necessary." The seller's loss is the buyer's gain and the total value is unaffected. If someone is swindled, this only means that a share of the value is illegitimately passed from one to another, but it doesn't affect the total value realised.

Further, labour of the average type, labour at the basic wage, is typical of a modern industrial capitalist economy, engaged in skinning chickens one day and packing parcels for Amazon the next. Marx calls this "abstract labour." It is "abstract" first of all, because it is an ideal lacking any concrete quality, and is simply measurable by time (for Marx, the number of working days, it being presumed that workers are made to work as long a working day as possible under existing conditions of labour). It is "abstract" as well in the sense that the act of purchase and sale, valuing a commodity at a certain sum of money, determines *post facto* the labour time which had been *socially necessary*, not the *actual* labour time expended. Here the entirety of existing social conditions come into play. The measurement by labour time is in that sense "abstract," but on *average*, across the economy, it will be quantitatively exact. Thus, money is the measure of "*socially necessary* labour time," under the conditions presumed in Volume 1, namely, long-term equilibrium and commodities bought and sold at their value. Putting this the other way around: *money is the appearance of abstract labour*. Or, as Moseley puts it:

> The 'value' of commodities in Marx's theory is a complicated concept which has three interrelated aspects: the *substance* of value (abstract labour), the *magnitude* of value (socially necessary labour time), and the *necessary form of appearance* of value (money and prices) (see the titles and the contents of the sections of Chapter 1 of Volume 1 of *Capital*). After Section 3 of Chapter 1, the 'value' of commodities when presented without further attribution usually refers to the third aspect – the form of appearance of value in terms of money and prices.
>
> 2016, p. 29

It is the interchangeability of labour time in a modern industrial economy which makes labour a universal and makes the adding up of labour time and the measurement of "abstract labour" a valid "practical abstraction." This kind of labour is essential to modern capitalism.

4   Circulation and Turnover Time of Capital

In Volume 1, Marx has already shown that banks do not create any additional surplus value by lending money to an industrial capitalist and charging interest. Nor do landlords create any additional surplus value by charging the industrial capitalist rent on the land they use. Interest and rent are merely claims to a *share* of the surplus already acquired by an industrial capitalist.

In addition to this, the industrial capitalist must pay the going price for the materials and machinery, etc., purchased from other industrial capitalists (constant capital) but this cost is passed on to their customers in the price of the product. Interest and rent on the other hand are paid out of the acquired surplus. How else?

Also affecting the annual rate of profit which is retained by the industrial capitalist is the consideration that all the calculations in Volume 1 concerned one circuit of capital, beginning with money, M, exchanged for labour-power and means of production, transformed in the process of production into commodities, and then realised again by returning the product to the market, realising a profit, ΔM. But the capitalist pays rent and interest *per annum* and his interest is only in the profit gained per annum. Consequently, the annual profit rate varies according to the circulation time, and it is the annual rate of surplus value which motivates the capitalist as the personification of capital.

Further, costs are associated with circulation, and in general, the industrial capitalist will have to lay out a portion of the surplus in order to pay for transporting the product to market, storing it and for the retailer to sell it. Thus, the transport and retail industries also claim a portion of the surplus. This is the means by which the surplus extracted by big capital is distributed to the other sections of the bourgeoisie.

These expenses, necessary for the realisation of capital but not adding to the value of the product, are dealt with in Volume 2, entailing the industrial capitalist sharing the surplus with other capitalists.

It is in the transactions with other industrial capitalists, both those selling means of production, and those involved in circulation, that the solution can be found to the paradox of a uniform rate of profit across the economy despite the variation in the composition of capital from one particular sector of the economy to another and the determination of value by labour time.

5   Equalisation of the Rate of Profit

Whereas it appears from Volumes 1 and 2, that every unit of industrial capital enjoys a different rate of profit, it is an empirical fact that the rate of profit tends to be equal across the economy. How can this be?

Moseley's notable contribution to the understanding of Marx's *Capital* is his decisive refutation of the claim that Marx failed to solve the problem of the "transformation" of values into prices – the so-called "transformation problem." This claim, according to Moseley, is based firstly on a failure to understand that the aim of Volume 1 is merely to determine the *total* surplus value under the assumption that goods are exchanged at their value. That is, that price is equal to value. This assumption is valid for the purpose of determining the total surplus value, as any gain from exchange for whatever reason is balanced by the equal loss for the other party, irrespective of its distribution. This assumption makes sense if one takes all the actors in the economy to be *independent producers paid for their work* by the sale of their product. However, producers who lack their own means of production (effectively all of them), sell their labour power to capitalists who use that labour-power to create *new* value, over and above the cost of wages and materials, etc., and become the owners of that product. The value of the product they have appropriated contains an element of surplus value which can be realised only by the sale of the product.

But the market in both capital and goods in such circumstances forces the capitalist to receive an *average* rate of profit when she sells the product. This must entail goods being exchanged at prices *differing* from their value, and thus a *portion* of the surplus extracted by use of the workers' labour capacity is either recovered by the employer and/or passed on to another capitalist via a reduced purchase price. Therefore it can no longer be presumed that value is the number of hours of socially necessary labour expended in production of the commodity. Products can no longer be presumed to be exchanged at their value determined by abstract labour time when capitalists are doing business with each other. If I understand Moseley correctly, once sold, the value of a commodity is realised as its price, as ever. So capitalist production necessarily entails the *sharing of the total surplus*, not thanks to swindling, but simply by selling according to different principles than those which applied in Volume 1. The total surplus remains the same, as determined in Volume 1, but portions of the surplus are passed back and forth by the capitalists according to commercial arrangements dictated by the market, the market in commodities and the capital market.

Just as the commodity market ensured commodities are sold at their value in Volume 1, the capital market ensures an equal rate of profit for all sectors of capital in Volume 3.

Failure to observe the difference between the simple commodity production and the market in commodities produced by capital, has led others to claim that throughout *Capital* there is a "duality" of price and value, the latter being taken as the socially necessary labour time embodied in each commodity. But capitalist production begins and ends with money, and the "historical" value-composition of the commodity (constant capital, wages paid, surplus value) is irrelevant once a product is purchased for money by a producer and the value of the product is realised. Only costs of production (including interest) matter for capital.

Certain sectors of the economy (the banks, state, landowners, the industrial capitalists themselves, and the transport, storage and retail industries) take a share of the surplus extracted by industrial capital, as accounted for in Volumes 1 and 2. Volume 3 deals with the fact that particular sectors of the economy have a different composition of capital and thus other things being equal they would generate a different rate of profit. By "sector" is meant the market in a particular use value which will have a characteristic necessary composition of capital associated with its particular production needs.

The subject matter of Volume 2 is the *reproduction of capital* and its particular component parts. Volume 2 also examines the distribution of surplus value among producers of inputs to industrial capital and among producers of means of subsistence and the luxury goods paid for by capitalists for their own personal consumption of surplus value – the complex picture of the circulation of particular portions of value (constant, variable or surplus) around the economy which ensures the ongoing reproduction of the relations of production.

In Volume 3, Marx does indeed deal with the "transformation" of values into prices, while maintaining the principle that value is once-for-all determined at the moment of sale. The result is the sharing of surplus-value amongst capitalists in different particular sectors.

Moseley shows that in Volume 3 a further distribution of the total surplus takes place between the particular sectors of the capitalist economy, this time between particular sectors of the economy with a greater or lesser composition of capital. In effect, those sectors with a lower organic composition of capital, and therefore, according to the arithmetic of Volume 1, higher rates of profit, have to share so much of their acquired surplus with other sectors as will bring their rate of profit up or down to the average, while those with a higher organic composition of capital and therefore a lower rate of profit receive a share of the total surplus which raises their rate of profit to the social average. This sharing of surplus value takes place through a combination of two processes: (1) the flow of capital between sectors of the economy via the capital markets, and (2) the products being sold below or above the values which would *appear* to follow from a calculation of added labour-time plus constant capital. The bourgeois myth of the productivity of capital imposes itself on the capitalist as a reality in the appearance of prices. A *real* illusion!

The first mechanism for this process of equalisation of the rate of profit is that the higher rate of profit enjoyed in one sector attracts capital invest-ment from another sector with a lower rate of profit, bringing about, effec-tively, over-capitalisation and under-investment in the respective industries. This movement of capital from one sector to another does not however affect the total surplus value accumulated by the capitalist class as a whole, other than secondary effects the movement has on the total capital investment. Marx claims that capital investment has an overall tendency to increase. This has an effect on the price of the means of subsistence, which Marx says has a tendency to decline along with a decline in the unit costs of production of con-sumer goods. In addition to this process, with capitalists in a profitable sector selling their products to other capitalists at a depressed price, they are effec-tively passing a share of that surplus on to other capitalists. It is the necessarily uniform rate of profit which drives both these processes, and which is also the outcome of the process. This also drives the going rate of interest on capital, which capitalists account as part of their costs of production.

Thus, equalisation of the rate of profit across sectors of the economy occurs by means of competition for capital investment and the free flow of capital in the capital markets, and the suppression or enhancement of the value of the products of different industries. This determines the distribution of capital between sectors of industry:

> Competition so distributes the social capital among the various spheres of production that the prices of production in each sphere take shape according to the model of the prices of production in these spheres of average composition.
>
> *Capital*, v 3, Ch. 10

Once a commodity is sold, then its value is realised in the given price. It is this price which enters into the cost of production for other units of capital, both constant and variable capital. A unit of capital in other sectors of the economy, by buying the products at this price in effect acquire or give up surplus value from/to the other unit of capital. By selling products relatively cheaply due to underinvestment and suppressed organic composition of capital, capitalists are in effect subsidising production in other sectors while still enjoying the average rate of profit – in effect sharing out surplus value to sectors which have been subject to overinvestment, equalising the rate of profit (see 2016, p. 50).

Moseley is a pains to point out the difference between a "simple commodity," such as was dealt with in Volume 1, and a commodity which is a product of capital:

> Marx discussed three important differences between commodities as products of capital and simple commodities. The first difference is that the labour which produces capitalist commodities is divided into paid labour and unpaid labour (i.e., the value of capitalist commodities contains surplus-value). The second difference is that the individual commodity is treated as an 'aliquot part' of the total commodity produced by a given capital, rather than an 'autonomous article', which means that the price of an individual commodity is not determined by the labour time required to produce this commodity (as with simple commodities), but is instead determined as a fractional part of the total price of all the commodities produced by a given capital, i.e., by dividing this total price by the quantity of commodities produced.
>
> 2016, pp. 140–141

The accumulation of surplus value by the capitalist class as a whole, as described in Volume 1, is unaffected by the equalising of the rate of profit which distributes that surplus value and secondarily drives the capital market.

In a capitalist enterprise, it is impossible to link any labour act to any one product. The production process in an enterprise can only be taken as a whole. This production process begins with a certain amount of money invested, *not* with a commodity with a certain amount of labour "embodied" in it. The price realised in the sale of the total product then recovers the money invested, M, and a profit ΔM, divided in some appropriate proportion between the prices of single products. The price of these products still represents the value of the product, but its price, and therefore value, is lower or higher thanks to the composition of capital and the effect of over- or under-investment of capital across the particular sector. All sectors tend towards the rate of profit applying to the sector with an average composition of capital.

The capital market thus tends to "distort" the distribution of labour and capital across the various sectors of the economy in the interests of accumulation of capital. One sector subsidises another by paying "higher" prices for their inputs or receiving lower prices for their products.

5.1   Long-Term Equilibrium

I think Moseley is right that Marx wrote *Capital* on the assumption of long-term equilibrium. This assumption is not intended to be factual, but as an analytical device to separate the dominant tendencies in capitalism from "noise." Nevertheless, such an assumption cannot be valid without demonstrating that there is a relevant real tendency towards equilibrium. In Volume 1, Marx observes that if a unit of capital adopts a technological improvement which reduces the cost of producing a product, then competition between units in the same trade obliges others to adopt the same improvement. The edge that the innovator gets allowing them to undercut their competitors in the same commodity market is soon wiped out, the organic composition of capital increases and the rate of profit tends to equalise at a lower rate across the sector. So the result is that capitalism is *not* in long-term equilibrium. Note that this observation would not make sense if Marx had presented his analysis in terms of a single economy-wide capital. Capital essentially exists as independent units; it is in the nature of capital that it exists in individual units. Price competition and the flow of capital across sectors of the economy does allow however for whole sectors to be treated as if they were a single enterprise for the purpose of determining the total of surplus value.

Equalisation of the rate of profit between different sectors of the economy is dependent on the flow of capital in the capital market. It is this capital market which really characterises what is meant by "the whole economy." Notwithstanding both Moseley and Marx, what makes capital in general *universal* is not the *sameness* of capital, not having some attribute in common across diverse units of production, but rather in the actual *flow* and metamorphosis of capital across individual units and particular trades through the financial system. The individual units of capital really exist simultaneously as a universal whole, like an organism whose cells are constantly renewing themselves.

This process derives, in my view, from the "two-fold character of labour embodied in commodities." This is the contradiction which Marx identified at the very beginning of *Capital* and can be seen to reshape capitalist society right through Volume 3.

Moseley mentions that equalisation of the rate of profit means distributing surplus value in proportion to the total capital invested by each unit, and that this is because it is only the rate of profit, not the rate of surplus value which motivates the capitalist, as a personification of capital and is what is considered by the lending bank. And Moseley is echoing Marx in this view.

> individual capitals are treated as shares of the total capital and they 'share' the total surplus-value according to their share of the total capital.
>
> 2016, p. 64

But it is not self-evident why pursuit of an annual profit should lead to equalisation of the rate of profit, and why the "hostile brothers" kindly treat each other *according to the share of each in the total capital* when distributing the total of surplus value. The practice of measuring profit relative to total capital derives from the banks having to divide the capital they hold between different investments. The proportionality of profit to capital invested by an Individual unit of capital (enacted in advance by a lending bank, though actually an outcome) determines that the sharing of surplus value will echo this presumption across all sectors of a capitalist economy.

The mechanism which restores equilibrium with a uniform rate of profit is that a higher rate of profit attracts capital to a unit insofar as there is free movement of capital, and thereby reduces that higher rate of profit to the general level. However, there is no end point to these adjustments. The movement of capital into trades in which labour-power is more productive of surplus produces ongoing changes in the distribution of capital across the economy.

6   The "Universal Individual" in Hegel

Moseley is one of the few who have recognised that Marx's *Capital* draws its structure from the third book of Hegel's *Logic*, the Concept Logic. The first section of the Concept Logic is what Hegel calls the "Subject," the *internal* development of the Subject, in this instance, capital, and this first section is marked by three "moments," namely, Universal, Particular and Individual. The preceding two books of the *Logic*, Being and Essence, do not form part of the exposition of the Subject, but represent its *genesis*, reflected in the prior development of economy itself and of the science of political economy.

> *Objective logic* therefore, which treats of *being* and *essence* constitutes properly the genetic exposition of the Concept.
>
> HEGEL, 1815, p. 577

I will elaborate on Hegel's method as exhibited by Marx in *Capital* in my own terms separately, but Moseley has made important discoveries in how Marx approached the use of Hegel's Concept Logic but has also made errors, in some of which he is echoing Marx himself as I see it.

The section of the *Science of Logic* entitled "The Idea of the True" is where Hegel explains his method of building any science. The relevant passage begins:

> The progress, proper to the Concept, from universal to particular, is the basis and the possibility of a synthetic science, of a system and of systematic cognition.
>
> HEGEL, 1816, p. 801

And this is exactly the approach Marx takes. As Moseley correctly points out, Volume 1 is entirely devoted to "capital in general," the Universal. However:

> *Capital in general* is defined by Marx as what capital essentially is – the *most essential properties which are common to all capitals* and which distinguish capital from simple commodities or money and other forms of wealth. ... the *production of surplus-value*.
>
> 2016, p. 43

"Common to all," may be a true definition of "capital in general," but is not a true definition of *universal* capital. Marx did subtitle Volume 1 "Capital in General," but it is clear enough that Marx began from the concept of capital as a Universal. The German language does not clearly distinguish these two concepts. See the Syllogism of Reflection (Hegel, 1831, §190) or the Syllogism of Allness (Hegel, 1816, p. 647) in Hegel's *Logic* for Hegel's explanation of the distinction.

Moseley (2015) gives a better definition than that given by Marx:

> The reason why Marx's theory begins with the general form of surplus-value is that it is based on the assumption that all particular forms of surplus-value *come from the same source* – the surplus value of workers.
>
> 2015, 122

As Ilyenkov (1983/1960, see p. 146 below) explained, it is that *other* to which all capitals relate in common which identifies them as capital, not a property of themselves which is held in common.

This definition is better because it defines the unit of capital in terms of the transformation of value elaborated in Part 2 of Volume 1, which constitutes a unit as part of the universal capital: M—C—M+ΔM, that is, the removal of money from circulation and its return to circulation thereby expanding itself. The further specification of capital in Part 3 of Volume 1, as *industrial* capital is the appropriation of surplus labour time of workers. It is not so much being "something in common" between units of capital which is important, but the characteristic *movement* of value which constitutes all units of capital as *part of the same universal capital.*

Moseley (2016, p. 47) cites Marx in the *Grundrisse*:

> Capital in general, as distinct from particular capitals, is an abstraction which grasps the specific characteristics which distinguish capital from all other forms of wealth.

and a little later:

> Capital in general is also defined as what all capitals have in common: "The introduction of *many* capitals must not interfere with the investigation here. The relation of the many will, rather, be explained after *what they all have in common*, the quality of being capital, has been examined."
> p. 48, citing MARX in the *Grundrisse*

It does seem that at times at least, both Moseley and Marx did not see the distinctive way in which Hegel understood "truly universal" as distinct from "merely general." This distinction is reflected in Hegel's comment on Rousseau:

> The aforementioned difference between the merely communal and the truly general is aptly expressed in Rousseau's well-known Contract social, in which it is said that the laws of a state must arise from the general will (the *volonté générale*), but need not therefore be the will of all (*volonté de tous*).
> HEGEL, 1831, §163

Words aside, this beginning with *Universal* capital is entirely consistent with analysing how the *total* surplus value exploited from a working class is accumulated, and this Marx does as Moseley has shown.

Volume 2 examines how each unit of capital shares the surplus value it acquires in the process of returning products to circulation and recovering money from circulation with a profit and the distribution of capital entailed in the reproduction of variable, constant and surplus value in the economy.

Volume 3 then deals with *Particular* forms of industrial capital. A unit of capital can constitute itself as capital only by exploiting labour in some particular way, in *some* trade. The relevant characteristic here is the specific market which the capital is serving. Each particular sector will determine a socially necessary composition of capital through competition *in that market*. Here the surplus value acquired by an entire sector of the economy, each individual capital competing with the others in the same trade, under the same technical conditions, becomes the Subject, doubtless represented politically by a peak industrial body. Moseley recognises that this phase of *Capital* is the Particular moment of Hegel's Concept Logic, and he provides quotes to indicate that Marx saw it that way, too. Rather annoyingly however, Moseley regularly refers to a sector of the economy not as Particular capital, but as "Individual" capital. But we are definitely not dealing with Individual capitals here, but all the individual capitals which realise their profits in the same particular market.

The Individual capital is the immediate, concrete, developed unit of capital, the individual firm or business. It is this *concreteness* that characterises "Individual" as Hegel sees it. It is clear enough that to complete *Capital* and make it a comprehensive text book of political economy further volumes on Individual capitals would be required. But equally Marx may have had little interest in, in effect, teaching capitalists how to make money, and further, the task of elaborating the science to this degree of detail is a task exceeding the capacities of one person, even Marx, at that point in the history of the science. However, Moseley cites Marx rejecting the need for an extension of the work to the Individual moment of capital for what strikes me as being a strange reason:

> Marx rejected Hegel's interpretation of singularity because the singularity of capital – interest-banking capital – is not the perfect embodiment of the inner nature of capital, but is instead the perfect 'obfuscation' of the inner nature of capital.
>
> 2016, p. 45

This could reflect Marx's opinion, but seemingly not Hegel's, because, for Hegel, the Individual (or Singular) is a single, *concrete* entity. Now it seems to me that Marx never solved the difficult quandary in analysis of capitalism which is reflected in this problem with the interpretation of Hegel's moments of the concept. On the whole, rich people, capitalists, do not own capital as such. They probably have large bank accounts, but fundamentally, they own companies or shares in companies. And it is companies which are the actors in the economy. It is companies which are the basic units of capital and the basic form of organisation of the capitalist class (Connell, 1977). But it is still individual persons who own capital through their shares (and such like) in companies, and it is those individuals who can trade in those shares on the capital market. It seems that there is a whole other layer of movement of capital entailed in *ownership* of capital over and above the *activity* of capital itself. In fact, Marx treats finance capital as the *pure* form of capital. However, finance capital forms an entirely new layer, above simple commodity production and industrial capital.

However, it is a general rule that the more abstract the appearance of an entity, the more powerful it is as a vehicle for objectification of social relations. Coinage has long failed to live up to the needs of capitalism for money; money is now almost entirely intangible. Marx goes on to remark on "particular forms of capital and surplus-value that develop out of the 'germ' of capital in general" (Moseley, 2016, p. 48). It is this development from a single germ cell and continued mutual transformation which marks what is universal, not what is common between them.

The "unit" of capital dealt with in Volume 1 is an *ideal*, not yet "the concrete individual," just as "universal" does not mean "general" or "what *all* have in common" but the *totality* of capital.

Moseley brings evidence from the *Grundrisse* which includes the interpretation of "Individual" (aka Singularity, depending on the translator), as the concrete, individual developed unit of capital, the individual firm or business. However, the fact that shares and such like are the means by which an individual *person* can *own* capital obfuscates the unit of capital itself. An individual person owns capital by owning a share in a company. But it is the company which is the Individual capital. An individual person's relation to the exploitation of labour-power is mediated by the company they work for or have shares in.

The Subject in Hegel's *Logic* can be interpreted as some species (Universal), including a range of varieties (Particulars) and Individual organisms. But the Subject here is capital, a social relation or form of activity, not a species. How to interpret the Concept Logic in terms of a social practice like capital? Moseley draws attention to a passage in the *Grundrisse* (Marx, 1973/1858, p. 275) where Marx is ruminating on different possible ways of interpreting the three moments of the subject as capital:

Capital.*

I.   Universality:

    (1)

        (a)   Emergence of capital out of money.

        (b)   Capital and labour (mediating itself through alien labour).

        (c)   The elements of capital, dissected according to their relation to labour (Product. Raw material. Instrument of labour.)

---

*   I have copied Moseley's formatting of the quote, but used the word "universal" rather than the translator's choice of "generality" for *allgemeine*. "Universal" is the conventional translation when referring to the moments of the Concept.

     (2)   Particularisation of capital:
         (a)   Capital *circulant*, capital *fixé*. Turnover of capital.
     (3)   Singularity of capital:
         Capital and profit.
         Capital and interest.
         Capital as *value*, distinct from itself as interest and profit.
III. Particularity:
     (1)   Accumulation of capitals.
     (2)   *Competition* of capitals.
     (3)   Concentration of capitals (quantitative distinction of capital as at same time qualitative, as *measure* of its size and influence).
VII. Singularity:
     (1)   Capital as credit.
     (2)   Capital as stock-capital.
     (3)   Capital as money market.

Here we see Marx experimenting, c. 1858, on how to render Hegel's moments of the Subject with the subject being capital, some time after he had committed himself to a plan of "reconstructing" capital by "rising from the abstract to the concrete" (*Grundrisse*, p. 100). Hegel never uses Universal, Particular and Individual in a tiered fashion like this. Nothing in Hegel's *Logic* suggests such a structure, but it does make sense. What we do see is how in the section "III. *Singularity*" Marx considered three possible ways in which an individual person can be an owner of capital. But a glance at the above plan reminds us that this is not in fact how Marx eventually proceeded in writing *Capital*.

In the end, Volume 1 was devoted to the Universal moment, capital in general.

A number of different approaches to Particularity are dealt with in the following two volumes. This is quite consistent with Hegel's Concept Logic. Volume 2 deals with distribution and circulation of capital between sectors of the economy producing capital goods, means of subsistence realised out of wages, and luxury goods ultimately purchased out of surplus value. And the distribution of the surplus value from the industrial capitalists to landlords, lenders, distributors and retailers. Altogether, the circulation of capital, and the problems which arise from the *realisation* and *reproduction* of the constant, variable and surplus value as determined in Volume 1.

Volume 3 goes to the capital market and exchange of products between industrial capitals, where the necessary equalisation of the rate of profit leads to surplus value being distributed between *particular* sectors of capital. The general schema of the Logic of the Subject is *not sufficient* to explain this. However, Moseley is right that Particularity is taken in Volume 3 in relation to the composition of capital allowing Marx to explain the equalisation of the rate of profit without abandoning the concept of value established in Volume 1, and he goes on to trace the further movement of that mass of surplus value in the finance system.

Looking back at Marx's early exploration of the moments of the concept in connection with capital, we see that Marx *could* have pursued an analysis of capital by means of examination of the various ways individual persons can *own* capital, but he did not take that path. Thanks to Moseley's examination of Marx's manuscripts, we can see the protracted process that eventually led Marx to a fruitful application of Hegelian logic to his analysis of political economy. His understanding of the *Logic* developed through his struggle with the subject matter over a period of ten years.

Moseley says:

> Marx criticised Hegel for surrounding his method in 'mysticism' (i.e., assuming that the universal is the Absolute Spirit), but Marx praised Hegel for correctly understanding the relation between the universal and the particular forms of the universal.
>
> 2016, p. 45

Moseley also says:

> For Hegel, the Universal substance is the Absolute Spirit, which incarnates itself in particular forms of objective reality. This is of course the idealist nature of Hegel's philosophy, which Marx completely rejected. For Marx, the universal substance is materialist – abstract labour.
>
> 2015, p. 119

Indeed Marx did criticise Hegel in such a way, but only Chris Arthur mentions the fact that *Capital* deals with only one Subject, capital, while the *Logic* is intended to cover how *multiple* subjects (family, church, state, etc.) interact with one subject, such as capital, merge with it and realise an entire social formation. The Universal is not the Absolute Spirit; it is the universal moment of one subject among many. And nor is the Absolute "abstract labour." Even in the most developed capitalism imaginable, there are still *other* subjects and *other* kinds of activity. Capital is not self-sustaining; capital relies on Nature and human communities to renew themselves despite the predation of capital. Such interactions are the subject matter of the remainder of the Concept Logic (Object and Idea), which are not within the scope of *Capital*. However, if you aspired to write the "unity of the capitalist state and economy," then the second phase of the Concept Logic, "The Object," is the relevant Logic. Marx did tackle the problem of how industrial capital interacts with *other sections of capital*, especially in Volume 2. How did Hegel inform Marx in his approach to *this* problem? The logic of the second chapter of the Concept Logic on the Object is very pertinent to this problem if one takes capital in one sector as Subject.

Marx had not yet fully solved the problem of how to interpret the subject matter of the *Logic* in a study of Political Economy, although he did prefigure it, in my view, in the very first article of his mature work, *Theses on Feuerbach*:

> All social life is essentially *practical*. All mysteries which lead theory to mysticism find their rational solution in human practice and in the comprehension of this practice.
>
> MARX, 1845

7   Marx's Starting Point

One aspect of Hegel's *Logic* which applied to the various sciences which Hegel outlined in the *Encyclopaedia* Marx figured out in the section of the *Grundrisse* called "Method of Political Economy." Marx drew the conclusion that every system of political economy (including his own) had first to identify "the simplest determinations" through analysis of the concrete data and an immanent critique of existing systems, then *reconstruct* capital concretely by a synthesis beginning from these "simplest determinations." That synthesis would be *Capital*. We know from notes he later wrote (1881) that rather than "value" he would begin from "the *simplest social form* in which the product of labour is presented in contemporary society, and this is 'the *commodity*.'"

I cannot say whether Marx had read the relevant passage in the *Science of Logic* explaining this method in "The Idea of the True" (the beginning of which was cited above). But this method is exhibited throughout various books of the *Encyclopaedia*, so it is possible that Marx figured it out whether or not he read the explanatory passage in the *Logic*.

> The progress, proper to the Concept, from universal to particular, is the basis and the possibility of a synthetic science, of a system and of systematic cognition.
>
> HEGEL, 1816, p. 801

The passage already cited above continues:

> The first requisite for this is, as we have shown, that the beginning be
> made with the subject matter in the form of a universal (*Allgemeinen*).
> In the sphere of actuality, whether of nature or spirit, it is the concrete
> individuality (*die konkrete Einzelheit*) that is given to subjective, natural
> cognition as the first; but in cognition that is a *comprehension*, at least to
> the extent that it has the form of the Concept for basis, the first must be
> on the contrary *something simple*, something *abstracted* from the con-
> crete, because in this form alone has the subject-matter the form of the
> self-related universal or of an immediate based on the Concept.
>
> HEGEL, 1816, p. 801.

So Hegel advises that a science must begin both from the Universal (capital in
general) *and* the simplest, individual unit (the commodity). Marx took it that
while the unifying content of Political Economy is value, capital, as the most
developed, "self-valorising" form of value, is the real subject matter. Volume 1
determines not only the total surplus value, but the total social product and its
division into constant, variable and surplus labour.

Part 1 of Volume 1 deals with the commodity (the simplest social form of
value) and Marx's application of this method in relation to his starting point
has been widely discussed in the literature. What is always overlooked however, is that Marx continued this approach (as did Hegel in the *Encyclopaedia*)
as he took up *successive key concepts of political economy*, only the first of which
was the commodity.

In Part 2, Marx introduces capital by means of Moneybags who buys in
order to sell at a profit.

> Our friend, Moneybags, who as yet is only an *embryo capitalist*, must buy
> his commodities at their value, must sell them at their value, and yet at
> the end of the process must withdraw more value from circulation than
> he threw into it at starting.
>
> *Capital, v. 1*, p. 176, my emphasis

This is the "germ cell" ("cell-form," to use the word Marx uses in the Preface
to the First German Edition, here "embryo"; *der Keim* was Hegel's term, the
"first" when beginning the synthesis of a new concrete concept). Moneybags's
buying-in-order-to-sell is the unit of capital which is to be understood as the
germ cell of a *single capitalist company*. A new *unit* of in the development of
value, the simplest form of capital.

It would have been utterly at odds with the method of the *Logic* for Marx to have *begun* with the total capital, total surplus value, etc., even though this is the intent of Volume 1 as Moseley has correctly identified. To do so would have represented capital as if it could be a single entity across the entire economy like the USSR aspired to be, whereas the concept of capital is precisely units like Moneybags which grow to become companies, but are always in competition with other units of capital like themselves.

While meticulously refuting those who take Volume 1 at "face value," so to speak, in which the subject matter is really individual capitalist firms, Moseley does not touch on why the Universal is represented as many individual units (*Einzelheiten*), which "in this form alone has the subject-matter the form of the self-related universal or of an immediate based on the Concept" (Hegel, 1816, p. 801).

As I have already mentioned, one important insight which Moseley brings to the Hegelian roots of *Capital* is his claim that Marx's logic is a logic of "sequential determination." He claims that others have interpreted the logic, including the algebraic representations of the logic of capital, as simultaneous determination in the manner of formal logic, and connected with this, interpreted capital as a self-replicating "system." But capital is not a "system" *in this sense*, because it is in its very essence subject to continual change through the spontaneous interaction of innumerable units. This is why the claim of "long term equilibrium" can only be a relative claim for analytical purposes. The contradiction between quantitative exchange-value and qualitative use value continuously drives the *reshaping* of the capitalist economy through competition, competition which, as Marx points out, is inherently self-cancelling.

But Hegel's *Logic* is also a logic of sequential determination and this is how Hegel introduced a sense of time into logic. It is this "sequential determination," exhibiting itself as "sublation" in the *Logic*, which distinguished Hegel's *Logic* from System Theory, and I am grateful to Moseley for this insight.

Moseley notes that:

> Marx added a quantitative dimension to Hegel's Logic of the Concept, because Marx's theory is a theory of capitalism, and quantity is the main thing about capitalism.
>
> 2016, p. 45

It is the judgments which buyers and sellers make every time they act in the economy, which reduces every social product to an exchange-value which makes this possible. And it is capital which makes this process of "practical abstraction" ubiquitous.

8   On Marx's Theory of Money

Moseley explains Marx's theory of money as follows.

Throughout, Marx assumes that money is in fact gold. Because of its physical properties and its relative scarcity, for centuries gold had functioned as money: as a store of value, as a means measurement of value, as a medium of exchange, and as capital. Nevertheless, paper currency was already commonplace in Marx's time. That is, money as an actual commodity was a germ cell of money from which the multiplicity of forms of money grew.

Gold embodies a definite quantity of abstract labour, being the average, socially necessary amount of labour-time required to find, mine and mint a given quantity of gold. However, since gold *is* money, it cannot be said to *have* a value, surplus or otherwise. As soon as the production cost of mining in a given gold mine generates a rate of profit below the going rate of profit, capital would be withdrawn from the mine, deployed elsewhere and gold mining would cease in the given mine. Thus the rate of profit in gold mining equals the general rate of profit.

However, Moseley says that it is widely agreed among Marxist political economists that it makes no difference to capitalism whether money is gold or whether it is paper money backed by the state or bank credit backed by a secure bank, so long as there is no uncertainty about the "abstract labour" represented by a unit of money. Gold is not the only option for this.

The downside of relying on gold mining for a money supply, is that the cycle of capitalist production begins from money; without the investment of new capital there can be no profit generated. Limiting the total capital available for production to the amount of available gold prevents the expansion of capital beyond very severe limits. Thus, so long as everyone trusts the central bank and the commercial banks to limit the issuing of capital to a level which maintains the going general rate of profit, a piece of their paper is as good as gold.

Another important conclusion of Moseley's study is that the average price of a commodity is not affected by changes in the price of labour-power.

> an increase or decrease in wages in this case leaves k + p [cost of production + general rate of profit] unaffected, just as it would leave the commodity's value unaffected, and simply brings about a corresponding converse movement, a decrease or increase, on the side of the profit-rate.
>
> p. 169, citing MARX in *Capital, v. 3*

Wage increases come at the cost of profits. All that is affected is the proportion between constant capital and variable capital. The movement of the total social capital between particular sectors of the economy will ensure that the profit rate will be equalised and the increased wage cost be absorbed by a reduction in the average rate of profit. This is, of course, an observation of great interest to the workers' movement.

9   Value of Labour Power

The cost of buying the means of subsistence for the working class may be greater or less than their value, as determined through the sharing of surplus value appropriately for the composition of capital in the sectors producing means of subsistence, presuming that these goods are to be purchased from capitalists.

> the prices of the means of subsistence and means of production are also equal to their prices of production, not their values.
>
> 2016, p. 133. See also pp. 154 & 168

But proletarians by definition have no capital, and do not own their own tools or the materials they work on. Consequently, under the rule of capital, they do not earn any rate of profit on exercise of their labour-power. Thus the production of the labour-power whose use they sell to the capitalist is "unproductive labour," i.e., it does not produce surplus value. Surplus value is produced by the *use* of labour-power and not its production. The vulnerability of proletarians to exploitation, in lacking their own means of production, allows this to happen. Under the rule of capital, even the self-employed artisan who competes with the employed proletarian will pay rent to the landlord and interest to the bank, absorbing the surplus value they create for capital leaving nothing for them, so long as they compete with proletarians.

Marx accepted that services, such as the labour of a schoolmaster, can be commodities, if they produce surplus value for a capitalist employer.

> outside the sphere of production of material objects, a schoolmaster is a productive labourer when, in addition to belabouring the heads of his scholars, he works like a horse to enrich the school proprietor.
>
> *Capital, v. 1*, p. 510

Marx regarded domestic labour as something capitalists purchased out of their share of the surplus value and had nothing to say about domestic services in working-class households, whether purchased from the market as they frequently are today or thanks to the unpaid labour of women. Marx had nothing to say about the labour component of producing labour-power and consequently Moseley has nothing to say about this in the book under consideration either.

Marx took the archetypal commodity to be a material object, rather than a service. This made sense in three ways. (1) in his day, services were largely luxuries purchased by capitalists out of their share of the surplus, (2) only things can be accumulated, not services, and (3) he needed this archetype against the view of some political economists that the worker, capitalist and landlord each received a share of the profit according to the value of their "service." But in principle, he was clear that services sold to capital for the extraction of surplus value can be commodities, too.

If the means of subsistence cost more than their value, then workers will be obliged to work longer than the necessary labour time in order to purchase their means of subsistence and must be paid accordingly by the employer. Producing labour-power is an industry like any other, except that it employs no capital and consequently earns no profit for its seller.

10   Conclusion to Chapter 4

Moseley has shown that the "production price" theory, as opposed to the idea of a quantity of "embodied labour" being *passed down* and *accumulated in the chain of production*, makes the equalisation of the rate of profit comprehensible while retaining the insights of Volume 1 determining the total quantity and source of surplus value in the unpaid labour of the working class. Equalisation of the rate of profit is achieved thanks to price competition and competition for capital between particular sections of the economy, distributing the total surplus value extracted from the working class in a manner that differs from the quantity of surplus value originating from each sector. This is ensured by the free movement of capital.

In Volume 1, it was assumed that every product is sold at its value (abstract labour), as in a hypothetical society of independent commodity producers where the impact of a capital market is left out of the picture.

On the other hand, given long-term equilibrium, every time a product is sold by a capitalist producer, the price is determined according to the necessary cost of production plus the going rate of profit. Competition between capitalists demands it, and the rule is enforced by the lending practices of the banks. However, the price of the product remains the *appearance* of its value. Surplus value is distributed among capitalists along the chain of production.

If the composition of a given capital unit were to be equal to the average across the economy, and the composition of capital in all the industries producing the means of subsistence likewise equal to its value (unlikely assumptions), then that firm would buy its inputs at value and sell its outputs at cost price plus profit which would likewise be equal to the value of the product as determined by embodied abstract labour. However, even given long-term equilibrium (in the sense which Moseley assumes), this is unlikely to be ever the case, because of the technical differences between diverse sectors of the economy.

The difference between the presumption of commodities sold at their value in Volume 1 determining rates of surplus value and profit for each unit, and the finding of Volume 3, that prices are determined by the general rate of profit and costs of production, is a difference arising in the course of the systematic, dialectical reconstruction of the capitalist economy. The analysis moves from *simple commodity production by independent producers*, to *commodity production by capital*, such that the rate of profit in every sector is invariant with respect to the composition of capital in each particular sector. Workers are paid for their labour-power, not any part of the product they are involved in producing, and are subject to exploitation. The abstraction of "simple commodity production," counterfactual in a time of industrial capital, is a valid abstraction because of the abstract nature of labour in developed industrial capitalism. It is not that workers have something in common which allows the theorist to form a concept of universal labour, but that all workers must sell their labour to capital and for capital any worker is interchangeable with any other. It is just abstract, featureless labour.

This is how I critically summarise the results of Moseley's meticulous reconstruction of Marx's thinking as he formulated what became the three volumes of *Capital*. Moseley's scholarship allows us to see that Marx did not begin with a clear conception, but rather, figured it out in the course of working through the theoretical and empirical data over a period of many years, at times hesitating or "misspeaking," but ultimately arriving at an analysis whose internal logic is impeccable.

While I have made, and will continue to make, criticisms of how Moseley and Marx himself understood the relation of the logic of *Capital* to Hegel's *Logic*, it is clear that Marx in many respects surpassed what Hegel was able to present in his *Logic*. It is important to grasp these differences, because we live in new conditions and face new problems and both writers have much to offer.

CHAPTER 5

Capital and the "Economic Germ Cell"

1   Introduction

As will be evident from the foregoing parts of this work, I believe that the writers who were inspired by Lenin's 1914 aphorism and the 1973 translation of the *Grundrisse* to reveal the Hegelian roots of Marx's *Capital* were mistaken in one way or another.

The first error was in seeking a "reflection" of the *Logic* in one positive science, Political Economy. The science of logic is distinct in its structure from all of the natural and human sciences. This is true not only of Hegel's approach, but *anyone* would agree that no positive science can be "like" logic. All the other sciences deal with facts, and all the transitions in the other sciences have a factual content: Logic does not.

The second error was in their insistence on seeing *Capital* as a *structural* science in which the study of the history could play no part. No one would seriously propose Biology without a theory of evolution, and you can't understand present-day political economy without understanding the history of the postwar economic arrangements. But there is an element of truth in this structuralism. In the final analysis, it is only the political economic system which we have before us here and now which is of real interest. But the study of history does guide how a science is built. For example, all of the original observations about impending crisis that Geert Reuten offered in his book were only thanks to the *observation* of historical tendencies in modern capitalism. The claim for a dichotomy between a structural dialectic and an historical dialectic is misconceived.

Third, all of the analyses of the relation between *Capital* and the *Logic* considered were either confined to the early chapters of *Capital* on simple commodity production, or were exceedingly general in how they traced the connection between *Capital* and the *Logic*, sometimes bending Hegel's text to fit. Fred Moseley is not guilty of this charge, and his treatment of Volume 3 was precise and detailed, but his claims were limited to the Universal and Particular moments of the Concept Logic. Key transitions in Volume 1 by which Marx introduced capital, surplus labour time, constant and variable capital and relative and absolute surplus value have been overlooked as seemingly irrelevant in the exercise of identifying Hegelian roots.

Finally, no one has taken seriously Marx's aphorism about the "value-form of the commodity" being "the economic cell-form" of bourgeois society. To help shed some light on these questions I shall review the work of one Soviet philosopher and one Soviet psychologist.

2   Evald Ilyenkov's "Abstract and Concrete in Marx's *Capital*"

The Soviet philosopher Evald Ilyenkov's study of the relationship of Marx's *Capital* to Hegel's *Logic* was published in English in 1982. However, it had been written in 1960, about five years after Ilyenkov published *Theses on the Question of the Interconnection of Philosophy and Knowledge of Nature and Society in the Process of their Historical Development*. This latter work announced Ilyenkov's dissent from orthodox Soviet Marxism, speaking for a current of Marxism initiated by the Psychologist Lev Vygotsky, long suppressed in Stalin's Soviet Union. Not only did Ilyenkov anticipate by almost 40 years the intense interest in the West in the relation between *Capital* and the *Logic*, but in my view is superior to most recent Western scholarship on this topic.

Ilyenkov's work differs from that of all the present-day writers on the topic because Ilyenkov approached the topic on the basis that:

> Marx's *Capital* is indeed the highest type of school for theoretical thinking. A scientist specialising in any field of knowledge can use it as a source of most valuable ideas with regard to the theoretical method of research.
> ILYENKOV, 1982, p. 289

Accordingly, Ilyenkov deals with the methodological issues as relevant to all the social sciences. The significance of Ilyenkov's study therefore goes beyond the reading and interpretation of *Capital*, aiming to enrich the Marxist approach to analysis of all social phenomena. This aligns with this author's aims in the study of current discourse on *Capital* and the *Logic*.

Ilyenkov addresses four questions: (1) the relation between the abstract and concrete, (2) the difference between the sequence of categories in cognition and in presentation, (3) the relationship between Hegel's Idealism and Marx's materialism with respect to methodology, and (4) the relation between the logical and the historical. The book deals exhaustively with these four questions, rather than merely seeking an homology or similarity between *Capital* and the *Logic* or aiming at a "reconstruction" of Marx's *Capital*.

Ilyenkov's views on the difference between Hegel's idealism and Marx's materialism goes to Marx's *critical* appropriation of British political economy which Hegel appropriated *un*critically, just as he uncritically appropriated the positive results of *all* the sciences in his *Encyclopaedia*. Ilyenkov differs with the present-day writers considered here on the question of the relation between the logical and the historical by 180 degrees.

In dealing with Ilyenkov's views on this matter I will address Ilyenkov's acceptance of the claim of universal applicability of the principles of "materialist dialectics" which he derived from the study of *Capital*, including the "dialectics of nature." This runs counter to present-day scepticism in relation to any such universal claims. To establish the limits of this claim to universality, I will draw from Marx's *Theses on Feuerbach* to establish the basis for appropriation of Hegel's *Logic* and its limits. The real subject matter of Hegel's *Logic* was always human practice, so it is clear that the scope of the *Logic* is that of human practice.

2.1 *The Abstract and the Concrete*

Ilyenkov approached all philosophical issues through an immanent critique of the history of philosophy, and his examination of the abstract and concrete was no different. Prior to Hegel, no consistent definition of abstract and concrete had withstood criticism, but I will not reprise his analysis of the earlier history of the problem.

Hegel agreed with Kant in understanding "abstractness" to mean that "a concept never expresses in its definitions the sensually contemplated reality in its entirety." Abstract is therefore like *extract*, in that it indicates that aspects of some reality have been extracted, removed from their connection to the whole of reality. Abstractness, then, refers to a paucity of connections to the full reality of the world. In that sense then, all concepts are to one degree or another, abstract. Thus, for Hegel, abstract referred to "anything general, any similarity expressed in word and concept, a simple identity of a number of things with one another."

Hegel was, Ilyenkov says, the first to define the concrete as "unity in diversity, as unity of different and opposing definitions, as the mental expression of organic links, of syncretism of the separate abstract definitenesses of an object within the given specific object" (Ilyenkov, 1982 pdf, p. 14).

The concreteness of a concept referred to the multiplicity of definitions simultaneously connecting the concept with other concepts. Abstractness on the other hand, refers to single properties of things, a feature exhibited in common by many different things, but failing to express any real connection between them. "Unity in diversity" implies the necessary and simultaneous connection of different definitions of something, not simply attributes combined by an "and" or an "or."

A word referring merely to the *abstract similarity* of a number of individual things, phenomena or mental images, then is not a *concept (Begriff)* for Hegel at all, merely an "abstractly general representation (*Vorstellung*)," a "pseudoconcept," which may allow you to recognise or refer to something, but which does not express a comprehension of the thing.

Reality itself is concrete, because every material object or phenomenon is connected by material threads to every other part of reality. But any everyday representation of any part of reality, its species, its size, its location, its present disposition, is bound to be abstract. "Everyday" concepts may be concrete where the concept in question is a part of someone's everyday life, the different aspects being unified in a person's practical experience. However, in everyday concepts borrowed from science, such as "atom" or "value," the connection between entities and phenomena is not reflected in any experience or *theory*. If a term is used which locates the concept in a theory, such as a scientific concept, then the relevant concept is to that degree concrete.

All concepts remain, of course, to a greater or lesser degree, abstract. But a concept which is part of some scientific theory or human practice necessarily entails connecting an object or phenomenon to many others simultaneously in a multiplicity of real and meaningful connections which cohere together. In line with Soviet practice, Ilyenkov restricts concreteness specifically to *scientific* concepts. I believe this restriction is unwarranted. To the extent that a theory expresses *more* than simply a categorisation of phenomena according to attributes held in common by a set of things, but is on the contrary connected to some real human practice, then we can talk of a concrete concept of a thing. It is these connections with other concepts are referred to by Hegel as the *content* of the concept.

Words can indicate concepts only to the extent they that belong to some theory, some system of concepts, which gives to each word a connection with other concepts. Taken out of the theory of which a word is a part, a word can only designate some object or, more exactly, some collection of features.

Thus, the concrete, essential nature of some problem is revealed by elaborating the content of a concept, the many interrelated definitions of the concept, and endeavouring to grasp the necessary *unity* of these abstract definitions, rather than by seeking a simple definition. That is what is meant by taking a problem concretely.

Practical human activity reveals the connections between things which make the basis of forming concrete concepts. Ilyenkov sees Hegel's idealism in his conception that it is thought alone which makes these connections, and which forms concrete concepts. But all phenomena are connected with each other by innumerable threads, and it is *practice* that reveals these connections. This idealism of Hegel can be countered so long as we understand "thought" as a subordinate but inseparable component of human practice.

The concreteness of a conception of some phenomenon is not *created* by mental reflection, but is a characteristic of the phenomenon itself. The task of cognition is, so far as possible, to *reproduce* this concreteness in conception. This concreteness is not necessarily preserved in the sensuous representation of a phenomenon or in a theoretical conception resting on sensuous representation alone. Concreteness is characteristic of rich, well-developed, profound and comprehensive knowledge, just as abstractness is characteristic of sensual knowledge which is poor, meagre and lopsided. The concreteness of a conceptual understanding of a phenomenon refers to the extent that abstract definitions retain their connections with each other:

> Each of the numerous definitions forming part of the conceptual system of a concrete science, loses its abstract character in it being filled with the sense and meaning of all the other definitions connected with it. Separate abstract definitions mutually complement each other, so that the abstractness of each of them, taken separately, is overcome.
>
> ILYENKOV, 1982, pdf, p. 22

Abstractness can also be a characteristic of real phenomena, most famously in the case of what Marx calls "abstract labour." "The reduction of different kinds of labour to uniform simple labour devoid of any distinctions 'is an abstraction which is made every day in the social process of production'. It is 'no less real (an abstraction) than the resolution of all organic bodies into air'." (pdf p. 19, citing Marx, 1859). Ilyenkov explains:

> 'The abstract' in this kind of context, very frequent in Marx, assumes the meaning of the 'simple', undeveloped, one-sided, fragmentary, 'pure' (i.e., uncomplicated by any deforming influences). It goes without saying that 'the abstract' in this sense can be an objective characteristic of real phenomena, and not only of phenomena of consciousness.
>
> 1982, pdf, p. 20

Thus "reduction to labour devoid of all differences appears here as an abstraction, but as a *real* abstraction" (pdf, p. 63). Thus both "abstract" and "concrete" can be descriptive of forms of development of nature, practice or thinking.

Ilyenkov illustrates the significance of concrete and abstract conceptions by contrasting the definition of humans as creatures with ear lobes (a feature shared by all humans) and Benjamin Franklin's definition of a human as "a being producing implements of labour." Ilyenkov calls Franklin's concept of the human "a concrete universal definition of a concept" (op. cit., p. 47). Very few people actually produce tools, but it is the practice of tool-making from which the diversity of human types can be comprehended, and in that sense it is a *concrete universal* characteristic of human beings, rather than an *abstract general* feature, like ear lobes. Thus the question of the universal character of a concept is transferred to another sphere, that of the study of the real *process of development*, rather than simply discerning a pattern in the variety which exists. It is not the concept as such which lends concreteness to a definition, but the process of development which can only be represented in a theory of that process of development.

What makes the concept of "commodity" or "value" concrete is not the concept of "commodity" or "value" as such, which can be revealed by a literary examination of the concept, but the economic concreteness sensuously exhibited in the ubiquitous practice of exchanging commodities. It is *the examination of this practice* from which the concreteness of the commodity relation can be appropriated. The *universality* of the category of value is first of all a characteristic not so much of the concept, of the mental abstraction, as of *the objective role* played by the commodity form in the emergence of capitalism. The words "commodity" and "value" were, after all, widely known and used long before and independently of the science of political economy. It was only with the attempt to create political economy as a *system*, beginning with William Petty, that the question of the *real source* of value, the *substance* of value, was posed. This led to the discovery that the substance of value was connected to social labour. This discovery was achieved by studying one practice alone, that of exchanging commodities, abstracted from its social and historical context.

Ilyenkov points out that entities interact not through an *identical* (internal) feature in them (in fact interaction is possible only thanks to *difference*), but in sharing a common relation to something *outside* of them, such as shared land or shared needs. It is in this – difference in commonality – that *concrete* links consist, recognising that a thing can be conceived concretely as one unit of a *concrete universal* substance. Concrete unity like this is the basis for real, objective connection between objects, rather than a person thinking about this concrete unity. It is this same unity-in-difference which distinguishes Darwin's theory of evolution from Linnaeus's taxonomy.

And it is in this sense that labour in general appears in political economy as a concrete universal substance, because each individual labour act is part of universal, social labour and each labourer merely an organ of that labour. Abstract labour, labour voided of all difference by the industrial system, is likewise a *real abstraction* and each individual commodity is a manifestation of this universal essence, but united in the common relation of all labour acts to capital.

This concept of concreteness is at the heart of how Ilyenkov identifies Marx's concept of the "cell":

> A concept, inasmuch as it is a real concept rather than merely a general notion expressed in a term, always expresses the *concretely universal,* not the abstractly universal, that is, it expresses a reality which, while being quite a particular phenomenon among other particular phenomena, is at the same time a genuinely universal, concretely universal element, a 'cell' in all the other particular phenomena.
>
> 1982, pdf, p. 50

Marx was able to form a concrete definition of 'value in general' or 'value as such' on the basis of concrete consideration of direct exchange of one commodity for another involving no money, abstracting from all other kinds of value, i.e., value based on surplus-value, profit, rent, interest, and so on. Marx began by limiting himself to *one* kind of value which proves to be elementary, primordial both logically and historically, constituting the generic essence of all the other particular categories of value. But it was only with capitalist development that value as such became the universal form of economic relation, displacing or incorporating all other pre-capitalist economic relations.

On the one hand, Ilyenkov shows how this approach to the definition of value echoes Hegel's definition of a geometric figure (which Aristotle showed is developed from the triangle, while the triangle simultaneously exists side by side with the other particular figures developed from it) and uses Hegel's inadequate definition of value in the *Philosophy of Right* to show how Hegelian dialectics was inadequate. However, it seems to me that Hegel could not, and made no effort to, create a scientific concept of value in line with the *Science of Logic*, but instead borrowed it without criticism from the Political Economists. It is surely *in this* above all that Hegel's idealism lies.

Ilyenkov's view of concepts presupposed an *historical* view of the object. Development can only take place through what is initially an exceptional individual instance of the entity (such as value), which develops to become a particular case alongside others, finally becoming the universal form, alongside others. Development can happen in no other way. This is in contrast, for example, to utopian visions in which the hoped-for universal form can never exist as an exceptional individual relation alongside others, and so remains a mere fantasy. This kind of historical study of *one* object, abstracted from all other relations, is like a genealogy, and differs from the conventional approach to historical investigation which considers an object only in its interconnection with everything else at one moment in time.

This historical approach is also at odds with the widespread conviction among writers in this discourse that Hegel thinks that a science should begin from an "empty concept." Rather, a science must set off from an immediate, concrete universal abstraction.

2.1.1 The Unity of the Abstract and the Concrete

Having identified the commodity as the cell of bourgeois society by considering the commodity *abstracted from* its relation to all the other phenomena of capitalist production, Marx was then able to express its unique form of dependence on the system of production relations as a whole. Because the commodity form proves to be the economically universal relation between people in capitalism, the purely abstract consideration of the commodity reveals at the same time a *"universal* theoretical definition of *the system as a whole."*

Another form of value, such as profit or rent, if considered in abstraction from other forms of economic connection, would fail to reveal the specific nature of capitalism. These other forms of value in capitalist society can only be analysed after surplus-value, money and commodity have been analysed first.

The point is to choose the starting point of the analysis such that the abstract consideration of that relation 'in itself' happens to *coincide directly* with a concrete consideration of the system as a whole. If any other relation, such as profit, is chosen as the starting point, then its consideration cannot lead to an understanding of the system as a whole, and you would have to start again with some other relation. Ilyenkov refers to this fact as the *dialectical unity* of abstract and concrete.

Another criterion for identifying the cell of a complex phenomenon which Ilyenkov observes is the mutual conditioning of the various interconnections with other aspects of the whole. This is manifested in the fact that the system continuously reproduces the cell as a condition for its own existence, and thus distinguishes an essential relation from relations entailed only in the original generation of the phenomenon. Capitalism not only grew out of the supply of impoverished workers resulting from the Enclosures, but *maintained* workers in that condition, ripe for exploitation, just as humans continue to make tools as a condition of their own existence. It is this process which transforms what may have been an isolated practice into a self-perpetuating system. This circularity of relations within a system presents problems for logical analysis; one appears to have a system of mutual interrelation in which neither is primary.

The only way to resolve this logical circle is through the study of history, how the system came into being and how it maintains itself.

Capitalism does not produce the natural resources needed for the labour force though it does *commodify* the labour force, making it available for exploitation; in fact, it uses up these resources. Other processes reproduce these conditions for capitalism. It is only the commodity form which is not only necessary for capitalism, but is continuously reproduced by it.

Although changes in the productive forces are well known to be a cause of the development of capitalism, Marx shows that capitalism is in turn a cause of development of the productive forces. Capitalism developed from *absolute* surplus value driving the production process, lengthening the working day, changing to *relative* surplus value as the driving force, reducing the cost of labour-power. This was brought about by the transformations in the labour process through the invention of new machinery. So it was the commodity relation itself which was the ultimate driver for development of the productive forces, which then became a cause of the development of capitalism. Thus capitalism is conceived as a system, governed by its own internal laws, rather than being essentially the product of other conditions.

It is the circularity in which customary and legal relations necessary for capitalism become a proximate cause of features of capitalism which lay behind Hegel's mistakenly taking law and custom to be the ultimate cause of changes in economic activity, rather than its product. It should also be clear from the above how important historical reflection is to the analysis of capitalism, in particular in determining the starting point for analysis. None of the writers considered earlier reflected on *why* Marx began from the commodity relation other than Reuten who said that Marx took this over from the Political Economists for the purpose of immanent critique, and Reuten then dropped it from his analysis.

2.2   *The Method of Investigation and the Method of Presentation*

Ilyenkov devotes a chapter to the question of ascent from the abstract to the concrete, relying on the famous passage on this topic in the *Grundrisse*, and points out that in rising to the concrete, the reverse process also constantly takes place; analysis and synthesis are closely interwoven.

That Marx uses the ascent from abstract to concrete in *Capital* and in his earlier economic works does not mean that the method of presentation differs from the method of investigation. If that were true, *Capital* would offer no guidance to scientific research at all, and the proper material to offer that would be his earlier drafts and numerous notebooks. Ilyenkov points out that the feature of *Capital* which makes it so important as a model for scientific research, is that Marx does not dogmatically present his ready-made results, "but rather goes through the entire process of obtaining these results, the entire investigation leading to them." But:

> Of course, the process of investigation is not reproduced in all the details and deviations of more than twenty-five years of research but only in those principal and decisive features which, as the study itself showed, really advanced thought along the path of concrete understanding. ... and the process of investigation appears in its genuine form free from accidental elements and deviations. ... the method of presentation of material in *Capital* is nothing but the 'corrected' method of its *investigation*.
>
> 1982, pdf, p. 94

Ilyenkov points out that the sensuously concrete which makes the starting point for investigation refers to "the entire mass of the socially accumulated empirical experiences, the entire colossal mass of empirical data available to the theoretician from books, reports, statistical tables, newspapers, and accounts" (1982, p. 97), and not Marx's personal observation of economic activity. These data of course contain all the abstract illusions of the writers of these documents according to their times, not the immediate reality of economic life as such. Thus, from the beginning, the researcher must appropriate this data *critically*.

2.3   Hegel's Idealism

Ilyenkov goes on to criticise Hegel's conception of concreteness on the basis that Hegel held that it is only in *thought* that concreteness existed. Further, Ilyenkov identifies Marx's materialism in his giving priority to economic life over the other "spiritual" forms of activity, while Hegel gave priority precisely to these "spiritual" forms of activity, such as law, religion and philosophy. But at the same time, in line with Soviet practice, Ilyenkov chides Hegel for failing to ascribe concreteness to Nature. I part ways with Ilyenkov here because the real subject matter of Hegel's philosophy is *practice*. Granted, the concreteness of human practice in its discovery of innumerable connections is governed by Nature and the infinite interconnectedness of matter. Nonetheless, Hegel's idealism lies in taking the "spiritual" aspect of human practice as the decisive one. Hegel here makes the error mentioned by Ilyenkov above, of failing to correctly resolve the "vicious circle" in which production relations determine themselves, while using legal and "spiritual" relations as a means. We should neither follow Hegel's error, nor ascribe to Nature the determining factor in human practice, but take *practice*, in its widest possible sense, as the real subject matter of Hegel's philosophy, albeit misconstrued by him as *thought*.

In Ilyenkov's own words:

> In reality, the immediate basis of the development of thought is not nature as such but precisely the transformation of nature by social man, that is, practice.
>
> 1982, p. 157

Revolutions in theory always begin with a critical reinterpretation of preceding theories. Analysis of the facts of economic development coincides with the critical analysis of the concepts developed by political economy in earlier times. A reinterpretation of the facts recorded by earlier writers entails the formation of new concepts through which such facts can be interpreted. It must be so because analysis and synthesis, induction and deduction are always internal opposites in the process of cognition at a definite stage in the historical development of a science. Every induction which leads to new concepts entails a renewal of the process of deduction in the light of new concepts, and a continual renewal of analysis and synthesis. This process is reflected first in the history of science and secondly as a consciously applied methodology.

Furthermore, generalisations always originate in the formulation of laws which arise from the analysis of a single case, rarely through the identification of common features in a multiplicity of instances. Equally, Marx established the principles for the application of Hegel's *Logic* to Science by his exhaustive examination of just one topic, political economy, in particular in Britain, where political economy could be studied in its purest and most developed form, thereby providing a *paradigm* for all the sciences. It is this aspect of Marx's *Capital* which is of central interest to this author.

2.4   *Logical Development and Concrete Historicism*

One of the problems of applying logical methods to a complex object such as political economy is that a real, historically emerging system, is, at any given point, only partially exhibiting its essential features. It is necessary to follow its ongoing change and crises.

> Marx demands from science that it should comprehend the economic system as a system that has emerged and developed, he demands that the logical development of categories should reproduce the actual history of the emergence and unfolding of the system.
>
> 1982, p. 198

The logical method must be closely linked to an historical enquiry and *vice versa*. The commodity form of value existed only as a *rare* and *exceptional* case in the past. Thus in criticising the categories of the science, it must be kept in mind that these categories were formulated on the basis of an object which was less developed. But it is pointless to criticise those categories on the basis of facts upon which they were based, which in any case are now long gone and available only through the writings of the time. The categories must be criticised on the basis of present-day reality, in which the object is more fully developed.

Nonetheless, it is necessary to make a detailed study of the past in order to understand how it prepared for the present state of affairs and thereby to better understand the present.

The history of a science holds up a kind of mirror to the history of the object itself. While the "abstract outlines" of the object remain the same throughout, the categories which were used in the earliest stages of a science disappear. Consequently, the logical mode of enquiry was for Marx the dominant one, while the historical mode of enquiry played an auxiliary role.

Marx says: 'To develop the laws of bourgeois economy, it is not necessary to write *the real history of the production relations*" (1973/1858, p. 460), so Ilyenkov poses the question as follows:

> why and in what way the theoretical analysis (analysis of facts through a critique of categories) proceeding from the results of the historical process, can in itself yield an essentially historical (though logical in form) expression of reality even where real (empirical) history leading to these results is not directly studied in detail.
>
> 1982, pdf, p. 139

The key is to proceed from the results of this history with the conviction that this result preserves its own history in changed, sublated form. Any real process of development begins from premises which were the outcome of different conditions. The new principle then grows to become a universal principle dominating the others, transforming them into secondary external forms, organs of its own body. The new form of interaction now generates by its own action what was previously created by the earlier practice. What was a precondition becomes a product. The essential feature of the new system emerges as a concrete abstraction carried out by the historical process itself.

In this way, Ilyenkov distinguishes between what he calls 'concrete historicism' and 'abstract historicism'.

When a researcher seeks to find the historical origins of some phenomenon the problem arises: how far to go back, where to begin and with what? It seems that one can prove anything by choosing a suitable starting point. For example, one might find the origins of capital in the first historical instance when a great deal of wealth was concentrated in the hands of one individual, whether by pillage or frugality. In such an instance the means of accumulation would have had not the remotest connection with modern capitalism, but rather reflected conditions of quite another time. Modern capital reproduces itself by the appropriation of the unpaid labour of free labourers whom it retains in a condition of penury through the wages system, ensuring a continued supply of labour-power. This practice was perfected only in the 19th century.

> The principle of *concrete historicism* ... imposes the requirement of establishing, in a strictly objective manner, the point at which the real history of the object under consideration begins, the genuinely concrete starting point of its origin.
>
> 1982, pdf, p. 144

A practice originates not so much when conditions make it possible to exist, but when the practice itself generates the condition for its own existence.

Concrete historicism requires that each concrete object (e.g. profit, rent, exchange-value, ...) must be considered in its own right, in contrast to "history in general," in which the entire system is considered in chronological sequence beginning from some arbitrary starting point. In considering each category on its own, the beginning must be made on the basis of its priority in the *resulting* formation, even if at the earlier time that category is marginal. It is not so easy to single out the historical development of a relation which was for a very long time *marginal*, but the aim must be to single out the *cardinal points*, crises in the development of that relation.

As Marx says: "It would be inexpedient and wrong therefore to present the economic categories successively in the order in which they have played the dominant role in history" (1859). Having made a beginning with what had turned out to be the universal in modern capitalism – exchange of commodities – other institutions and practices must then be presented in the logical order in which they are produced by the dominant relation. In general, this order is the *opposite* of the order in which such relations were dominant in the historical development of the object as a whole.

Observe the contradiction here: the presently *dominant* relation which marks the *beginning* of the analysis existed *long ago*, marginal but nonetheless laying the groundwork for the present system. On the other hand, the historical succession of relations which are dominant is *inverted* in the logical development, the most ancient institutions coming last. What was dominant long ago becomes marginal in the present. This principle is true not only of the development of capitalism as a whole, but also applies to transient crises and other phenomena within capitalism. – underlying causes tend to come to light only after the dust has settled.

> The 'historically anterior' continually becomes the 'logically posterior' in the course of development.
>
> 1982, pdf, p. 147

The principle of concrete historicism can also be applied to historical development itself. In Marx's famous words:

> There is in every social formation a particular branch of production which determines the position and importance of all the others, and the relations obtaining in this branch accordingly determine the relations of all other branches as well. It is as though light of a particular hue were cast upon everything, tingeing all other colours and modifying their specific features.
>
> MARX, 1859

The point is that the history of each distinct industry or practice must be studied in its own right, so that its place in the developed system can be comprehended. Cardinal moments arise when one institution or practice moves from a subordinate to a dominant position, and transforms the whole social formation as it does so.

2.4.1 Ascent from the Abstract to the Concrete in Marx's *Capital*

Ilyenkov defines his aims in analysing *Capital*:

> Our task is that of singling out the universal logical elements of Marx's treatment of economic materials, the logical forms that are applicable, due to their universality, to any other theoretical discipline.
>
> 1982, pdf, p. 150

Capital begins with an analysis of *value*, because value is the "real form of economic relations that is the universal and elementary form of the being of capital" (loc. cit.). However, the immediate subject of analysis is the unmediated exchange of commodities, in the capitalism of Marx's times a rare practice.

Profit, money, wages and rent are not addressed initially. Nevertheless, this analysis reveals "the objectively universal form of all phenomena and categories of developed capitalism without exception" (loc. cit.).

Value is not abstracted as a common feature of profit, wages, etc. "The concrete universal concept registers a real objective elementary form of the existence of the entire system rather than an empty abstraction" (loc. cit.).

The proposition 'the substance of value is labour' is not contradicted by the fact that not all labour creates value (labour may be fruitless) and not all historical forms of labour create value (such as that of the subsistence farmer), far less does labour necessarily produce capital. Each form of value has to be traced through its real emergence and relations of mutual dependence as it emerged historically, beginning from the simplest form of value, the direct exchange of commodities. This process Ilyenkov calls 'genetic deduction'.

2.5   Contradiction

After a reflection on contradiction in the history of science and philosophy, Ilyenkov points to the most significant contradiction which Marx had to confront in the writing of *Capital*: the specific empirical fact of the uniformity of the rate of profit stands in contradiction to the law of value and exchange of commodities at their value, which implies a variation in the rate of profit according to the organic composition of capital.

> It is impossible to bring them into agreement exactly because such an agreement does not exist in the economic reality itself.
>
> 1982, pdf, p. 164

Average or natural prices correspond to embodied labour only in the instance where independent producers (not capitalists) directly exchange their products. When capital enters the scene, the price at which commodities are exchanged vary from their values (in the manner exhaustively explained by Fred Moseley, in line with Marx's explanation), once one takes into account that labour-power is a commodity which produces surplus value for the consumer of that labour-power. Once the purchase and sale of labour-power by capitalists enters the scene, and production entails purchase and sale of commodities *between* capitalists, then commodities are *no longer exchanged at their value*, and prices are explained by Marx *on the basis of the operation of the law of value in respect to labour-power* and the *expropriation of surplus value by capitalists*.

A uniform average rate of profit co-exists with the labour theory of value in the same way that a universal co-exists with its particulars. However, this conception is admissible only in the case that Hegel's conception of the concept is accepted, rather than the formal logical concept of concept based solely on the shared features of individual instantiations of the concept, and on the basis of the necessary labour-time as the foundation for the value of all commodities, including labour-power. Such a distinction between labour and the value of labour-power makes no sense in the circumstance of a hypothetical society of producers directly exchanging their products. The determination of prices via costs of production is *made necessary by new facts*, namely, the exploitation of wage labour by capital. The point was *not to eliminate the contradiction* between the law of value and the uniform rate of profit but to *express* that contradiction in the theory of production prices. Resolution of the contradiction in the law of value was addressed by *new facts*, which had not yet become dominant in the times of Adam Smith, David Ricardo or Hegel, the capital market.

2.6   Summary

In his study of Marx's *Capital* Ilyenkov is constantly engaged with Hegel, but nowhere does he look for or find *parallels* of the kind which have obsessed some Marxists in recent times. His attention was focussed chiefly on how Marx determined the starting point of *Capital* (the concrete universal in its simplest social form considered abstractly) and the manner of its elaboration from this starting point (from abstract to concrete, from universal to particular), introducing new concepts as required by the intrusion of *new facts* into those principles.

Like this writer, Ilyenkov's interest lay in trying to determine the basic philosophical principles of *Capital* as a work of science such that they could be generalised to deal with other issues.

3   Lev Vygotsky's Psychology

Ilyenkov was a philosopher, but part of a line of Soviet Psychologists initiated by Lev Vygotsky (1896–1934). Vygotsky's work was inspired by Marxism, but not, like others of his time, by stringing together isolated quotes from Marx and Engels. In 1927, he defined his relation to Marx in these terms, referring to the 1867 Preface to *Capital*:

> Marx ... compares abstraction with a microscope and chemical reactions in the natural sciences. The whole of *Das Kapital* is written according to this method. Marx analyses the "cell" of bourgeois society – the form of

the commodity value – and shows that a mature body can be more easily studied than a cell. He discerns the structure of the whole social order and all economical formations in this cell. ... we must create our *own Das Kapital*.

1927, pp. 320, 330

He read Lenin's "Annotations" on Hegel's *Logic* as soon as it was published in 1929 and frequently cited it. In 1930, Vygotsky worked closely with Fingert and Shirvindt, supporters of the Hegel scholar, Abram Deborin, and from this point on Vygotsky exhibited a Hegelian understanding of "concept" and developed the method of research based on the identification of a "germ cell." He applied this method to make revolutions in several different fields of psychology.

What Vygotsky did was to produce *one* study (*Thinking and Speech*, 1934) which would function as an exemplar for research in Psychology; that one study addressed the age-old problem of the relation between thinking and speech, that is, the intellect, and by solving this *one problem* in an exemplary fashion, he created a paradigm for research in all domains of Psychology, and as a matter of fact, in *all* the sciences. Vygotsky left us as many as *five* different exemplars of analysis by units.

Vygotsky learnt the idea from Marx's *Capital*, but its origins are much older.

3.1   Origins of the Concept of "Cell" as a Method of Analysis

The idea of the 'cell' originates with Johann Gottfried Herder (1744–1803), often recognised as the founder of Anthropology. In his effort to understand the differences between peoples, Herder introduced the idea of a *Schwerpunkt* ('strong point'). This idea is probably better known nowadays in its formulation by Marx already cited: "There is in every social formation a particular branch of production etc." (1858, pp. 106–7). Herder's friend, Johann Wolfgang von Goethe (1749–1832), sought to utilise the idea in his study of Botany during his Italian journey in 1786, to understand the continuity and differences between the plants found in different parts of the country.

Goethe came to the idea of an *Urphänomen* – not a law or principle, but a simple, archetypal phenomenon in which all the essential features of a whole complex process are manifested. In Goethe's own words:

> The *Urphänomen* is not to be regarded as a basic theorem leading to a variety of consequences, but rather as a basic manifestation enveloping the specifications of form for the beholder.
>
> 1988, p. 106

Empirical observation must first teach us what parts are common to all animals, and how these parts differ. *The idea must govern the whole*, it must abstract the general picture in a genetic way. Once such an *Urphänomen* is established, even if only provisionally, we may test it quite adequately by applying the customary methods of comparison.

1996, p. 118

This 'delicate empiricism' meant that in order to understand a complex process as an integral whole or *Gestalt*, we have to identify and understand just its smallest part – a radical departure from the 'Newtonian' approach to science based on discovering intangible forces and hidden laws.

It is widely agreed that the idea which Goethe was working towards was the *cell* of an organism, but it wasn't until microscopes became powerful enough to reveal the microstructure of organisms that Schleiden and Schwann were able to formulate the cell theory of biology in 1839. The cell is the unit of analysis of biology, and alongside Darwin's theory of evolution by natural selection, constitutes the foundation of biology.

3.2   *Hegel's Formulation of the Idea*

The philosopher, Hegel, took up Goethe's idea and gave it a firm logical foundation in his *Science of Logic*, in which the place of the cell was now taken by the *Concept*, the unit of a 'formation of consciousness', initially its simplest unit. The *Logic* describes the formation and development of concepts in three Books. Book One, known as the Logic of Being, describes the process in which the basic regularities are abstracted from the flow of immediate perception in the form of measures. Book Two, the Logic of Essence, describes the emergence of theories trying to make sense of this data, with each theory being contested by opposing theories and both then being overtaken by others, digging successively deeper, and building up a theoretical picture of the phenomenon, until ... Book Three, the Logic of the Concept, begins when, in a kind of Aha! moment, an abstract concept is identified which captures the phenomenon as a whole at its simplest and most abstract level. Beginning from this abstract concept: the 'cell', the phenomenon is then reconstructed as a *Gestalt* – an entire 'organism' – by unfolding the contradictions inherent in this cell, as it develops internally and interacts with other cells.

Note that each of these three phases has the form of a movement from abstract to concrete, (abstract in the sense of simple and isolated) *and* from concrete to abstract (concrete in the sense of immediate and real). Being: from perceptions to measures, Essence: from Identity to a concept; Concept: from a simple cell to a rich and concrete concept of the whole.

In the section of the *Science of Logic* on The Idea, Hegel outlined the methods of analytic and synthetic cognition. Synthetic cognition relies on the division of the subject matter of the science carried out according to the inner nature of the subject matter itself, rather than by an arbitrary, subjective scheme imposed from without. Each division of the science requires the definition of a starting point which allows a synthetic reconstruction of the whole.

Here is the key passage from "The Idea of the True" in the *Science of Logic*:

> The progress, proper to the Concept (*Begriff*), from universal to particular, is the basis and the possibility of a *synthetic science*, of a *system* and of *systematic cognition*. The first requisite for this is, as we have shown, that the beginning be made with the subject matter in the form of a *universal* (*Allgemeinen*).
>
> In the sphere of actuality, whether of nature or spirit, it is the **concrete individuality** (*die konkrete Einzelheit*) that is given to **subjective, natural** cognition as the *first* (*das Erste*); but in cognition that is a *comprehension*, at least to the extent that it has the form of the Concept for basis, the *first* must be on the contrary *something simple* (*das Einfache*), **something *abstracted* from the concrete**, because in this form alone has the subject-matter the form of the **self-related universal** or of an **immediate based on the Concept.**
>
> HEGEL 1816/1969, p. 801, S 779. HEGEL's italics, my bold

The first is the concept from which each science is to begin – the 'cell'.

Hegel is saying firstly that the *synthetic* phase of a science must begin with this "*something simple.*" This prescription applies to "actuality, whether of nature or spirit" – i.e., the natural and social sciences, not necessarily the Logic.

Second, Hegel describes this "*something simple*" (*das Einfache*) as "the concrete individuality that is given to subjective, *natural* cognition." *Einzel* means "single," so *Einzelheit* means a "single instance," something immediate and distinctive, an "individuality." "Natural cognition" refers to the common sense or normative perception of a process within a given social formation from which the science arises, prior to critical analysis or synthetic cognition. "Cognition, once it has begun, always proceeds from the known to the unknown" (Hegel, 1816, §1707).

Note that *Einzelheit* differs from *Einzelne*, usually translated as the Individual, the third moment of the Subject in the Concept Logic. Vygotsky adopted the word "unit" for this *Einzelheit*.

For Hegel, 'concrete' means the intersection or unity of two distinct concepts. For example, Hegel says (1831, §§87–88) that, whereas Being and

Nothing are *abstractions*, Becoming is the first concrete concept because it is the organic unity of Being and Nothing. As an organic unity of opposites, there is an internal contradiction which is what drives development as the content of the 'concrete individuality' unfolds. Without that internal contradiction, the concept cannot be a true concept capable of grasping a whole. Sometimes this internal contradiction arises from the concept representing the intersection of two processes having independent roots.

The *Erste* (the first) is a product of analytical cognition. "Ordinary thought is presupposed to be acquainted with it" (1816, p. 803). At nodal points in the development of a science a corresponding "simple something" is abstracted from concrete of experience, and subjected to *synthetic cognition*, that is, the dialectical unfolding or reconstruction of a whole process, the whole 'circle' of the particular science. These nodal points mark out the alternation between analytical cognition and synthetic cognition in the concretisation of the concept.

This "something simple" must be "*abstracted* from the concrete" by analysis. So the beginning of a science requires the abstraction of such a concrete individuality from the whole concrete field of experience which can be made the starting point for a synthetic reconstruction of the concrete in theoretical form. This act of abstraction requires an acquaintance with the whole process:

> analytic cognition ... starts from a *presupposed*, and therefore individual (*einzeln*), *concrete* subject matter; this may be an object already *complete in itself* for ordinary thought, or it may be a *problem*, that is to say, given only in its circumstances and conditions, but not yet disengaged from them and presented on its own account in simple self-subsistence.
>
> HEGEL 1816/1969, p. 787, S. 753

Hegel said that "the first requisite for this is, as we have shown, that the beginning be made with the subject matter in the form of a *universal*." That is, the concrete *individuality* which is the product of analysis is simultaneously *the universal*, that is to say, it is an *archetype* or "germ cell" of the entire organism which is to be synthesised in theory. "Concrete individuality," for Hegel, means that the cell is internally contradictory (like the exchange-value and use-value of a commodity), the coincidence of two antithetical concepts which can be exhibited by analysis, and it is by the unfolding of this internal, implicit contradiction, that synthetic cognition unfolds the whole circle of phenomena which make up the science in question. Many foundational units arise from the intersection of processes with independent roots, and this may provide the contradiction encapsulated in the unit.

This process of searching for a germ cell is represented in the first volume of the Logic: Being and Essence. Its discovery is the founding point of the Concept Logic. The judgments and syllogisms in the Subject section of the Concept Logic express the contradictions implicit in the germ cell.

Note that the "something simple" is an *individuality*, something definite, and must be represented by a countable noun. This is the difference between, for example, Morality and moral *actions*, or between Art and a *work* of art. An individuality is discrete and bounded, and not continuous and uncountable, a countable noun which has a plural form, a particle rather than matter, a something rather than stuff, an action rather than activeness.

According to Hegel, an exposition of the science following the path of synthetic cognition begins from this concrete individuality which is abstract (i.e., simple, and abstracted from its concrete circumstances) instance of the Universal – the phenomenon which is the subject matter of the whole science, and proceeds from there to the various particular forms of the universal. This phase of the science is demonstrated in the Concept Logic: a *concept* of a concrete individuality is taken up, and clarified through analysis, and then subjected to immanent critique, successively surpassing its limits, exploring the particular forms implicit in it, until arriving at a contradiction which can be resolved in actuality only by a new concrete individuality, and with that a new branch of science.

It should be noted that Hegel never believed that the natural and human sciences could be elaborated by logic alone, without reference to observation and experiment:

> Their [the sciences'] commencement, though rational at bottom, yields to the influence of fortuitousness, when they have to bring their universal truth into contact with *actual facts* and the *single phenomena of experience*. In this region of chance and change, the adequate notion of science must yield its place to reasons or grounds of explanation.
>
> HEGEL, 1830, §16. S. 70, my emphasis

When a new fact intervenes in the subject matter, then the researcher must incorporate this new fact in the same way, through a "simple something," marking out divisions in the subject matter as it is concretised with the intervention of new facts.

The *synthetic* phase of the science – the development from the cell to an organism – *also* necessarily relies on observation of the development of the subject matter itself and the theorist's intervention in the subject matter, rather than by merely logical critique by a philosopher, that is, by thought alone.

In the *Logic*, the simple concepts which mark the beginning of each Book are, respectively: Being, Reflection and Abstract Concept. These logical categories are *in the context of Logic* also "simple somethings," and the development of each offers the model of synthetic science to be applied in the natural and human sciences.

The remainder of the *Encyclopaedia* demonstrates the use of "simple somethings" which have the form of the self-related universal, including for example:

– The first book of the Philosophy of Nature ostensibly begins with "Space," but much more determinate concepts are its immediate beginning: the Point, the Line, and the Surface (enclosing a space).
– The second book of the Philosophy of Nature, "Mechanics," actually begins from the Particle. "Organic Physics," nominally about "Life," actually begins from an Organism.
– The three books of the Philosophy of Subjective Spirit are "Soul," beginning with Feelings, "Consciousness" beginning with Sensations, and the Finite Mind.
– In the Philosophy of Objective Spirit, "Abstract Right," goes through: Possession (Taking Possession, Use & Alienation); "Contract" (Gift, Exchange & Pledge) and "Wrong" (a Non-malicious Wrong, Fraud & Crime).
– "Morality" goes through: Purpose, Goal, Means, Intention, Welfare, the Good, among others, and
– "Ethical Life" goes through: Family, Market, Public Authorities, Corporations, and State.
– In the Philosophy of Absolute Spirit, Art is ostensibly about the "shape of beauty", but begins from the Work of Art; Revealed Religion begins from the 'Concrete Individuality' (*konrete Einzelheit*); and Philosophy from the Syllogism.
– 36 examples of 'cells' used by Hegel in the various sciences he outlined.

3.3 *Marx's Appropriation of Hegel*

Marx acknowledged his debt to Goethe and Hegel in the first Preface to *Capital*, where he says:

> The human mind has for more than 2,000 years sought in vain to get to the bottom of it, whilst on the other hand, to the successful analysis of much more composite and complex forms, there has been at least an approximation. Why? Because the body, as an organic whole, is more easy of study than are the cells of that body. In the analysis of economic forms, moreover, neither microscopes nor chemical reagents are of use. The force of abstraction must replace both. But in bourgeois society, the

commodity form of the product of labour – or value-form of the commodity – is the economic cell-form.

MARX, 1996/1867, p. 8

Marx further indicated his debt to Hegel's *Logic* in the famous passage of the
Grundrisse, "The method of political economy," in which he described the history of political economy in terms of two phases: first an analytical phase in
which the economic data is analysed and represented in a succession of theories until arriving at abstractions, such as 'value', from which the whole phenomenon is reconstructed synthetically as a 'system'.

> Along the first path the full conception was evaporated to yield an
> abstract determination; along the second, the abstract determinations
> lead towards a reproduction of the concrete by way of thought.
>
> MARX, 1973/1858, p. 100

The first phase corresponds to the time Marx spent in the *immanent critique* of
the theories of political economy leading to the identification of the 'cell'; the
second phase is the *dialectical reconstruction* of political economy in *Capital*,
beginning from analysis of the cell, exchange of commodities, in Chapter I.

In his 1881 Notes on Adolph Wagner Marx says:

> I did not start out from the 'concept of value' ... What I start out from is
> the simplest social form in which the labour product is presented in con-
> temporary society, and this is 'the commodity'.
>
> 1881, p. 544

The commodity is a *form* of value, but 'value' is an intangible, neither "a geo-
metrical, a chemical, or any other natural property" (Marx 1867, p. 47) – but a
suprasensible quality of commodities, and as such is unsuited for the role of
cell. As a *social relation*, value can *only* be grasped conceptually. Nonetheless,
the commodity is a form of value which, thanks to everyday experience, *can
be grasped viscerally*. This means that the critique of the concept of commodity works upon relations which can be grasped viscerally by reader and writer
alike. By beginning with the (concept of) commodity Marx mobilises the readers' natural understanding of commodities, and as he leads us through each
successive relation, so long as that relation exists in social practice, then not
only is the writer's intuition validated by the *existence* of that relation, but it
also allows the reader to securely grasp the logical exposition.

Marx's decision to begin not with 'value' but with the 'simplest social form of value', the 'commodity', illustrates Marx's debt to Goethe as well as Hegel. Further, he insisted on tracing the emergence of every relation in economic life, rather than in claiming to derive them from logic, thus recovering the *empirical* moment in Goethe's original idea, before it was taken up as a *logical* category by Hegel.

Only Part I, Chapters 1 to 3 of *Capital*, deal with simple commodity production, which Marx represented symbolically as C–M–C. In Chapter 4, Marx derives the first, abstract concept of *capital* which is to be the real subject matter of the book: M—C—M' – buying in order to sell at a profit. This action is the basic unit and embryo of capital, and is personified as Moneybags and reified as a capitalist firm. While capital is an aggregate of commodity relations, it is a distinctive unit. Capital accumulation gives a new direction to the development of economic life, and the remaining chapters are concerned with new facts which demand the modification of the concept of bourgeois society.

4   The Development of Science

Marx had been able to appropriate Hegel's method, but neither the naturalist-poet Goethe, nor the philosopher Hegel nor the communist Marx could have a significant impact on the course of natural scientific activity during the nineteenth century. How could this achievement of Classical German Philosophy be transformed into methods for the resolution of the problems in the various branches of science?

Science proceeded piecemeal, and not according to the grand plan of Hegel's *Encyclopaedia of the Philosophical Sciences*, and certainly not according to the ideas of the communist revolutionary Karl Marx. The natural sciences were in general able to make progress by problem solving in the separate disciplines, with occasional breakthroughs. Such breakthroughs along with the unceasing development of instruments and other technology would have their impact on other sciences. But there has never been any overall conception guiding the work of scientists. It took almost a century from Hegel's death in 1831, through the efforts of German natural science, French social theory and the American Pragmatism, before a practical, laboratory method for understanding how individual human beings appropriated the cultural practices of their time in the development of their activity and consciousness was finally accomplished by Lev Vygotsky, thanks to the methodological conquests of Hegel and Marx, and the cultural conditions created in the wake of the Russian Revolution.

5   Hegel on Mediation and Immediacy

Before moving to look at how Vygotsky appropriated and used the idea of 'cell' for psychology, I must recall a key concept with which Hegel framed his entire philosophy: mediation. He writes in an Introduction to the *Science of Logic*:

> there is nothing, nothing in heaven, or in nature or in mind or anywhere else which does not equally contain both immediacy and mediation, so that these two determinations reveal themselves to be unseparated and inseparable.
>
> 1816/1969, p. 68

In the introduction to his *Encyclopaedia*, Hegel characterises the history of post-Enlightenment philosophy in terms of a struggle between, on the one hand, the various philosophies of *immediate* knowledge: Descartes' Rationalism, the Empiricism of the natural sciences, and Jacobi's reliance on Faith, and on the other hand, Kant's philosophy which held that things in themselves could not be objects of experience, and consequently knowledge of things in themselves was impossible; all knowledge was *mediated*.

Hegel's entire philosophy was built on what is sometimes called by followers of Vygotsky "double stimulation." In Hegel's words:

> The relationship of *immediacy* and *mediation within consciousness* will have to be discussed explicitly and in detail below. At this point, it suffices to point out that, although both moments *appear* to be distinct, *neither of them* may be absent and they form an *inseparable* combination.
>
> 1831, §12n

5.1   *The Method of Double Stimulation*

Until Vygotsky's breakthrough, psychology had been split between those, like Helmholtz, who approached psychology with 'brass instruments' as if it were a branch of the natural sciences, and those like Dilthey who studied cultural phenomena as if psychology was a branch of the 'human sciences'. Recognising that the mind was formed by the joint actions of physiology and culture, Wundt had even proposed that there be two separate psychologies: one carried out in the laboratory with the aid of introspection, the other through the study of literature and art. In the twentieth century, psychology was split between Behaviourists who denied the existence of consciousness and saw psychology in terms of reflexes, and 'empirical psychologists' who studied the mind by means of introspection. The 'brass instrument' methods hitherto employed in psychology laboratories were capable of investigating only the most trivial and primitive reflexes which humans have in common with the animals, while introspection was incapable of providing objective access to consciousness. Contra Behaviourism, human behaviour cannot be understood without reference to consciousness; but consciousness (like history) cannot be observed *directly*, but only as mediated through its connection with physiology, behaviour and artefacts, each of which is subject to objective observation.

Vygotsky solved these problems with the experimental method of dual stimulation.

The method of double stimulation was first formulated by Vygotsky in conjunction with Alexander Luria in 1928 (See Luria 1928 & Vygotsky 1928). An experimental subject, typically a child, would be presented with a problem, such as memorising a series of words, and as they were trying to solve it, the researcher would present them with an artefact, perhaps a picture-card, to use as a means in solving the problem. In this simple scenario, we have the *germ cell* of cultural development and activity. In the diagram below:

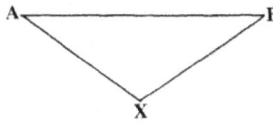

FIGURE 1

A represents a person who confronts an object or problem, *B*, and *X* is a sign, an artefact introduced into the scenario by a collaborator, as a means of solving the problem. This simple germ cell captures the essential relation of people to their culture: a problem set by another person is solved by using an artefact (in this case, a sign) drawn from the cultural environment. In the process of appropriating the use of the given artefact, the subject's psychology is enhanced by the creation of a new reflex, associating *X* with *B*. Vygotsky has set up here an extremely simple scenario, which can be sensuously experienced and grasped viscerally, without the need of a pre-existing overarching theory. But in this simple set-up we have both the immediate situation of an individual confronting a problem, and the entire cultural history of the subject's environment represented in the artefact-solution. This is the prototype of a *unit of analysis* in which both the individual psyche and an entire cultural history are present.

The meaning of the term 'dual stimulation' is illustrated in the diagram. *A* is subject to two stimuli at the same time, both the object itself, $A \to B$, and the auxiliary stimulus, $A \to X$, which is associated with the object, $X \to B$. Thus the subject responds to the object *B* in two ways *at once*, the immediate perception of the object $A \to B$, and the sign $A \to X$. Each of these reactions is a natural reflex. It is the mediated reaction $A \to X \to B$, which is *socially constructed* and which gives *meaning* to the object, B, a meaning acquired from the culture, thanks to the collaboration with another person, in this case, the researcher. X may be an image on a card which reminds the subject of the word to be remembered, for example, or it may be a written word giving the name of the object. This idea, in which all our relations to the environment are taken to be *mediated*, is directly linked to Hegel's *dictum* (1816, §92) cited above, that everything is both immediate and mediated. It is by using cultural signs and tools, to solve problems thrown up in life in collaboration with others, that people learn and become cultured citizens of their community, introducing mediating signs and other artefacts to control their interaction with their immediate environment.

Using this experimental set-up, Vygotsky was able to observe, for example, whether and how children of different ages were able to use which kind of memory-cards to improve their performance in memorising tasks, and by this means demonstrated, for example, the qualitative difference between how small children remember and how older children remember. And so on. By appropriating elements of their culture in the course of their development, people restructure their consciousness and activity.

The above representation of a mediated-immediate relation between subject and object is an prototype for the units which Vygotsky identified and used to revolutionise a number of fields of psychology. In itself it is too general to be itself such a unit. To function as a unit, a more definite mode of action is needed.

This first unit of analysis, the *artefact-mediated action*, was the first germ-cell developed for psychological research by Vygotsky. It is however only a schema for a unit. For the solution of any particular problem in psychology, X must be replaced by some more restricted class of sign, artefact, action or activity.

5.2   *Word Meaning*

Around 1931, Vygotsky came to the conclusion that not just any artefact, but *the spoken word*, was the *archetypal* cultural artefact through which people appropriated the culture of their community. After all, every physiologically able child spontaneously learns to speak while many never master literacy, and speech had emerged contemporaneously with labour (the use of tool-artefacts) in the very evolution of the human species. Signs, such as the written word, were a later invention, based on the development of technology, and corresponding to the transition to class society and nation-states. It was with this conviction that Vygotsky composed his last and definitive work, *Thinking and Speech* (1934).

In the first chapter of *Thinking and Speech* Vygotsky presents his one and only exposition of analysis by units, and in this instance his chosen unit is *word meaning*: a unity of speech and thinking, of sound and meaning. A word is a unity of sound and meaning because a sound without a meaning is not a word and nor is a meaning without a physical sign a word: to be a word means to be both. Word meaning is equally a unity of generalisation and social interaction, of thinking and communication. Word meaning is a unit because it is the smallest, discrete instance of such a unity.

The internal contradictions within word meaning arise from the fact that thinking has its origin in both pre-lingual intelligence and pre-intellectual speech. This unit is very fruitful. As a unity of generalisation and social interaction, the word is connected with a person's social connections as well as their thinking. Each of these aspects of the activity of an individual has separate roots, each with its own path of development, linked together in the development of word meaning. (Compare this approach to Reuten's attempt to theorise the capitalist state and the capitalist economy in a single development, ignoring the fact that the state and bourgeois society have separate roots).

This unit can be understood as an instance of a *sign-mediated action*, though Vygotsky insisted that word meaning is not a *subset* of the larger category of 'artefact-mediated actions', which would have the effect of subsuming communicative action, including speech, under labour activity. Rather, the relation between tool-use and sign-use is genetic. The archetype of a 'sign', according to Vygotsky, is a mnemonic symbol, such as a knot in a handkerchief or a notch in a message stick, and these signs, he claimed, developed into the written word in several parts if the world a few thousand years ago. Sign-mediated actions, such as the use of written words, arose historically as an extension of tool-mediated actions. *Speech* however, arose in close connection with the development of labour in the very process of human evolution. The use of symbolic artefacts, such as writing, therefore has to be understood as something phylogenetically and ontogenetically distinct from speech which co-evolved with tools and the human hand as part of the labour process (tool-use and tool-making) which, according to Engels (1876) drove the evolution of the human species. A tool is an existent concept.

In his discussion of tool use, Vygotsky distinguished between 'technical tools' and 'psychological tools'. Tools in the normal sense, technical tools, are used to operate upon matter, whereas psychological tools are used to work on the mind, and these include "language, different forms of numeration and counting, mnemotechnic techniques, algebraic symbolism, works of art, writing, schemes, diagrams, maps, blueprints, all sorts of conventional signs, etc." (Vygotsky 1930, p. 85). Using a (technical) tool has profound psychological effects because tool use widens the scope of a person's activity and expands their horizon of experience, but it does not 'work on the mind' directly as does a psychological tool. Psychological tools developed alongside of and as an extension of the development of technical tools.

It is important to emphasise that to speak, that is to say to act with a word, is an *action*; to *mean* something. That is, word-meaning is an action. 'Word meaning' does not refer to an entry in the dictionary, it is the *action* in which an intention is carried out using a meaningful word as a means. Consequently, there is always a moment of volition in every word meaning. As Hegel says: "The subjective Idea is in the first instance an *urge*" (Hegel, 1816, p. 783).

Just as Marx analysed the commodity as early as 1843, but took until 1859 to realise that the commodity had to be taken as a unit of analysis or germ cell, Vygotsky pointed to the importance of analysing speech in his first published work (1924) but took a further decade to settle on the spoken word, the simplest act of 'psychological exchange', as the *unit of analysis* for the work which would become the paradigm for his method of "analysis by units."

Using this unit of analysis, Vygotsky analysed the development of the *intellect*, that is, of symbolic thinking. The unit of 'practical intellect' is a tool-use, and has a distinct path of development, side by side with (verbal) intellect, whose unit is a word meaning. The word is also a 'germ cell' in the sense that it is the cell which can grow into an entire science, an entire field of theory and practice, just like a cell can grow into an organism.

5.3   *Concepts as Units of the Intellect*

Although word meaning is the basic unit of the intellect, a larger, 'molar' unit is required to understand the structure and development of the intellect. This molar unit is the *concept*, which is an aggregate of many word meanings. The central concern of Vygotsky's analysis in *Thinking and Speech*, is the formation of concepts, which in his day only reached a fully developed form in late adolescence with entry into adult life. Vygotsky's task then was to trace the development of the intellect from infancy to adulthood, by observing the development of speech. It is the intellect which is the real subject matter of *Thinking and Speech*, just as it is capital not commodity exchange which is the real subject matter of Marx's *Capital*. Word meaning is the simplest social form of the intellect.

Vygotsky traced the changes in word meaning from the first emergence of speech in the form of *unconscious expressive* speech, to communicative speech, calling upon adults for assistance, to *egocentric* speech in which the child gives itself audible instructions or commentary, with the child taking the place of the adult in commanding their own behaviour, to egocentric speech which becomes more and more curtailed and predicative passing over into *inner* speech, and later, as he notes in the final chapter of *Thinking and Speech*, thinking which goes *beyond* speech with the most developed forms of thinking which are no longer tied to putting one word after another. The changing form of word-meaning allowed Vygotsky to trace the emergence and construction of the verbal intellect and thereby understand its essential nature.

The development of thinking and speech takes the form of a double-helix:

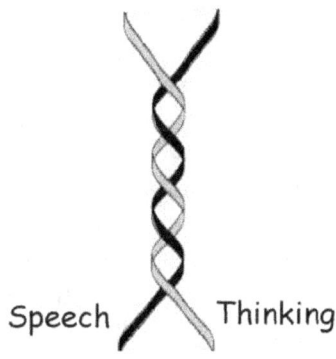

Speech   Thinking

FIGURE 2

This model of co-development is used throughout by Vygotsky in understanding the complex development of all the higher forms of activity acquired by human beings.

By the use of a germ cell which is open to observation, and tracing its internalisation as it is gradually transformed into something private and inaccessible to observation, Vygotsky created an objective scientific basis for Cultural Psychology. This was an astounding achievement.

5.4 The Formation of Concepts
In his study of the formation of concepts in the fifth and sixth chapters of "Thinking and Speech," Vygotsky describes experiments using the method of dual stimulation by setting children sorting tasks. Children were invited to sort a variety of different sized, shaped and coloured blocks into groups that were

'the same'. The problem could be solved by looking at nonsense words written on the base of the blocks. The children were only gradually introduced to these clues so that the researchers could observe the children's actions in forming better and better groups, aided by reference to the signs. Vygotsky was able to describe a number of discrete types of concepts, according to the different ways children sorted the blocks.

Vygotsky identified each of these concepts as a *form of action*, rather than as a logical structure, as Hegel might have categorised them. Nor did Vygotsky reify them as mental functions or capacities; they were just forms of action. Thus, by using sign mediated actions as his unit, Vygotsky was able to study the emergence of concepts, the units of the intellect. These concepts, constructed in the laboratory on the basis of features of the objects being sorted, were not yet truly concepts, but exhibited the type of concepts which arise among children who have not yet left the family home and entered the world of adult concerns.

True concepts, acquired through instruction in some real-world institution and actual concepts developed through participation in everyday life, are yet different forms of activity. These Vygotsky investigated through experiments involving speech; typically young people would be asked to complete a narrative sentence with "because ..." or "although ..." observing their efforts to verbalise causal relations with which they were practically speaking well-accustomed, but with conscious awareness. The insight behind these experiments is that a child, or even a domesticated animal, can learn to respond rationally to a situation, demonstrating an implicit understanding of the relevant causal connections between events, that is, they can develop a practical intellect. However, the ability to isolate this relation in a form of thought, and with conscious awareness use the concept as a unit in reasoning, is something characteristically human: conceptual thought. True concepts are transmitted through the generations by cultural institutions, professions and so on, and are carried chiefly by words which are part of a real language. So a concept is the conscious awareness of a culturally transmitted form of activity organised around a word or other meaningful artefact.

By characterising concepts in this way, as forms of sign-mediated activity, Vygotsky laid the basis for an interdisciplinary science. Social formations are made up of a variety of forms of activity, each of which is apprehended as a concept, and these concepts together constitute the culture of the given community. Vygotsky has given us a down-to-earth laboratory method for studying how people acquire these concepts and construct institutions and social movements.

Note that just as Marx did not take value as some intangible quality, but rather began with a specific type of social action, commodity exchange, Vygotsky did not take 'concept' to be some intangible mental entity, but rather a specific type of social action. And this is true of all Vygotsky's units of analysis – they are definite, observable forms of activity.

Note that in the above we have seen *two* units: word meaning and concept. The 'larger', or molar unit, concept, arises on the basis of the 'smaller' or molecular unit, word meaning. Words only exhibit their full meaning as part of a system of meanings constituted by the concept they evoke, and conversely, concepts exist only in and through the word meanings and other artefact-mediated actions associated with them. Nonetheless, Vygotsky showed that children learn to use words in correct contexts long before they master conceptual thinking, at which point their speech activity is transformed.

This process whereby a molar unit of activity arises on the basis of a molecular unit of action, is a common feature of the analysis of processes by units. It is found in Marx's critique of political economy with commodity and then capital, and in Activity Theory where the molecular unit is an artefact-mediated action and the molar unit is an activity, i.e., a practice. The method of analysis by units allows the researcher to trace step by step show how the more developed unit emerges out of the action of the fundamental units, which can be grasped viscerally out of the existing conditions, i.e., practical intelligence.

5.5   *Germ Cell and Unit of Analysis*

The term Marx used for the concept of 'cell-form' is referred to by followers of Vygotsky by two different terms: *unit of analysis*, and *germ cell*. These are two different expressions for the same concept, but indicate two different aspects of the same concept. All referencing the terms used by Hegel in the excerpt from "The Idea of the True" cited above: *das Erste* (the first) and *der Keim* (the germ cell, used by Hegel in the same sense in the chapter preceding "The Idea of the True") and *Einzelheit* (single instance, unit of analysis).

"Germ cell" indicates the germ from which more complex forms develop, just as the cell grows into an organ or organism. For example, actual exchange of commodities is rarely seen in modern capitalist society, where everything is bought and sold, not literally traded. But Marx showed how, historically, once a community starts producing commodities for exchange, perhaps on its borders or with passing merchants or in the towns, it is more or less inevitably drawn into the world market, and with that the need for a universal measure of value. But he had to isolate commodity exchange, and study it in its purest form, abstracted from the historical conditions in which it existed. Thus, a universal commodity, emerges; gold, paper money, credit and so forth all 'unfold' themselves from the original simple exchange. This first unit, C–C, through the mediation of money, opens up into C–M–C in which a person sells in order to buy. From this mediating element there arises a whole class of people who buy in order to sell at a profit: M—C—M', and thus arises *capital*, a new unit of value, a new social relation which arises on the basis of the 'logic' of that simple relation, *exchange*. With the emergence of capital – firms buying in order to sell at a profit – economic life is reorganised, with production of commodities now subsumed under capital (rather than under pre-existing feudal or ancient relations) and reoriented towards the accumulation of capital rather than simply the cooperative provision of human needs. The 'germ-cell' of capital, M—C—M', exhibits this course of development in embryo.

Likewise, in psychology, simple word meaning, when developed in the course of discourse, gives rise to more developed forms of thinking and speech, namely concepts. "Germ cell" emphasises this aspect of *development*, the relation between the simple undeveloped relation, on the one hand, and on the other hand, the mature, concrete relation.

The difference between how Vygotsky uses the term and how it was used in sociology in his time, is that he recognised that the unit of analysis already represented a *concept of the whole*. That is, he merged this analytical concept from contemporary sociology with Goethe's idea of the *Urphänomen* as a representation of a Gestalt.

I will illustrate how the idea of a unit of analysis figured in Marx's work. The young Marx was outraged by the treatment of the poor, by censorship and other social issues, but realised that he knew nothing of the root causes of these phenomena. Thus he turned to a study of political economy. 25 years later, when he wrote *Capital*, 'bourgeois society' was now conceived of as an integral whole, a market place – just millions and millions of commodity exchanges, and nothing else. Other phenomena, such as censorship, political corruption, cruelty, now came to be seen as *inessential* and contingent. By taking commodity exchange as the unit, the whole, the *Gestalt* was now redefined and was not coextensive with his original conception of the whole. This is the other aspect to the concept of 'cell': it means taking the whole process to be nothing other than millions and millions of this one simple relation, a relation which can be grasped viscerally, without the need for abstract theories and forces and so on. The "unit of analysis" expresses the results of analysis in terms of a relation between the whole and the part; the whole is *nothing but* millions and millions of the same unit of analysis. For example, it is possible to see the water cycle – rain, rivers, ocean, evaporation, clouds and back down again as rain – as one whole process, a *Gestalt*, because all these are nothing but billions and billions of the same unit: water molecules. And this was known before we knew that water molecules were H_2O.

So when we gain a certain insight into a complex process with an *Aha!* moment, that the process is nothing but such and such a simple action or relation, then this is the *starting point* for a truly scientific understanding of the process, an understanding which allows us to understand not just as a process with this or that features, but as a whole, as a *Gestalt*.

Thus the germ-cell and the unit of analysis are one and the same thing – be it a commodity exchange or a meaningful word – but in one case the developmental aspect is emphasised, and in the other case the analytical aspect is emphasised.

5.6   *Five Applications by Vygotsky of the Method of Analysis by Units*

'Unit of analysis' is a relative term: analysis of what? A unit of analysis is always used for the analysis of some specific problem or fact. Frequently, writers only ever analyse one phenomenon and devote their lives to that one issue. For example, among philosophers Kant takes the judgment as the unit of experience, Frege takes the smallest expression to which pragmatic force can be attached as a unit, and Wittgenstein takes the smallest expression whose utterance makes a move in a language game and Robert Brandom takes the proposition as his unit of analysis.

Vygotsky's work covered *five different domains* of psychological research. He used the unit of *sign-mediated actions* to analyse a range of distinct psychological functions, such as will, attention, memory, personal development and more. And he used *word meaning* to study verbal intelligence and concept formation. In addition to these, Vygotsky found a unit of analysis for three other areas of research.

5.6.1   Perezhivanie

Perezhivanie is an untranslatable Russian word meaning 'an experience' together with the 'catharsis' entailed in surviving and processing that experience. One and the same event does not have the same significance for every person, so *perezhivaniya* are 'lived experiences' which depend not only on characteristics of the event itself, but also on characteristics of the individual. Vygotsky wrote that alongside heredity, it was *perezhivaniya* which formed the personality. Understanding the personality as a process rather than a product, he claimed that *perezhivaniya* were units of the personality. *Perezhivaniya* stand out from the general background of experience, have a beginning, a middle and an end and throughout the course of the experience, have a unity and a certain intense emotional colour. *Perezhivaniya* have a definite psychological form. Reflect on your own life, remember those seminal experiences, the daring moves you got away with, the public humiliations you suffered, the reprimands, injustices or accolades you received. Your personality is an aggregate structure of all these *perezhivaniya*, what happened and how you handled them and survived, and analysis of them would give a therapist or prospective partner insight into your personality. It is these *perezhivaniya* which make up the story you tell yourself of your own life, your identity.

Vygotsky dealt only briefly with *perezhivanie* in a lecture called "The Problem of the Environment" (1934a) in which he defines a *perezhivanie* as a "unity of environmental and personal features." This expression has been the source of much confusion. A personal feature might be a child's age and an environmental feature might be the school-entry age; neither of these features by themselves shape the personality of a child. However, *taken together* – whether at school age the child is *ready* to attend school – is self-evidently a factor in the forming of the child's personality. Further, *perezhivanie* is often translated as "lived experience," which in contemporary social science is taken to be entirely subjective, whereas *perezhivaniya* are both objective and subjective. *Perezhivanie* does not mean 'experience' – for which the Russian word is *opit*, because *perezhivaniya* are discrete episodes which stand out from the background of experience and include the active contribution of the subject and its aesthetic character. *Perezhivaniya* are units of personality (development).

5.6.2   Defect-Compensation

Vygotsky devoted much of his efforts to work with children affected with a variety of disabilities. In those days, the Soviet government grouped all kinds of disabilities together under the heading of Defectology. But Vygotsky did not see the defect as being on the side of the subject; rather the defect was in the relation between the subject and the cultural environment, including the failure of the community to provide for the full participation of the subject in social life.

For every defect, there is a compensation. That compensation is a combination of measures on the part of the community to facilitate the participation of the subject, and the psychological adjustment made on the part of the subject to overcome the barrier to their participation. Vygotsky took the unit of analysis for defectology as the unity of the defect and the compensation – the "defect-compensation." Vygotsky's writing on defectology is in Volume 2 of his Collected Works.

5.6.3   Social Situation of Development

In his work on child development, Vygotsky developed the concept of 'social situation of development'. Vygotsky insisted that the social situation is not just a series of factors – age of mother, salary and occupation of father, number of siblings, etc. – it is a specific situation or predicament. Each of these situations has a definite name in a given culture, such as 'infant' or 'primary school child', etc. Each of these situations entails certain expectations placed on the child and their specific needs are met in a corresponding appropriate way. The child is more or less obliged to fit into this role. In the process of normal development however, at a certain point, the child develops needs and desires which cannot be met within the current social situation, and a crisis breaks out in the family group, both the child and its carers. The child may become difficult and rebellious, and if the family and carers respond, the child and the whole situation will undergo a transformation and a new social situation will be established, with the child occupying a new social position: an infant becomes a toddler, etc. Child development is constituted by this specific series of *situations*, with both family and child going through a series of culturally specific transformations in which the child eventually develops into an independent adult. The social situation of development is a unity of the child and its carers in a culturally specific caring relationship.

In each of the areas of psychological research into which Vygotsky went, his aim was to establish a unit of analysis characterising the field. He was not always successful, and for example, his study of the emotions failed to arrive at a unit of analysis before his death in 1934. But he did discover five units: sign- and tool-mediated actions, word meaning, *perezhivaniya*, defect-compensations, and social situations of development.

Readers might mistakenly presume that Vygotsky represents some now long-forgotten episode in the early USSR. Not so. There are certainly many more people using Vygotsky's ideas in Education, Child Development, Disability Services and Youth Health than there are studying the Marx-Hegel relation. And moreover, students of Vygotsky are invariably engaged in the practical application of these ideas.

5.6.4   Activities

The Activity Theorists, who continued Vygotsky's work, particularly contributed to the notion of 'germ cell' as an agent of social and psychological change.

A.N. Leontyev also famously defined a hierarchy of three units of analysis: (1) The *operation*, a form of action which can be done without conscious awareness by adapting to conditions, (2) The *artefact mediated action*, and (3) The *activity* (or project or form of practice). Note that here 'activity' means a discrete aggregate of actions all having a common motive, but each having a distinct goal differing from the shared motive, and possibly executed by different individuals. Every action thus harbours this contradiction between a goal which differs from its motive. The concept of "an activity" is distinct from the notion of activity, referring to the generalised substance of human life. Activities as units of analysis is a rendering in terms of social action rather than in psychological terms of Vygotsky's unit of *concepts*. Indeed, it is important to remember that the motive of an activity is usually a concept belonging to the culture as a whole, some norm, even though the object of the activity is at the same time, some definite situation in the larger objective social formation. Hegel used the same idea in his *Philosophy of Right*, in the section on Morality. (See my essay "Mediation and Intention in Hegel's Theory of Action," 2019).

5.7   *The Importance of Vygotsky for Social Theory*

Hegel, Marx and Vygotsky each made an important development on the methodology invented by Goethe. Hegel replaced the *Urphänomen* with the abstract concept which could be the subject of reasoning, rather than merely intuition. Marx insisted that the real subject was social practice rather than "thought," and criticism could only reconstruct what was given in social practice. Consequently, rather than an abstract concept such as 'value', the germ-cell would be an action, an artefact-mediated action in fact – a commodity exchange.

Each of the germ cells or units of analysis identified by Vygotsky can be expressed either as some activity (an aggregate of many actions sharing the same motivation) or as an artefact mediated action, a characteristic element of some action such as the relevant artefact.

In his critique of psychology, Vygotsky showed that this germ cell had to be a discrete, finite, observable interaction. Whereas Marx left us only *Capital*, Vygotsky applied the method to the solution of five different problems, and provided five different instances of a 'germ-cell', thus making the idea explicit and the method reproducible.

Vygotsky was a psychologist, in particular, a Cultural Psychologist, not a social theorist. He approached the cultural formation of the psyche, as mentioned above, by means of a study of the collaborative use of artefacts which originate in the wider culture, in some social situation, also the product of the wider culture. But he did not investigate the processes of formation of the social environment itself. These were problems that were taken up by the Activity Theorists who followed on from Vygotsky's work. Although the Activity Theorists made important developments, none of them were able to consistently maintain Vygotsky's method of analysis by units. Their contributions to social theory were often laughable.

Nonetheless, through the method of analysis by units, and in particular through the unit, tool- or sign-mediated action, Vygotsky has given social theorists an approach which can fully integrate the sciences of the individual and the social and historical sciences.

6   Conclusion to Chapter 5

Marx and Vygotsky both set out to create a science based on the method first described by Hegel, but rather than, like Hegel, just rationalising existing theories on political economy or psychology respectively, they used the method of *immanent critique* exemplified by Hegel in his *Logic*.

I think recent writers on Marx's *Capital* and Hegel's *Logic* have proved the fruitlessness of trying to write "our own *Das Kapital*" by taking *Capital* to be an "mirror" of the *Logic*, or taking the *Logic* to be a coded version of *Capital*. I believe we would be more successful by following Ilyenkov and Vygotsky's example of appropriating the method shared by *Capital* and the *Logic*. How to apply this method to the natural and social sciences is explained by Hegel in the section entitled "The Idea of the True."

Quoting the same 1927 passage in which Vygotsky advocated that Psychology emulate *Das Kapital*, having in mind colleagues who wanted to construct a "Marxist Psychology" by assembling quotes from Marx and Engels:

> In order to create [a general science], we must reveal the *essence* of the given area of phenomena, the laws of their change, their qualitative and quantitative characteristics, their causality, we must create categories and concepts appropriate to it, in short, we must create our *own Das Kapital*. It suffices to imagine Marx operating with the general principles and categories of dialectics, like quantity-quality, the triad, the universal connection, the knot, the leap etc.
>
> VYGOTSKY, 1997/1927, p. 330

This imagined method, descriptive of how "Marxist Psychologists" approached their work in Vygotsky's time, is in effect just what those casting *Capital* as an "mirror" of the *Logic* are doing. Where is the positive content of the science of *economics* in such a work?

It is worth noting that when Lenin read the *Logic*, he annotated or underlined 38 different passages from "The Idea of Cognition," between pp. 783 and 823, almost every page, including "The Idea of the True," in Hegel's *Science of Logic*. So when he wrote "without having thoroughly studied and understood the *whole* of Hegel's *Logic*," he meant it.

CHAPTER 6

Conclusion

The recent flurry of interest in the relationship between Hegel's *Logic* and Marx's *Capital*, or Marx's first economic manuscript, the *Grundrisse*, has added little to what was already known about that relationship.

If Marx did indeed follow the *Logic* paragraph by paragraph from beginning to end in writing the *Grundrisse*, it is clear that this was simply an exercise. Every time Marx launched into a new field of study, he went to Hegel as his teacher. Even as late as 1881, when he took up the study of calculus, he chose as his teacher not one of the brilliant French mathematicians of the day, but Hegel. In any case, very little of the structure of *Grundrisse* remained in the 1859 draft of *Capital* which he wrote immediately after completing the *Grundrisse* or in *Capital* itself.

Marx did understand that if he were to follow Hegel's approach in his immanent critique of political economy then that meant creating a *concrete concept of capital*, which in turn meant beginning from an elementary concept of capital represented by some simple "universal individual." The outcome of his critical analysis of political economy was that he took the commodity to be that "simple something" from which to make a beginning. The commodity relation was the "universal individual" instance of bourgeois society, the commodity the "universal individual" instance of wealth in bourgeois society.

The choice of this starting point is the first and most important instance of the influence of the *Logic* on Marx in his work on *Capital*.

Bourgeois society had not existed as a self-governing social formation prior to the mid-nineteenth century. Prior to the emergence of capital as the ruling power in society, bourgeois society only ever existed in the margins of earlier state forms. So "bourgeois society" is an analytical abstraction, abstracting "civil society" from the states and historical communities of which it was a part.

"Capitalism" is a concept distinct from "bourgeois society," and a scientific study of capitalism requires more than a scientific study of bourgeois society. The emergence of capital, particularly finance capital, as a ruling power in bourgeois society and in the state at large was a new fact the significance of which the Political Economists had had no experience. The creation of a capital market introduced a new ethos overlaying the bourgeois society which had been the object of study of Adam Smith and David Ricardo.

The ongoing maintenance of a permanent pool of penurious labour available for exploitation in wage labour is also a fact which needed to be accounted for.

Why do writers in this present-day discourse think that these facts were *logical* phenomena which could be derived from or described by Hegel's *Logic*?

None of the present-day writings examined have provided a satisfactory answer to the question of *why* Marx began with the commodity. In almost every case, it is not even asked.

Marx knew his Hegel, and many of the concepts and transitions found in *Capital* are reminiscent of concepts and transitions in the *Logic*. The overall structure of *Capital*, beginning from an "universal individual" and becoming more and more concrete as it progresses, is strikingly evocative of Hegel's *Logic* and the *Encyclopaedia*.

But the fact is that no natural or social science is "the same as" logic. Logic differs from any positive science in that it must make its beginning from an empty concept. Logic must have no presuppositions beyond the presumption of a readership capable of understanding logic. This insight was one of Hegel's achievements and was manifested in his analysis of the concept of Being, showing that if correctly understood it was an empty concept. This contrasted with the appeal to axioms which had provided the starting point for formal logic.

Science on the other hand always makes its beginning from an observation – some distinctive fact which has to be explained in a way which is consistent with other observations, or some problem which has arisen in practice. Every science aims to reconstruct some phenomenon beginning from its most simple fact, some fact which in itself can be recognised without the aid of some specialised theory, and can be analytically isolated from its context and must be provided with an explanation by means of which the observation can be comprehended. Only such a simple something can provide a secure and rational starting point for a science.

All those who try to use metaphors and homologies to discover hidden meanings in the Logic ignore this simple truth. Science is concerned with facts! It is odd that present-day writers seem comfortable with the idea that Hegel was unaware of this obvious truth. Have they naturalised capitalism to such an extent that *they* think that capitalism is simply "logical"? Or are they willing to suppose that Hegel was such a fool as to believe so, and then followed his example?

Hegel constructed his *Encyclopaedia* on the principle that each science sets off from some "simple something." But Hegel never did any actual research himself. He simply rationalised and "arranged" the natural science of his day in logical order. The natural science of his times had no theory of the evolution of species (Lamarck's theory he rightly rejected as being unable to explain the real variety of creatures on the planet) and no scientific theory of the evolution of the solar system. Only the evolution of the continents became known in his lifetime.

Consequently, the idea of Nature as timeless was incontrovertible. In this circumstance, to modern eyes Hegel's Philosophy of Nature and Subjective Spirit resembles the now denigrated Natural Philosophy. But the concept of Nature as invariant is absolutely valid. The theory of the Big Bang, for example, relies on the presupposition of the invariance of the basic laws of physics. But it is far from obvious what is essential and stable and what is contingent and transient if one ponders the cosmos without a theory of the development of the Universe.

Hegel's knowledge of non-European cultures was also limited, being reliant on reports of missionaries and the literature of Christianity and ancient Greece. This meant that the only application of his *Logic* to a real science which had any chance of standing up to modern criticism was his *Philosophy of Right*. This we know Marx turned to even before beginning his work on the *Grundrisse*. Even here, Hegel's misogyny led him to naturalise the gender relations of his time, and never having witnessed a movement of the proletariat he had reason to regard movements of the oppressed as a social problem rather than as a progressive force in society. (The exception was the anti-slavery movement and the Haitian Revolution which he supported.) So it is easy to see how it is that the only work of Hegel's which has withstood the test of time is his *Logic*, and the rest of his works are largely discounted by Marxists.

But ignoring the *Encyclopaedia* is a mistake which has led to widespread misunderstanding of the *Logic* itself. To understand the *Logic*, you need to see how he used it in the *Encyclopaedia* where it is applied to the positive sciences.

Logic is a science unlike any other in having no presuppositions. Hegel knew this, and he knew that every positive natural or social science had to make its beginning from some *experience* and always had to do with the contingencies of the external world. And as I have demonstrated, Hegel made this clear in the *Logic*, so long as you read the whole book.

It is possible to make a theory of ecology, for example, without recourse to a theory of evolution. System theory can work very well as a rationalisation of how things are here and now, without any theory of how things come to be the way they are. But how does one distinguish contingency from necessity? It is in fact impossible to rationally perceive the present moment in isolation from its history. No one can "see" a social system. And in order to be able to imagine the world in some way other than how it is, one must have a theory of its historical development, of how things come to be the way they are and how they can become otherwise. Oddly, it is Hegel's *Logic* which, once the starting point is determined, exhibits a capacity to comprehend objects, systems and processes in their development, because of its structure of *successive determination*.

A familiarity with the various chapters of the *Encyclopaedia* is necessary to grasp how the *Logic* is used in the positive sciences, the natural and social sciences.

What is it about this conjuncture that a generation of Marxists should be prepared to cast *Capital* as a work of logic immune to the ceaseless tides of history which have risen up and brought down every social formation in turn? Has capitalism become so powerful as to appear logically necessary?

But enough of such generalisation! The point here and now is just to understand how Hegel's *Logic* was in fact used by Marx in writing *Capital*.

Fred Moseley was right in his claim that Volume 1 of *Capital* is about "Capital in General," the Universal moment of capital. But if that is the case, why did Marx choose to make a beginning from the *commodity* and not capital? The only one of the present-day protagonists in this debate who addressed this question was Geert Reuten. Reuten claimed that Marx simply appropriated the commodity from the Political Economists and because everyone based themselves on the analysis of the commodity and since Marx wanted to do an immanent critique of Political Economy, he would have to start from the same point. But nowadays Economists do not start from the commodity, so there is no longer any need to start from the commodity, Reuten reasoned. Instead Reuten made his beginning from an abstract system characteristic, namely dissociation. In effect, presuming what was to be proved and abandoning Marx's method from the outset.

Actual commodity exchange was no more common in Marx's day than it is in ours. Marx's choice of the commodity was certainly informed by the work of the Political Economists, but it was also historical reflections which determined Marx to begin from the commodity. It is an open question as to whether further historical reflection would cause a present-day writer of *Capital* to revise Marx's logical and historical analysis in relation to the starting point. I remain to be convinced that a present-day writer of *Capital* would make their beginning from some concept other than the commodity. The more so because no one in the present discourse grasped the process which led to Marx choosing the commodity as his starting point for an analysis of capital.

Hegel began his critique of Logic from Being, which was the central principle of the first ancient European philosophy. The determination of this starting point required an investigation which was both logical and historical. Hegel held that earlier speculations about the nature of reality did not warrant the name of 'philosophy'. Philosophy properly so-called began with the Eleatics who made Being the Absolute. But it wasn't enough to just begin from Being. Hegel subjected Being to a critique, producing the well-known series of concepts Being, Nothing, Becoming, Determinate Being and the One.

The synthetic unfolding of the Logic of Being begins from the One. This is tantamount to saying that the science of pure quantities and qualities make their beginning when some definite something is distinguished from its background and the possibility of counting them arises. The idea of a One is the nearest the Logic comes to identifying a "simple something" from which a science must begin. The One is also, like Being, a formal concept, lacking any real content ensuring that no extraneous content is imported into the Logic. In the case of any positive Science this starting point must be a *definite something* or real problem, not an empty concept. Otherwise, the science which is built on this foundation is entirely without positive content. It would just be a Logic.

Nevertheless, Marx never did explain why he chose to make a beginning from the commodity and we must examine whether this decision is still appropriate. I have elaborated on Hegel's directions in "The Idea of the True," to begin a science from a "universal individual" and explained how this led to the choice of the commodity. But not just any commodity. Marx took the "commodity" to be an industrial product, not a service. Is this still appropriate in this post-industrial age? For Marx the commodity relation excluded rent and interest, unlike for the Political Economists who accepted rent and interest as equals alongside profit on enterprise. But services are nowadays central to the production process itself. What would it mean to expand the industrial commodity to include service-commodities? Should advertising and marketing which are the main sources of income for the platforms – the core business of the wealthiest capitalists – be treated in the same way as retailing and distribution were treated by Marx as *costs* imposed on the surplus extracted by the producer of the product being advertised? Are retailers like Amazon to be excluded as sources of surplus value, as retailers and distributors were treated by Marx? It would seem strange in a post-industrial age if all these sectors which have accumulated the largest masses of capital are themselves to be seen as merely deductions from surplus value, not its producers. But perhaps it is so. It should not be ignored that platforms like Amazon, Uber, Facebook and so on, like AI, are the products of enormous amounts of wage labour, both to produce them in the first place and to maintain them. Wage labour is alive and well in the age of the internet.

But writing two generations after the final abandonment of the Gold Standard, at a time when governments routinely inject billions of dollars of credit into the banking system and even manual workers carry out their everyday purchases with a card and rely on superannuation funds for their pension, Marx's theory of money may need some further development. "Quantitative easing" and controlled inflation are routine instruments of capitalist rule nowadays. Consequently, in reconsidering the first couple of chapters of *Capital* it will be necessary to re-examine and perhaps extend this theory.

What are the implications of a "post-industrial" age? Is it still appropriate to base the concept of the exploitation of the working class on "unpaid labour time"? And what is the significance of Hegel's *Logic* in Marx's introduction of "unpaid labour time" in his analysis of surplus value? To answer this question it will be useful to study the *Encyclopaedia* rather than restricting ourselves to the *Logic*. Not of course to look for a mirror of political economy in some part of the *Encyclopaedia*, but to see how Hegel applied the *Logic* as *new facts* enter into the development of a science. How is the sequence in which new concepts are introduced regulated?

We will see that in unfolding a given science it is not possible to complete the task with a *single* germ cell. The "simplest determinations," plural, have to be selected and introduced into the derivation as suggested by Marx's synopsis of the *Logic* in "Method of Political Economy." What governs the sequence in which other concepts are introduced into the exposition?

The idea of "unpaid labour time" was a crucial and novel concept without which Marx could not have made it clear that surplus value was accumulated by expropriating unpaid labour from the workers. In a methodological review, it is not acceptable to gloss over such innovations. Does it still make sense to talk of unpaid labour time? Platforms like Facebook and X manage to operate with relatively small labour forces only because they allow fraud, hate speech and misinformation to run wild on their platforms. If they were to be required to exercise social responsibility in running their businesses their wage bills would be far greater. As it is, no platform can exist without a labour force continuously engaged in combating viruses and hackers as well as development. Amazon is notorious for its stinginess with labour time. It is easy to underestimate the amount of labour-time which these businesses demand; think of the labour time Uber requires to maintain its street maps.

The distinction between the rate of surplus value and the rate of profit generated contradictions which have befuddled many of Marx's readers. Reuten's contribution suggests that the whole of Volume 1 of *Capital* in which value represents abstract labour time could have been avoided by taking it from the beginning that costs of production determine price. This is unacceptable. *Capital* is not a how-to manual for capitalists, but exposes the fact that the wealth of the capitalist class is gained by exploitation of the working class, and as Moseley has demonstrated, measures the extent of that exploitation and the quantity of surplus value that the finance capitalists have to play with.

Volume 1 of *Capital* seems to be based on a counterfactual society of independent commodity producers exchanging the products of their labour with each other. This vision is counterfactual, but it expresses the situation where one person's labour is equivalent to that of any other producer. I pay for your product the equivalent of what it would take for me or someone else to produce the same product, in the existing social conditions. Your labour is interchangeable with mine. The equality of all human labour per unit time reflects the nature of industrial labour in the modern factory system in which all labour is of one uniform kind, differing only in duration and intensity. The factory system mimics the ethos of universal equality of labour because it treats all labour as interchangeable. What an irony: the ethical equivalence of Proudhon's bourgeois Utopia and the Dystopia of its reality!

In Volume 3 of *Capital* it is predominantly the capitalists who are selling products to one another. Capital is supplied by a bank which judges how much an individual capital will receive on loan on the basis of their ability to pay the going rate of interest. Under these circumstances a new ethos has not supplanted so much as overlain the ethos of the equality of all human labour: the proportional equality of all capitals, expressed in the equal rate of profit, enforced by the capital market.

The labour process has so changed in the 130 years since the publication of *Capital* Volume 3! The changing labour process brings about radical changes in social consciousness, but does it change the fact that capital appropriates a sum total of surplus value by the appropriation of unpaid labour from the working class, which it then distributes via the financial system and petty enterprise? Is there any new ethos at work which warrants a rethink of the conclusions of Volume 3? We shall see.

Marx's critical appropriation from political economy of the idea of value as abstract labour time allowed Marx to highlight distinction between the distribution of social labour and the distribution of capital and to determine the sum of surplus value available for distribution by the capitalists amongst themselves. In what sense can we say that this is an example of Marx's use of "Hegelian logic"?

The way in which two different ethoses overlay one another in *Capital* is similar to the logical construction of the *Philosophy of Right*. Ethical Life is the product of both Abstract Right belonging equally to all citizens, and Morality, in which every person makes independent decisions based on their position in society – two different ethoses providing the complex and agonistic basis for Ethical Life.

The idea of "relative and absolute surplus value" was important for the use of Marx's political economy by the labour movement in the way it focussed attention on the class conflict over the length of the working day, a conflict which continues unabated despite the great progress that has been made since the inauguration of the "Eight-Hour Movement" in 1856. In what way does the introduction of this insight into the exposition reflect Hegel's *Logic?*

Look at how Marx has divided Volume 1 into parts and the names given to successive parts: 1. Commodities and Money, 2. Transformation of Money into Capital, 3. Production of Absolute Surplus Value, 4. Production of Relative Surplus Value, 5. The Production of Absolute and of Relative Surplus-Value, 6.

Wages, 7. Accumulation of Capital. Hegel says "division presents itself as disjunction of the universal as the first" (1816, p. 801). That is, when something enters into the analysis which makes a break from the first (*das Erste*), then the researcher should open a new division and define a new first, a new germ cell. Does this division of the subject matter reflect Hegel's advice in the *Logic*? The remaining parts are explicitly on historical subject matters.

I believe that Marx saw each of these Parts of Volume 1 as introducing and concretising new facets of the development of value. In what way is Marx following the way Hegel built the *Encyclopaedia*? Whereas Hegel merely outlined the existing sciences, but did not challenge them, Marx was challenging some aspect of political economy in each of these parts of Volume 1.

Volume 2 of *Capital* has received relatively little attention by current commentators and correspondingly I have said little about Volume 2 myself. There are some difficult technical aspects dealt with in this volume such as the move from aliquot parts of value to time rates. But also there is the question of the interpretation of the Particular and Individual moments of capital. Fred Moseley has identified that the Particular moment is taken up in Volume 3. In Volume 3, "Particular" is determined by differing organic composition of capital in different industries. Capital intensive industries demand a greater share of the social surplus if they are to enjoy the going rate of profit and the capital market ensures that they receive it.

But in Volume 2, "Particular" has several *different* senses. Capital engaged in production of means of production and capital engaged in production of the means of personal consumption must be differentiated as particular moments of capital from capital engaged in the realisation of surplus value. Likewise, Marx differentiates between producers of subsistence goods and producers of luxury goods. The proportions between the various departments of capital are necessary for social reproduction. Where does this leave us in understanding the "Particular" moment of the Concept? Are multiple criteria for the identification of Particular moments consistent with Hegel's *Logic* or was Marx making an innovation in Logic here?

This brings us to the question of the Individual moment. Marx never definitively resolved this question of interpretation. I am firmly of the view that "Individual capital," in the context of a scientific study of capital, means *the individual capitalist firm* or company. Marx exhibited however, in the *Grundrisse*, his interest in interpreting this as the capital held by an *individual person*, and Tony Smith suggests with good reason, that Marx may have meant that finance capital is the Individual moment of capital (See p. 89 above).

It appears to me that the individual capital emerges in Chapter 5, as Moneybags, "Moneybags, who as yet is only an embryo capitalist" (Marx, 1996/1867, p. 176). But the historical reality was even then that companies like

the East India Company amassed capital through commerce and landed aristo-
crats amassed family capital through the Enclosures. Nowadays, in full-blown
capitalism, capital is overwhelmingly owned by companies. Individual wealthy
people own capital only mediately by means of owning shares in companies.
The individual capitalist proprietor is the exception not the rule. Moneybags
is just a germ cell of the capitalist company. A large proportion of capital is
"owned" by retired workers through their pension schemes, though they have
no say in the management of that capital which is exclusively the role of
large financial companies who make decisions (sometimes legally mandated)
according to the profit motive alone. Wealthy individuals do play the Stock
Market though, and by this means a larger or smaller portion of the social capital is placed into the hands of one or another company. The will of a company
is the aggregate of many individual wills. Granted all sorts of skulduggery goes
on with wealthy individuals and "shell companies" but the principle is unal-
tered it seems to me. The Individual capital is a company. At this moment I
have no idea how the various kinds of fraud involving the creation of companies sits with a study of *Capital.*

The "germ cell" of the capital form of value is the capitalist firm, beginning
with the owner of a sum of money, buying labour power and materials, over-
seeing production, and then selling the product at a profit. Whether the owner
is an individual or a corporation is neither here nor there.

So it seems that with the "individual" moment we are faced with a duality:
individual companies and individual people. Nowadays, Moneybags is largely
replaced in small business by franchise holders who seem to be little different
economically than an employee of the company owning the franchise. Elon
Musk and Jeff Bezos own the largest shares of the companies in which they
have an interest, but the relevant capital is still owned by the company: they
just have a larger vote. In a Hegelian reflection on *Capital* I will have to examine this problem. Which is an Individual capital: Amazon or Jeff Bezos's share
in Amazon?

What I do *not* intend to do, however, is to copy and paste a logical concept
into political economy as if economic relations had no content other than
Logic. But at the same time, it will not be possible to enter into this project
without laying out my interpretation of what the *Logic* is. What is the real subject matter of the *Logic*. Any logic is, including but not limited to Hegel's *Logic*,
the logic *of* something. In my view, Hegel's *Logic* is the logic of human practices
(Note the plural).

One of the questions which arises from such an analysis of Logic is this:
what is the significance of starting from "the commodity" rather than *action* of

"exchange of commodities." That is, does it matter whether the germ cell is a *form of action* or an *artefact* defined by its place in a form of action?

A final observation.

I have shown that Volume 1 of *Capital* reflects the modern bourgeois ethos, the equivalence of all human labour. This ethos is expressed in the Utopian society of independent commodity producers, and perversely in the reduction of labour to abstract labour by the factory system. The Political Economists sensed this ethos and made it the basis of their science, but were unable to carry it through consistently. This Marx did.

Marx further showed how the capitalist ethos expressed in the equal rate of profit apportioned to each capital modifies the distribution of value amongst the capitalists. Thus one ethos overlays another ethos expressing the basic classes of capitalist society and the conflict between them. Capital is as much a work of Ethics as of Science.

The Physiocrats had held that the soil is the source of all wealth and attempted to write political economy accordingly. This assertion is logically consistent and expresses the ethos of the landowner who believes that he is responsible, with his land, for all the wealth manifested in the towns, where the burgers and artisans simply divided the produce of the land among themselves. Transparently, this theory of value expresses the interests of the landowning class. Equally, it can be seen that the labour theory of value expresses the standpoint of the modern proletariat and the production price theory together with the equality of the rate of profit expresses the ethos of capital. Have the changes in the production process generated any new ethos expressing new class interests, those of the "platform capitalists"? Or the interests of the "knowledge class"? It is still capitalism, but it will be necessary to look closely at the changes which have taken place in the labour process over the past 130 years to grasp what *Capital* has to tell us about post-neo-liberal capital.

A companion volume to this book, demonstrating a Hegelian interpretation of *Capital*, has been published.

References

Abazari, A. (2020). *The Ontology of Power. The structure of social domination in capitalism*. Cambridge, UK: Cambridge University Press.

Arthur, C. (2011). The New Dialectic. In *Towards a Systematic Dialectic of Capital*. https://chrisarthur.net/.

Arthur, C. (2011). *Towards a Systematic Dialectic of Capital*. https://chrisarthur.net/wp-content/uploads/2017/12/towards-a-systematic-dialectic-of-capital.pdf.

Arthur, C. (2015). Marx, Hegel and the Value Form. In *Marx's Capital and Hegel's Logic. A Reexamination*, edited by Fred Moseley and Tony Smith. Chicago, IL: Haymarket Books.

Blunden, A. (2019). *Mediation and Intention in Hegel's Theory of Action*, https://www.ethicalpolitics.org/ablunden/pdfs/Article_on_Mediation+Intention.pdf.

Blunden, A. (2021). *What is the difference between Hegel and Marx?* https://www.ethicalpolitics.org/ablunden/pdfs/1-difference.pdf.

Connell, R. (1977). *Ruling Class, Ruling Culture*. Cambridge University Press.

Engels (1859). Karl Marx, "A Review of 'Contribution to the Critique of Political economy'," *Das Volk*, Nos. 14 & 16. https://www.marxists.org/archive/marx/works/1859/critique-pol-economy/appx2.htm.

Engels, F. (1876). The part played by labour in the transition from ape to man. In *MECW* vol. 25, pp. 452–64. https://www.marxists.org/archive/marx/works/1876/part-played-labour/index.htm.

Fineschi, R. (2014). On Hegel's Methodological Legacy in Marx. In *Marx's Capital and Hegel's Logic*, ed. Fred Moseley and Tony Smith. Chicago, IL: Haymarket Books.

Goethe, J.W. v. (1988). *The Collected Works, vol. 12. Scientific Studies*. Ed. and tr. D. Miller. Princeton, NJ: Princeton University Press.

Goethe, J.W. v. (1795/1988). Outline for a General Introduction to Comparative Anatomy In *The Collected Works, Scientific Studies, vol. 12*, tr. Douglas Miller.

Goethe on Science (1827/1996). *An Anthology of Goethe's Scientific Writings*, selected and introduced by Jeremy Naydler, with a foreword by Henri Bortoft. Edinburgh, UK: Floris Books.

Hanzel, I. (2014). The Circular Course of Our Representation In *Marx's Capital and Hegel's Logic*, ed. Fred Moseley and Tony Smith. Chicago, IL: Haymarket Books.

Hegel, G.W.F., (1816/1969). *The Science of Logic*, trans. A.V. Miller, London UK: George Allen & Unwin. https://www.marxists.org/reference/archive/hegel/works/hl/hl000.htm.

Hegel, G.W.F. (1821/1967). *Philosophy of Right*. trans. T.M. Knox. Clarendon Press. https://www.marxists.org/reference/archive/hegel/works/pr/prconten.htm.

Hegel, G.W.F., (1831/2010). *The Encyclopaedia of The Philosophical Sciences in Basic Outline. Part 1: Logic*, trans. Brinkmann & Dahstrom, London UK: Cambridge University Press. https://www.marxists.org/reference/archive/hegel/sl_index.htm.

Hegel, G.W.F. (1837/1902). *The Philosophy of History*. trans. J. Sibree. American Home Library Co.

Ilyenkov, E. (1960/1982). *The Dialectics of the Abstract and Concrete in Marx's* Capital, Moscow, Progress Publications. https://www.marxists.org/archive/ilyenkov/works/abstract/dialectics-capital.pdf.

Kant, I. (1787). *Critique of Pure Reason*. https://www.marxists.org/reference/subject/ethics/kant/reason/ch01.htm.

Loyn, H.R. (1984). The Governance of Anglo-Saxon England, 500–1087.

Lenin, V.I. (1914/1972). Conspectus of Hegel's Logic. *Lenin Collected Works, vol. 38*. Moscow, Russia: Progress Publishers.

Luria, A. (1928/1994). The problem of the cultural behaviour of the child, in R. van der Veer & J. Valsiner, eds., *The Vygotsky reader* (pp. 46–56). Oxford: Blackwell. https://www.marxists.org/archive/vygotsky/works/reader/p046.pdf.

Marx (1974/1844). *Economic and Philosophical Manuscripts*. tr. Martin Milligan. Moscow, Russia: Progress Publishers. https://www.marxists.org/archive/marx/works/1844/epm/index.htm.

Marx (1845). Theses on Feuerbach. pp. 6–8. *MECW, vol. 5*. https://www.marxists.org/archive/marx/works/1845/theses/index.htm.

Marx (1845a). German Ideology. *MECW, vol. 5*. https://www.marxists.org/archive/marx/works/1845/ german-ideology/ch01.htm.

Marx, K. (1858/1973). *The Grundrisse*. Translated by M. Nicolaus, Penguin. https://www.marxists.org/archive/marx/works/1857/grundrisse/index.htm.

Marx, K. (1867/1996). Capital, Volume 1, *MECW vol. 35*. London, UK: Lawrence & Wishart. https://www.marxists.org/archive/marx/works/1867-c1/index.htm.

Marx, K. (1859/1977). *A Contribution to the Critique of Political Economy*. P Moscow, Russia: Progress Publishers. https://www.marxists.org/archive/marx/works/1859/critique-pol-economy/index.htm.

Marx, K. (1867/1983). *Das Kapital. Kritik der politischen Ökonomie, Band 1*, in *MECW vol. 35*. https://www.marxists.org/archive/marx/works/1867-c1/index.htm.

Marx, K. (1867/1996). *Capital. A Critique of Political Economy*, in *MEGA* $II^2/5$. http://www.mlwerke.de/me/me23/me23_161.htm.

Marx, K. (1868/1988). Letter to Kugelmann, 11 July 1968, pp. 67–70, *MECW vol. 43*. New York: International Publishers. https://www.marxists.org/archive/marx/works/1868/letters/68_07_11-abs.htm.

Marx, K. (1881/1989). Marginal Notes on Adolph Wagner, in *MECW vol. 24*, 531–559. New York: International Publishers. https://www.marxists.org/archive/marx/works/1881/01/wagner.htm.

Marx, K. (1894/1981). Capital Volume 3, *MECW vol. 37*. New York, NY: International Publishers. https://www.marxists.org/archive/marx/works/1867-c1/untermann/volume-3.pdf.

Moseley, F. (2016). *Money and Totality*. Leiden, NL: Brill, https://resistir.info/livros/money_and_totality.pdf.

Moseley, F. & Smith, T. (2014). *Marx's Capital and Hegel's Logic. A Reexamination*. Chicago, IL: Haymarket Books.

Postone, M. (1993). *Time, Labour, and social domination*. Cambridge, UK: Cambridge University Press. https://files.libcom.org/files/Moishe%20Postone%20-%20Time,%20Labor,%20and%20Social%20Domination.pdf.

Reuten, G. (2019). *The Unity of the Capitalist Economy and State*. Brill. https://www.researchgate.net/publication/330152819.

Rosdolsky, R. (1977). *The Making of Marx's Capital*. trans. P. Burgess. London: Pluto Press.

Rubin, I.I. (1972/1928). *Essays on Marx's Theory of Value*. Moscow: Gosudasrstvennoe Izdatel'stvo. https://www.marxists.org/archive/rubin/value/index.htm.

Smith, Tony (2014). "Hegel, Marx and the Comprehension of Capitalism" https://www.academia.edu/12001215/. In *Marx's Capital and Hegel's Logic*, ed. Fred Moseley and Tony Smith. Chicago, IL: Haymarket Books.

Smith, T. & Moseley, F. (2015). *Marx's Capital and Hegel's Logic. A Reexamination*, edited by Fred Moseley and Tony Smith. Chicago, IL: Haymarket Books.

Spencer, L.A. (2023). *Marx and Engels on Bonapartism. Selected Journalism, 1851–59*, ed. Leonard A. Spencer. Lanham, MD: Rowman and Littlefield.

Trotsky, L. (1936). *Revolution Betrayed*. https://www.marxists.org/archive/trotsky/1936/revbet/ch04.htm.

Uchida, H. (1988). *Marx's* Grundrisse *and Hegel's* Logic, edited by Terrell Carver. London, UK: Routledge.

Vygotsky, L.S., (1924/1997). The methods of reflexological and psychological investigation, *Collected Works of L. S. Vygotsky, vol. 3*. New York: Plenum Press, pp. 35–50. https://www.marxists.org/archive/vygotsky/works/1925/reflexology.htm.

Vygotsky, L. (1927/1997). The Historical Meaning of the Crisis in Psychology: A Methodological Investigation. In *The Collected Works of L. S. Vygotsky, vol. 3*, (pp. 233–344). New York: Plenum Press. https://www.marxists.org/archive/vygotsky/works/crisis/psycri13.htm.

Vygotsky, L. (1928/1994). The problem of the cultural development of the child, in R. van der Veer & J. Valsiner, eds., *The Vygotsky reader* (pp. 57–72). Oxford: Blackwell. https://www.marxists.org/archive/vygotsky/works/1929/cultural_development.htm.

Vygotsky, L. (1934/1987). Thinking and Speech, in *The Collected Works of L. S. Vygotsky, vol. 1*, (pp. 39–288). New York: Plenum Press. https://www.marxists.org/archive/vygotsky/works/words/Thinking-and-Speech.pdf.

Vygotsky, L. (1934a/1994). The problem of the environment, in R. van der Veer & J. Valsiner, eds., *The Vygotsky reader* (pp. 338–54). Oxford: Blackwell. https://www.marxists.org/archive/vygotsky/works/1934/environment.htm.

Index